Baltic Biographies at Historical Crossroads

This book brings together life stories from five generations of Balts, living through the diverse and recurring transformations of the twentieth century; occupations, war, independence, totalitarianism, democratic rule, and market economy. The twentieth-century history of the Baltic countries has often been deeply tragic. Lying on the coastline of the Baltic Sea, these rather small but strategically well-located territories have historically found themselves in the middle of many power struggles between larger states, empires, and other power-holders: the Teutonic Knights, Swedish kings, Tsarist Russia, Nazi Germany, and the Soviet Union. Today, they are once again forced to stand up to the Russian Federation.

Biographical interviewing is a field focused on individuals, and on how those individuals choose to recreate and present their lived lives, make meaning of it through the narratives they tell. To interpret the biographical narrations of Lithuanians, Latvians, and Estonians, shaped by complex and controversial historical background, the authors use Pierre Bourdieu's concept of social and cultural capitals, the principles of Erving Goffman's framing analysis and Alessandro Portelli's distinction of private and public spheres, Anton Steen's investigations of post-socialist elites and Piotr Sztompka's theory of cultural trauma, etc. Given analyses of particular biographical narrations are supplemented by brief historical and sociological overviews, which allow the reader to better understand the contexts of lived lives, and the mental atmosphere in which the interviews were conducted.

Aili Aarelaid-Tart is Research Professor and head of the Centre for Contemporary Cultural Studies, Tallinn University, Estonia.

Li Bennich-Björkman is Skytte Professor of Political Science and Eloquence at Uppsala University, Sweden.

Routledge/European sociological association studies in European societies

Series editors: Thomas P. Boje, Max Haller, Martin Kohli and Alison Woodward

1 **European Societies**
Fusion or fission?
Edited by Thomas P. Boje, Bart van Steebergen and Sylvia Walby

2 **The Myth of Generational Conflict**
The family and State in ageing societies
Edited by Sara Arber and Claudine Attias-Donfut

3 **The End of the Welfare State?**
Responses to State retrenchment
Edited by Peter Taylor-Gooby and Stefan Svallfors

4 **Will Europe Work?**
Integration, employment and the social order
Edited by Martin Kohli and Mojca Novak

5 **Inclusions and Exclusions in European Societies**
Edited by Martin Kohli and Alison Woodward

6 **Young Europeans, Work and Family**
Futures in transition
Edited by Julia Brannen, Suzan Lewis, Ann Nilsen and Janet Smithsen

7 **Autobiographies of Transformation**
Lives in Central and Eastern Europe
Edited by Mike Keen and Janusz Mucha

8 **Europe and Asia Beyond East and West**
Edited by Gerard Delanty

9 **Cultural Overstretch**
Differences between old and new member states of the EU and Turkey
Edited by Jürgen Gerhards

10 **Social Class in Europe**
An introduction to the European socio-economic classification
Edited by David Rose and Eric Harrison

11 **Conflict, Citizenship and Civil Society**
Edited by Patrick Baert, Sokratis M. Koniordos, Giovanna Procacci and Carlo Ruzza

12 **Muslims in 21st Century Europe**
Structural and cultural perspectives
Edited by Anna Triandafyllidou

13 **Internationalisation of Social Sciences in Central and Eastern Europe**
The 'catching up' – a myth or a strategy?
Edited by Ilona Pálné Kovács and Dagmar Kutsar

14 **Baltic Biographies at Historical Crossroads**
Edited by Aili Aarelaid-Tart and Li Bennich-Björkman

Baltic Biographies at Historical Crossroads

Edited by Aili Aarelaid-Tart and Li Bennich-Björkman

Routledge
Taylor & Francis Group
LONDON AND NEW YORK

First published 2012
by Routledge
2 Park Square, Milton Park, Abingdon, Oxon OX14 4RN

Simultaneously published in the USA and Canada
by Routledge
711 Third Avenue, New York, NY10017

Routledge is an imprint of the Taylor & Francis Group, an informa business

First issued in paperback 2014

British Library Cataloguing in Publication Data
A catalogue record for this book is available from the British Library

Library of Congress Cataloging in Publication Data
Baltic biographies at historical crossroads/edited by Aili Aarelaid-Tart and Li Bennich-Björkman.
p. cm.
1. Baltic States–History–20th century. 2. Balts (Indo-European people)–History–20th century. 3. Balts (Indo-European people)–Biography. 4. Balts (Indo-European people)–Interviews. 5. Collective memory–Baltic States. I. Aarelaid-Tart, Aili. II. Bennich-Björkman, Li. DK502.73. B355 2012
920.0479–dc23

2011027430

ISBN: 978-0-415-68110-0 (hbk)
ISBN: 978-1-138-01997-3 (pbk)
ISBN: 978-0-203-80523-7 (ebk)

Typeset in Times New Roman
by Wearset Ltd, Boldon, Tyne and Wear

Contents

Figures and tables

Figures

Tables

Contributors

Aili Aarelaid-Tart is a Research Professor and a head of the Centre for Contemporary Cultural Studies at Tallinn University, Estonia. She holds an MA in history, a Ph.D. in philosophy (Leningrad University) and a Ph.D. in social sciences (Helsinki University). She started to take an interest in biographical research in 1996, at first interviewing Estonian intellectuals about their mentalities during the period of Soviet occupation. This fieldwork was concluded in *Still Thinking about Culture*, which was written and published in Estonian in Tallinn 1998. Next she worked on comparing the life stories of Russian colonists in Estonia and Estonian exiles in Sweden. The English-language monograph *Cultural Trauma and Life Stories* (Helsinki, 2006) is a summary of 10 years of her theoretical and empirical research. Articles of Aarelaid-Tart have appeared in *Sociological Perspectives* (2000), *Socis* (2003, 2004, 2006), *Acta Historica Tallinnensia* (2004, 2008, 2009), *Journal of Baltic Studies* (2008) and *Trames* (2010). She has published articles in the edited volumes of *Biographical Research in Eastern Europe: Altered Lives and Broken Biographies* (London: Ashgate, 2002) and *Soldiers of Memory: World War II and its Aftermath in Estonian Post-Soviet Life Stories* (Amsterdam and New York: Rodopi, 2011). Aarelaid-Tart is a member of the boards of the Biographical Perspectives on European Societies Research Network of the European Sociological Association and the Estonian Life Stories Society.

Laura Assmuth is currently Associate Research Fellow at the Department of Social Research, University of Helsinki, Finland. She holds a Ph.D. in social anthropology, and is adjunct professor in sociology and social anthropology. She has carried out ethnographic fieldwork in southern Italy and Sardinia, and more recently in Estonia, Latvia, north-west Russia and eastern Finland. Assmuth is the author of the monograph *Women's Work, Women's Worth: Changing Life-Courses in Highland Sardinia* (Finnish Anthropological Society, 1997). She has directed several international research projects on rapid cultural and social change in post-socialist Baltic countries and adjacent areas in Russia. She has published widely on these studies; for example in *Focaal: European Journal of Anthropology* (2003) and the edited volume *Culture and Power at the Edges of the State: National Support and Subversion in*

European Border Regions, Lit-Verlag (2005). Assmuth's ongoing research interests are: the study of post-socialism; gender; life course; ethnic, national, religious and linguistic identities; state borders; and migration. Until 2011 she was the principal investigator in the research project *Rural Futures: Ethnographies of Transformation from Finland, Estonia, Russia and Ukraine*, funded by the Academy of Finland.

Baiba Bela is docent in sociology and social anthropology at the University of Latvia. She has been doing research within the Latvian National Oral History project (Institute of Philosophy and Sociology, University of Latvia). Her doctoral dissertation 'Life story as social message' (2004) was about the social and cultural construction of life stories and the analysis was based on biographical interviews from a small rural borderland village. Currently she is engaged in the research of individual and collective identities of exiled Latvians in Sweden. Research interests are connected with oral history, narrative analysis memory and identity. Bela is the author of 35 articles in journals, books, and collected articles, mainly in Latvian. Articles of Baiba Bela have appeared in *Pro Ethnologia* (2003), *ELORE* (2006), *Suomen Antropologi* (2007), *Humanities and Social Sciences of Latvia* (2008). Bela has with Ieva Garda analysed the cultural vernacular of life stories, paying particular attention to elements of Latvian literary ballads in the article 'The link between real-life experiences and the Latvian literary ballad', which was published in *Singing the Nations: Herder's Legacy* (2008). She is a member of the board of the Biographical Perspectives on European Societies Research Network of the European Sociological Association, member of the board of the Association of Latvian Anthropologists and a member of the Life Story Society.

Li Bennich-Björkman is Johan Skytte professor in political science at the University of Uppsala, Sweden. She has published on the organization of creativity, *Organising Innovative Research* (Elsevier/Pergamon Press, 1997), educational policies, integration, and political culture. A dominant theme in her present research on eastern Europe and post-Soviet states has been how historical and cultural legacies relate to the divergent post-communist trajectories. A particular focus has been on the three Baltic states. Within this framework, the Ukraine has been included. Recent research activities have concerned the impact of the European Union on elite values and political culture in the Ukraine, Bulgaria, and Romania. Her latest publication is a monograph published with Palgrave/Macmillan, *Political Culture under Institutional Pressure: How Institutional Change Transforms Early Socialization* (2007), dealing mainly with the Estonian Diaspora. Articles have appeared in the *Journal of Baltic Studies* (2006), *East European Politics and Societies* (2007) and *Nationalities Papers* (2007) as well as *Higher Education Quarterly* (2007). Comparative state-building in Estonia and Latvia was addressed in a recently published volume on *Building Democracy East of the Elbe* (Routledge/Sage: 2006).

Aida Hachaturyan is a researcher at the Centre for Contemporary Cultural Studies, Tallinn University, Estonia. She holds a Ph.D. on Russian Philology (2006). Since 2002 she has participated in different projects of the Estonian Scientific Fund: 'Cultural trauma of the 1990s – historical parallels and coping strategies: the text of Tallinn in Russian culture and 'Factor of culture and sustainable development of Estonia in global risk society'. Her main research interests are problems of the Estonia's Russian-speaking community self-identification, coping strategies, and patterns during the rapid cultural changes in re-independent Estonia. She has been an editor of the Russian language issue *Dialogues of Culture* (Tallinn, 2007). Her articles have appeared in the *Pro Ethnologia* (2003), *Socis* (2006), *Toronto Slavic Quarterly* (2006).

Kirsti Jõesalu is a researcher at the Centre of Excellence of Cultural Theory at the University of Tartu. She is currently working on her Ph.D. thesis in ethnology at the University of Tartu and has completed her Mag.phil at the University of Tartu (2004). Her main fields of research are memory of socialism, study of socialist everyday life, and oral history. She has been working on biographical research since 2001, at first interviewing Estonian young elites about the 'national movement' of the 1980s. Her current research interest is connected to the memory politics of socialism. She has published in *Pro Ethnologia* (2003), *Bulgarska etnologia* (2008) and chapters in several books, e.g., 'Arbeit im Sozialismus – Arbeit im Postsozialismus' (2004) and 'Arbeitswelt-Lebenswelt' (2006, both Lit-Verlag).

Ene Kõresaar is Senior Researcher of Memory Culture Studies at the University of Tartu, Institute of Journalism and Communication. Her main fields of research are the study of socialist everyday life, oral history and memory of socialism and the Second World War. She has been working on memory politics and life story-telling since 1998 focusing on Estonian post-Soviet narrative memory of the twentieth century (a book publication *Ideologies of Life: Collective Memory and Autobiographical Meaning-making of the Past in Estonian life Stories*, 2005, in Estonian). She has been a co-editor and co-author of several books and special journal issues on post-socialism and memory including *She Who Remembers, Survives: Interpreting Estonian Women's Post-Soviet Life Stories* (2004, Tartu UP); *Memory between Disciplines: Inter and Trans-Disciplinary Perspectives in Current Memory Studies* (2008, Trames), *Burden of Remembering. Recollections and Representations of Twentieth Century Memories* (2009, SKS), and *Soldiers of Memory: World War II and Its Aftermath in Estonian Post-Soviet Life Stories* (2011, Rodopi).

Raili Nugin works as a researcher at the Centre for Contemporary Cultural Studies in Tallinn University, Estonia. She holds an MA in history at the Central European University in Budapest (2001) and recently completed a Ph.D. in Sociology at Tallinn University. The main research interest of the Centre is the cultural change in Estonia during the transition after the fall of communism. Raili Nugin's main research area is transition to adulthood, its conceptualization, and its change during recent decades in Estonia. She has published in several journals, including *Young: Nordic Journal of Youth Research* (2008) and *Journal of Baltic Studies* (2010). Nugin is a member of the board of the Youth Research Network of the European Sociological Association.

Vaida Obelenė is a postdoctoral researcher at the Uppsala Centre for Russian and Eurasian Studies (UCRS). She holds a Ph.D. in Political and Social Sciences of the European University Institute. Her thesis entitled 'Discontinuity in elite formation: former Komsomol functionaries in the period of postcommunist transition in Lithuania and Belarus' sought to contribute to the area of social stratification by studying social mobility of former communist functionaries both during communism and post-communism. The study was based on narrative biographical interviews with former communist functionaries in the two countries. Her publication 'Expert versus researcher: ethical considerations in the process of bargaining a study' endeavoured to reflect the experiences of interviewing powerful and knowledgeable research subjects, and appears in Bogner, A., Littig, B. and Menz, W. (eds) (2009) *Interviewing Experts*, Palgrave Macmillan. Prior to her Ph.D. research, she worked as a researcher with Lithuanian and international organizations, predominantly in the fields of education and social policy and third-sector development. Her publications from that period include *Making a Difference with Minority Youth in Europe* (2004), published by the Council of Europe, Strasbourg; *Jugendpolitik in Ländern des Übergangs – welchen Beitrag kann sie zur Zivilgesellschaft in Europa leisten?* (2004), co-authored with H. Reiter in Otten, H. and Lauritzen, P. (eds) *Jugendarbeit und Jugendpolitik in Europa, Verlag für Sozialwissenschaften*, Wiesbaden; and *Youth Policy in Transformation. Lithuanian Youth Policy Review* (2002), co-authored with H. Reiter, published by the State Council of Youth Affairs, Vilnius.

Herwig Reiter holds a Ph.D. in Political and Social Sciences of the European University Institute and is currently a research fellow at the German Youth Institute, Munich, Germany. His main areas of interest include the sociology of youth, work and unemployment, life course and biography, post-communism and transformation, as well as qualitative methodology and methods. His interest in the post-communist transformation and the Baltic countries in particular goes back to the year 2000 when he was a member of the Council of Europe expert group for the International Youth Policy Review of Estonia. Since then, he has participated in several youth policy missions to the Baltic countries and in 2008 prepared the report on 'Youth policy in Latvia'. In the context of his Ph.D. project about the meaning of unemployment among young people in Lithuania ('Dangerous transitions in the '"New West" – youth, work, and unemployment in post-Soviet Lithuania') he had the opportunity to complement this policy expertise in the region with an academic perspective. Currently, he extends his research of post-communist societies to the Balkan area as part of the new periphery of the European

Union. Articles have appeared in *Young* (2003), *Sociological Problems* (2008), *Journal of International Relations and Development* (2009), *BIOS – Zeitschrift für Biographieforschung, Oral History und Lebensverlaufsanalysen* (2009), the *Annals for Istrian and Mediterranean Studies* (2010), and the *Journal of Baltic Studies* (2010). Herwig Reiter is a member of the European Sociological Association and the International Sociological Association.

Maija Runcis is associate professor in History at Stockholm University and Södertörn University (Centre for Baltic and East European Studies, CBEES). She published her doctoral thesis about the Swedish sterilization programme in spring 1998. Later she became a member of the research project 'Welfare state, media and modernization' and published two monographs: *Sweden is not the Whole World* (2001) concerns the education of immigrants in Sweden through radio and television programmes; *Neither Fish nor Fowl: Education Broadcasting in Sweden 1930–2000* (2006) was published in English in 2011. Other monographs include *The Power Over the Children* (2007). In her ongoing research work, she focuses on the conflicting issue of 'the (not) liberated woman' in a 'disciplining communist state' and the Latvian family in Soviet Latvia by investigating the relationship between the family and the state in post-war Soviet Latvia. The aim is to explain the complex issues of 'the strong state' and 'the emancipated woman' by investigating the relationship between the family and the state in Soviet Latvia. The main questions to be answered are: Whether or not Latvian family privacy was regarded as a shelter from the collectivistic Soviet state system and ideology. What implications did the sovietization of family life have on the Latvian people.

Vieda Skultans is Emerita Professor of social anthropology at the University of Bristol. Her research career spans some four decades but her early work was an ethnographic study of spiritualist healing groups in south Wales which was subsequently published as a monograph *Intimacy and Ritual* (Routledge, 1974). Much of her career was spent in the Department of Mental Health at the University of Bristol. Here she developed an interest in the history of psychiatry and in cross-cultural psychiatry, culminating in work in a healing temple in Maharashtra and with healers in the Kathmandu Valley. Over the past two decades her work has focused on eastern Europe, in particular Latvia and the Ukraine. The particular theoretical interest has been on narrative memory and mental distress. Vieda Skultans has written four books (sole author), edited one volume, co-edited two volumes, and edited three journal issues: Skultans, Vieda (1998) *The Testimony of Lives: Narrative and Memory in Post Soviet Latvia*, London and New York: Routledge; Hurwitz, Brian, Trisha Greenhalgh and Vieda Skultans (eds) (2004) *Narrative Research in Health and Illness* Oxford: Blackwell and *BMJ* books; Skultans, Vieda (2007) *Empathy and Healing: Essays in Narrative and Medical Anthropology*, New York and Oxford: Berghahn. Skultans has published in the *Journal of the Royal Anthropological Institute, Social Science and Medicine, Psychological Medicine, Culture Medicine and Psychiatry, The Lancet,*

History of the Human Sciences, Anthropology and Medicine, Anthropology Today, History Workshop Journal, Oral History Journal, Auto/biography, Sociology of Health and Illness, Ethnos and *Transcultural Psychiatry.*

Indrek Tart is a senior researcher at the Centre for Contemporary Cultural Studies, Tallinn University, Estonia. His Ph.D. dissertation in comparative literary studies field dealt with analyses of poetry publishing dynamics in Estonia 1637–2000. His main interests over the years have been bibliometric studies in the literary field, the re-emerging civil society in Estonia, and the Internet as a new social and cultural environment. In the last 10 years he has been deeply involved with a theoretical and empirical study of the system of basic human values in Europe with a particular emphasis on east-central Europe and especially the Baltic countries. He has been a long time contributor to the Estonian Human Development Report series. He has published articles in Estonian, English, and Russian. His last publication is from 2010: 'Basic human values and identity research in Estonia, Latvia and Lithuania after 1989', in H. Best and A. Wenninger (eds) *Landmark 1989: Central and Eastern European Societies Twenty Years After System Change,* Berlin: LIT-Verlag. He is a member of the European Sociological Association and the International Sociological Association. Indrek Tart is also known in Estonia as a poet, poetry translator, and literary critic, and is a member of the Estonian Writers' Union.

Foreword

There are few regions in the world where recent political history has so fundamentally affected people's everyday life histories as the Baltic republics. Parts of larger entities, they became independent for two decades after the Second World War, were then occupied successively by the Soviet Union, then by the German Reich and again by the Soviet Union, to finally become free through the collapse of the Soviet empire, which left them with sizeable Russian minorities. During recent years, they have decisively entered the western European community, with special emphasis of a stance against Russia. Furthermore, one must not forget their very different early histories, from the Lithuanian–Polish Commonwealth to Estonia's and Latvia's histories of being constant battlegrounds with very short periods of independence.

Now the three Baltic countries are entering a completely new stage. In essence, they form an experiment of how former relatively equal socialist (state-controlled) countries embark on an extremely liberal free-market model scarcely known elsewhere in Europe and in particular in opposition to the Nordic welfare state model of their closest Western neighbours, Finland and Sweden. They have allowed social and economic inequalities, and poverty, to explode and have subjected their people to a drastic economic cure of extreme proportions in order to be able to be accepted into the Euro zone. I expect all this will yet have dramatic consequences in the Baltic people's life histories, comparable to the catastrophe experienced by Ireland or Iceland in recent years. As one of the biographies of the book describes it, the Baltic countries have entered the period of the irresponsible state, a state which only demands but gives nothing in return, and ignores the consequences for weaker individuals.

It is surely not misleading to speak of a cultural trauma when discussing the past and the present in the Baltic countries. The people in these countries have experienced very turbulent times, and only the very young have not personally experienced the Soviet period. For the majority of people, this period is still an important part of their lives, if we believe in the Mannheimian generation theory which assumes that the formative generational events have taken place in one's early youth. For most of the people, we can speak of a trauma in the sense that this period contains important events and changes, which for many reasons are not now regarded as pleasant. In addition, the rapidity of changes must create its own difficulties. We know that on the scale of stressful events, fairly commonplace activities such as divorce, moving house, and unemployment rank highly. The unusual situation of simultaneous changes in the national political context, in the social system, in the economic situation, etc. must be extremely stressful. But it should be noted that both positive and negative events can be traumatic in the short run. The most recent events in the Baltic countries are an interesting example of a mix of extremely positive (independence, freedom, opening of possibilities) and negative (radical economic changes and crises, poverty, upheavals) and of events to which the term 'globally positive' could be applied.

Yet it must be remembered that in the European contexts, the Baltic states have huge ethnic minorities. When we speak of multiculturalism and its problems, the Baltic states are an extreme example, which all European countries should take seriously. For the Russian minorities, the changes in 1991 have meant a clear loss of status. Transition from a superior situation to being second-class citizens is not easy, although the Russians are a heterogeneous group and many of them came to share in the spoils of the relative success of the Baltic republics inside the Soviet Union, and almost became the ethnic majority in Latvia. The different situations and life changes of this very large minority has had and will have important consequences. In all Baltic countries, everything Russian is now viewed as quite negative and this has obvious consequences in the treatment of the Russian minorities, especially those who completely resist tolerance and integration.

Biographies of uneventful lives may be interesting but typically they can be passed in two or three sentences. Not so in this book. We have a juxtaposition of large changes both in everyday lives and great upheavals. The recent attention received by the Finnish–Estonian author Sofi Oksanen's novel *Purge* is interesting in this respect. While the Estonians themselves may not be so enthusiastic about the book, it has conquered the European scene (and especially the French) by a storm. Yet there is no need to create fiction about dramatic adventures and events if you look at the Baltic history. Ordinary people's lives are quite sufficient and this book contains stories no less fascinating than those invented by Oksanen. Or let us say that here we see how enormous the variation in life stories really can be: from pre-war police to forest brother, from non-party director of a company which has extensive connections with nomenklatura to Baltic exiles in the Sweden with shady pasts, from Russian speakers with very ordinary lives in their new homelands to young communists who become entrepreneurs in the new Lithuania. Indeed, this book mainly describes the rather more dramatic life course changes.

It is therefore an important event that a group of mostly young researchers have written a book about these momentous events from a biographical perspective. Almost immediately after the inception of the social sciences, the Chicago School's biographical approach became one of the first clearly identified sociological research approaches. In the post-Second World War decades, biographical studies lost their importance but were revived in the 1970s. Their aspect of being exceptionally suitable for examining events where constant change and upheaval during a generation's lifetime is the rule has ensured that biographical studies have now become a permanent part of the research panoply. As one of those who participated enthusiastically in the new wave of life story research in the 1970s, and a founding member of the Estonian biography movement, I am extremely happy to see a group of young, gifted researchers continuing this tradition and using it in such a productive manner.

The last chapter by Indrek Tart describes the enormous value changes experienced by people in the Baltic countries, as compared to the simultaneous changes in Sweden. This kind of dramatic value change in connection with equally dramatic changes in the general life situation is truly exceptional. So, reader, prepare for a roller-coaster of extreme ups and downs. You will not be the same after finishing it!

Professor J.P. Roos
University of Helsinki
Department of Social Science Research

Acknowledgements

This book is the result of a special Baltic life stories workshop inside RN3 'Biographical Perspectives on European Societies' at the 8th European Sociological Association (ESA) conference held in Glasgow on 3–6 September 2007. This book is arguably, therefore, a 'child' of ESA: many of the authors are members of ESA; the idea for the book and the subsequent outline were discussed during ESA conferences and annual interim meetings; and *Baltic Biographies At Historical Crossroads* will be published under the ESA book series 'Studies in European Societies'. The book would not have been possible without the support and contributions of many people, not least the contributors of the individual chapters who have written, and with great patience, rewritten their contributions. The book is mainly sponsored by Grant Number 7030 (partly by 7614 and 8190) from the Estonian Scientific Fund, which we hereby gratefully acknowledge. All members of Estonian team are participants in the inter-university (University of Tartu and Tallinn University), intellectually wealthy and advanced environment of the Centre of Excellence of Cultural Theory, which is supported by the European Regional Fund. Numerous grants from the Royal Academy of Letters in Sweden and the Academy of Sciences in Estonia made it possible for both editors to travel between Tallinn and Uppsala to work on the book. Many individuals deserve gratitude for making this project a reality. Marie-Thérèse Letablier at the European Sociological Association, as chair of the book's publishing committee, kindly helped us at a decisive moment in the reviewing period. We would also like to extend special gratitude to Lauri Tart for a first edit of all the chapters by the Baltic authors, and to Marcus Denton of OÜ Derettens for his excellent work as our native language editor. Finally, our home departments and environments must be mentioned. The Estonian Humanitarian Institute at Tallinn University and The Department of Government at Uppsala University, and their many inspiring and knowledgeable colleagues always provide intellectual challenges. The Uppsala Centre for Russian and Eurasian Studies (UCRS) has during the last year provided a stimulating environment, not least for the advancement of Baltic Studies.

1 Introduction

On living through the twentieth century in the Baltic states

Aili Aarelaid-Tart and Li Bennich-Björkman

Baltic memories of a turbulent past

The Baltic countries are filled with contrasting memories just waiting to be expressed. Our book is an attempt to give voice to these memories, and to do so within a framework based on the latest findings in the fields of biographical and memory research (Borneman 1995; Skultans 1998; Breckner *et al.* 2000; Humphrey *et al.* 2003; Bertaux *et al.* 2004; Balint *et al.* 2007; Leinarte 2010). By writing this book we want to bring to life the dramatic twentieth-century history of the Baltic countries. Lying on the eastern coastline of the Baltic Sea, these rather small but strategically located territories have historically found themselves in the middle of numerous power struggles between larger states, empires, and other power-holders: Teutonic Knights, Swedish kings, Tsarist Russia, Nazi Germany, the Soviet Union. The Russian Federation is currently the Baltic countries' main concern. The last century in Baltic history has been fickle and filled with political turmoil. Within the last 90 years they have experienced declarations of independence in 1917–1918, loss of independence in 1940, the triple occupations between 1940 and 1944 by Russian, German, and lastly Russian forces, Stalin's terror between 1944 and 1953, the consolidation of Communism from the 1960s to the 1980s, and, finally, the restoration of national independence in 1991. The controversial history of Europe in the twentieth century has thus been an everyday experience for those on Baltic soil, with occupations, deportations, and loss of independent statehood causing periods of profound sorrow and even terror, but also moments of intense joy and national pride when independence was declared once again.

Our goal is not to write yet another book about the history of the Baltic countries, as such books already exist (Rauch 1970; Küng 1980; Crowe 1993; Gerner and Hedlund 1993; Branch 1999; Nørgaard *et al.* 1999; Raun 2001; Smith *et al.* 2002; Kõll 2003; Mertelsmann 2003; Kelertas 2006; Misiunas and Taagepera 2006; Kasekamp 2010). Instead, we have shaken the historical kaleidoscope in order to glance at a new picture. A picture in which it becomes possible to see history in the making, through the eyes and minds of those who experienced it, whose lives were rapidly changed by decisions made at the 1919 summit in Versailles, at policy-makers' desks in Berlin and Moscow in 1939, or in the relaxed conference atmosphere of the Crimean palace of Livadia, in Yalta, 1945. Official history is one thing, everyday life as it unfolded for people in the Baltics in the midst of world events is a completely separate matter.

In our book we try to interpret the multifaceted course of Baltic history through the eyes of its real carriers: individual people with their life stories. The analyses of the life stories presented in this book ponder mechanisms for coping with swift historical turning points, as remembered by five generations and several micro birth cohorts (for a similar classification see Kraniauskienė 2004a). First, we have the Republican generation born in the 1920s, which fragmented into various segments during the triple Russian–German–Russian occupations in 1940–1944. Members of this generation are the carriers of the memory communities of exiled people, of people deported to Siberia, of young men conscripted into the Russian and German armies – but of also those who were overtly eager to collaborate with the (new) Soviet power. Second, there is the birth cohort 1930–1945 of children and teenagers from the period of warfare, deportations, and terror, whom Wulf (2008) calls the 'fatherless generation', because their fathers were killed or imprisoned, or fled abroad or were simply permanently out of contact. Members of this generation were often afraid to show who they really were (being children of the 'wrong' kind of people). They were later forced to become 'the average builders of communism', which they could never be in earnestness. The first true post-war generation that grew up under the conditions shaped by Soviet mentality forms our third generation, mostly born around the 1950s. The pre-war experiences of their parents were kept secret from them, since traumatized relatives were afraid to tell them the truth about their countries' lost independence (Aarelaid-Tart 2006). Some of them maintained leading positions in the communist system, whereas some of them were involved in rebellions against it (Soviet dissidents came primarily from this age cohort). Teenagers of the 1980s (born around 1970) form the fourth generation, whose formative years coincided with the destabilization and subsequent collapse of (Soviet) socialism. A new era, beyond the reach of their parents, opened up for them. The challenges of the new era were met brilliantly by many members of this birth cohort, while others faced total failure. This generation did not reflect much on the trauma of the collapse of socialism, but referred to the Soviet period as 'interesting', 'fascinating', and 'fun' (Nugin 2008: 198). Finally, children born from 1991 onwards in the independent Baltic states, now young adults beginning to make their own decisions, form our fifth generation. Their life stories are currently more like CVs than stories. The central problems for this generation relate to the more risk-prone and uncertain social environment, and the problems of an emerging economy in an increasingly globalizing world.

All of these generations have had their own experiences with living under two or more opposing mental, ideological, and economic systems. This also means that generations in the Baltics have often been cut off from the normal parent-to-child transmission of useful practices, tacit knowledge, and advice on how to maneuvre in society. Each generation has encountered a new, not only informally but also formally reformed 'environment' of institutions. History and nationalism have instead become the common glue. For the surviving memory communities (and for biographers as their carriers), this contrast means a life that encompasses the two considerably different value constellations of their Western neighbours and Russia. During the Soviet period, northern Estonia had a 'window' to the West through Finnish TV stations and a few, but not very intense, cultural contacts with central Europe and Sweden. Lithuania was involved in the Catholic resistance against Soviet ideology (Kasekamp 2010: 153) alongside its larger neighbour Poland. For example, people there continuously erected new wayside shrines in place of those the officials demolished (Clemens 2003: 36–38). Latvia was less fortunate. Sharing its borders with Estonia in the north, Lithuania in the south, and Russia in the east, Latvia had fewer links to 'outside influences' than the other two Baltic states. Furthermore, Latvia was not only the most heavily Sovietized of the three countries, but also the headquarters of the Soviet Baltic Military District were located in Riga. When the Baltics regained their independence in 1991, their storytelling tradition was firmly anchored in the inter-war period. In the ensuing years, thousands of life stories were collected by researchers, deposited in memory archives, and analysed in an increasing number of texts on biographical research within ethnology, cultural studies, and sociology. In the 1990s, biographical studies in ethnic languages were considered the best method of restoring the national memories that were partially lost under Soviet pressure. Consequently, the majority of the corpus has been published in the Estonian, Latvian, and Lithuanian languages (Hinrikus 2000, 2006b; Kraniauskienė 2004b; 2006b; Šutinienė 2008), but not exclusively. We intend, through this book, to contribute to the English-language corpus of Baltic memory studies, as one of our goals is to make Baltic biographies more accessible to an international audience by theorizing and analysing them in English (Kirss *et al.* 2004; Kõresaar *et al.* 2009; Stiver-Lie *et al.* 2006; Kirss and Hinrikus 2009; Leinarte 2010; Kõresaar 2011).

The Baltic region's historical position between northern-central Europe and Russia

A crucial issue for all national self-reflection is that of who we have been throughout history. Did we constitute the rulers or those being ruled, a nation with its own kings, aristocracy, and upper classes; or one mostly consisting of peasants under foreign power-holders? Knowledge of the national past is usually moulded by the official education system and individuals usually take such knowledge for granted.

While it is not always evident, the backdrop of biographical interviewing always includes the awareness that the respondent is a carrier of national memory. Baltic peoples, like others, cling to specific 'symbols – musical, literary, and sacred places – that reminded them of their community and that strengthened common bonds' (Clemens 2003: 19). Estonians place great value in their tradition of song festivals and many life stories describe interesting details about the respondents' personal involvement in this prestigious nation-wide activity. Lithuanians consider the rituals of the Catholic Church to be vitally important and the researcher of their biographies must keep this in mind. Rural roots of Latvians often inspire public places such as restaurants and cafés, even in the 'post-modern' era of the twenty-first century. Thus an introduction to Baltic biographies requires a short historical overview.

Estonia, Latvia, and Lithuania are often lumped together in a much too simplistic manner. Even though their twentieth-century trajectories share considerable similarities, they carry with them different historical legacies and identities. The history of the Baltic states is a blend of struggles over territory and local dominance. The account is exciting, complicated, and tragic, interwoven with foreign cultural influences and power-plays. Historically, the territories presently constituting Latvia and Estonia were a remote part of Europe, a distant pagan spot on the north-eastern periphery. It was only in the late Middle Ages that this geographical area was recognized, particularly by German merchants, who also founded the Hanseatic League (Bilmanis 1944: 51). Heightened interest in Estonian and Livonian provinces was spurred in particular by their favourable geographical position on the important crossroads between East and West (Jackson 1940: 52). The Baltics were the last areas of Europe to be incorporated into Western Christendom in the thirteenth century. It was through the efforts of clergy, German Teutonic crusaders, and Danish and Swedish kings that the people of Latvia and Estonia became part of the Christian milieu. Under their native chief Mindaugas, later King of Lithuania, the Lithuanians were baptized, but after his assassination in 1263, society returned to the pagan customs of their ancestors (Misiunas and Taagepera 2006: 2). In 1386, Prince Jogaila (Jagiełło) converted Lithuanians to Christianity following his accession to the Polish throne. From a cultural perspective it is important to note that in the sixteenth century Estonia and Latvia became adherents of the Reformation and Protestantism without major social unrest or strife, while the southern parts of present-day east Latvia (Latgale) and Lithuania stayed Catholic. Protestantism, the preserve of the German land-holding classes did not begin to influence the peasants until the mid-seventeenth century. The effects of enforced Christianization on the local peasantry were similar among all the Baltic people: they were mostly serfs and ruled by nobles who could not speak their languages. However, religious sentiment has never played as crucial a role among the Estonians and Latvians as it has in Lithuania where Catholicism prevailed.

As in other parts of eastern Europe, a grand-scale national awakening took place in these territories in the mid-to-late nineteenth century. At the time, Estland, Livland, and Kurland were still provinces of the Tsarist Russian Empire, but local power was held by the Baltic German nobility, who were, however, isolated from their German Fatherland. Lithuania was for a long time in a personal union with Poland (the Commonwealth) and had been one of the principal powers of central Europe. After the partition of Poland in the eighteenth century, Lithuania became part of the Russian Empire and experienced very strong Russification in the second part of the nineteenth century. The Lithuanians' golden past, however distant, has had a profound effect on their nation-building. First, it affected their early movement for national survival, the establishment of the independent Republic of Lithuania, and the bloom of nation-wide consolidation in the inter-war period. Second, it influenced the country's transition to democracy in the late 1980s, when the Lithuanians boldly emphasized their tradition of independent sovereignty. Compensating for a lack of a similarly remarkable past, Estonians and Latvians have instead had a tendency to depict their countries as nations of suffering peasants that long endured the oppression of their neighbours, but, at last, heroically regained their freedom (Boldane and Snitnikovs 2006).

The Baltics have always felt a cultural affinity with, and a closeness to Europe due to their geographical location. Estonia in particular has maintained close ties to the Nordic countries, such as Finland and Sweden. As for Finland, not only does it share with Estonia the historical experience of being a Tsarist Russian province up to 1918, but there is a high degree of linguistic closeness as both speak Finno-Ugric languages. Latvian and Lithuanian belong to the same Baltic subgroup of Indo-European languages but, as described above, the nations' historical experiences differ. Riga, as the capital of Latvia, had been the religious and military centre of the Baltic German nobility since the Middle Ages. Lithuania borders with Poland, as well as with western Ukraine and Belarus, and has historically belonged to the mostly Slavonic Central European culture and thinking. Throughout history Vilna (Vilnius) has been a renowned hub of Polish, as well as Jewish, culture. The Baltic area became an active independent political entity in the international arena only after the First World War. During the Soviet period these three annexed republics were collectively labeled 'Pribaltica' and informally dubbed the 'Soviet West'.

The Baltic states in the inter-war period

Members of the oldest generation of our respondents were children in the inter-war Baltic states. After the restoration of independence in 1991 they were eager to tell their life stories, with an emphasis on the brilliant beginning suddenly interrupted by the brutal Soviet occupation (Anepaio 2001; Kõresaar 2004). Such a broken-up style of biography-making has been formative: contrasting the 'bad' Soviet period with the 'good' pre-war period is quite characteristic even of generations born in the 1940s and 1950s. When telling their life stories, Balts both in their homeland and in exile describe the years before 1940 as a 'golden era' without significant social problems and full of positive nationalist sentiments and patriotic events. The fact that the inter-war period has taken on the character of something of a 'paradise lost' could colour the respondents' memories (Bennich-Björkman 2007: 40), and gives interviewers cause to be cautious. Researchers of biographical material should necessarily clarify how well told stories match lived lives and how much the memories of the idealized reality are adequate.

Thus, a more detailed description of the period becomes inevitable because several of today's political issues, social conflicts and national sentiments are deeply rooted in that period and are reflected in the life stories of our respondents in one way or another. Indeed, a definitive and symbolic turning point in the history and collective memories of the Baltic peoples is the emergence of independent nation-states. The three Baltic states were formed as a result of the dissolution of the Tsarist Russian Empire and the defeat of Germany in the First World War. Victory over these two historically hated power-holders opened up a new era for the native peoples, for their national consciousness and for new fields of political, cultural and economic experience. Even though their transition to independence was similar, the Baltic states developed in quite distinct directions during their two decades of sovereign existence (the 1920s and 1930s). Estonia and Latvia in the 1920s were clearly societies that valued individual achievement, and the ideal of the self-made man played a significant role. In contrast, the Lithuanian regime from 1926 to 1940 was one based on profoundly anchored perceptions of collectivism and order.

The social differentiation within the indigenous populations was fairly insignificant, and the degree of urbanization was quite low. In 1930, 17.4 per cent of Estonian, 13.5 per cent of Latvian, and only 6 per cent of the Lithuanian labour force was engaged in industry (Misiunas and Taagepera 2006: 11). After substantial land reforms in the early 1920s in Estonia and Latvia, the expropriated land from the Baltic German landowners was redistributed to the then landless indigenous farmers (Rauch 1970: 87; Smith *et al.* 2002: 13). These reforms established a new, independent agrarian middle class (Kasekamp 2010: 114) and the former political elite, the Baltic German land-owning nobility, was deprived of its influence. The land reform in Lithuania, where the local polonized nobility had been considerably more repressed in Tsarist times, was less sweeping (Misiunas and Taagepera 2006: 10). The success of these political and land reforms, which eliminated the major socio-economic antagonism, made these people the most egalitarian societies in Europe (Kasekamp 2010: 114). The establishment of new egalitarian social structures induced a relatively high right-wing mentality common to all three Baltic states. Self-conscious farmers and property-owning townspeople had an ever-increasing suspicion towards all left-wing parties in general and the Communist Party in particular. Many of the stories of today's older respondents underlined the gradual growth of anti-communist sentiments in conjunction with the flourishing of patriotic feelings. The respondents recall that although many members of their social networks were not rich at all, most of them intensely disliked the Communists.

In Estonia and Latvia, association membership was quite lively during these inter-war years, including organizations such as the Boy Scouts, the Young Eagles, the Home Daughters and the Women's Home Guard. There were many cultural societies in villages and small towns, involving choral singing, orchestras, folk dancing, gymnastics and drama performances. A network of adult education groups (Nordic-style 'folk universities') developed; co-operative practices spread among agricultural producers, which required a certain level of social trust, interaction and co-operation. From the 1920s until the first half of the 1930s, around 12,000 organizations were registered in both Estonia and Latvia.

These years saw the establishment of the all-Estonian and all-Latvian umbrella organizations and their involvement in international, mainly Scandinavian, associations (Ruutsoo 2002: 74–75). In Lithuania the voluntary associations were larger but weaker; a number of mass organizations were created and supported by the state in order to consolidate the nation around the one-dimensional ideology of an 'organic state'. From the initial years of national independence, the associations in Lithuania developed into a corporative framework of religious communities, and militarized and paramilitary institutions (Ruutsoo 2002: 77). In the stories of republican generation there are a lot of nostalgic motifs of singing and dancing together in village societies, learning together in youth educational societies or participation in pro-patriotic defence organizations. The storytellers did not retain memories of the political atmosphere surrounding their voluntary activities. Thus, the remembrance of collective engagement into patriotically inclined associations were to them more important than the democratic or authoritarian framing of their social activities.

The inter-war period can be divided into two: democratic and authoritarian. Democratic governments prevailed in Lithuania until 1926 and in Estonia and Latvia until 1934, after which they were replaced by elected authoritarian political leaders: Antanas Smetona in Lithuania, Kãrlis Ulmanis in Latvia and Konstantin Päts in Estonia. There are those who claim that the Latvian dictatorship of Ulmanis was the harshest and most undemocratic in the three Baltic states, severely suppressing the formerly lively civil society and prevalent pluralism (Ruutsoo 2002: 53; Smith *et al.* 2002: 22). Konstantin Päts and his authoritarian regime in Estonia were more modest in comparison. A conservative State Elder ('riigivanem'), Päts was in permanent opposition with another 'Founding Father' of the Estonian state, the liberal Jaan Tõnisson who was the editor of the free-thinking Tartu-based newspaper *Postimees* (Rauch 1970: 159; Smith *et al.* 2002: 19–20). So, even though Päts had banned all political parties, some strands of pluralism still existed, contributing to a less suppressed political climate.

The period of democratic rule in Lithuania was very short, lasting for just six years. A *coup d'état* by Antanas Smetona, the influential politician and leader of Tautininkai (the Nationalist Party), effectively ended parliamentary democracy. Therefore, like its neighbour Poland under Josef Piłsudski, Lithuania was significantly shaped by the authoritarian period. The initial democratic years of Lithuanian independence strongly resembled Estonia and Latvia in their emphasis on the rule of law and the separation of powers. But the later years prior to the Soviet occupation in 1940 had a more lasting, formative impact and created an ideological tradition exuding collectivism and Lithuanian nationalism, much like in Mussolini's Italy. In Smetona's ideology of the organic state, individualism was subordinated to the demands of the nation; discipline, and conformity to the national will, superseded personal freedom; everything alien to the Lithuanian 'soul', such as parliamentary democracy, was rejected; national consciousness and love for the fatherland were paramount; the leaders' will was supreme; the key to national survival was to mobilize and drill the nation like an army (Smith *et al.* 2002: 27).

The German and Russian armed forces demolished those three sovereign states, as they did with many countries in eastern and central Europe. Biographies generally recall the two decades of independence favourably, idealize national unity and deem the actions of the authoritarian presidents were necessary to reinforce the state. In life stories, the comprehensive land reforms and the consequent creation of large numbers of new farmsteads are converted into pastoral tales of childhood homes in beautiful natural surroundings. The children of the time echo the development of civil society by either recounting their own participation in the Boy Scouts and similar patriotic youth organizations, or by remembering their parents' involvement in local associations. The republican generation had only a brief period to become politically mature and their comprehension of world affairs was undercut by the destruction of their nation-state. Most respondents consider the change of regime in 1940 was also a watershed in their personal lives, a moment when the earlier safety of childhood and adolescence was replaced by a harsh, unknown reality.

The Baltic states under Soviet occupation

The outbreak of the Second World War marked a new historical turning point for the Baltics. The infamous Molotov–Ribbentrop pact between Germany and the Soviet Union sealed the fate of the region. The Russians annexed the Baltic states in 1940, were forced out by the German forces in 1941 and retook the area again in 1944. The war took a heavy toll: total war casualties are estimated at 4–5 per cent of the population, and a further 12–15 per cent suffered from later Soviet repressions (Mertelsmann 2008). The first deportations undertaken by the Soviet authorities in 1941 decimated the populaces and created profound resentment and fear, and consequently many people seemed to welcome the arrival of German troops (Mertelsmann 2003: 12). When the Red Army returned in the autumn of 1944, thousands of Estonians, Latvians and Lithuanians decided to flee westward and, over time, formed substantial exile communities in Canada, the United States, Australia, the United Kingdom, Sweden and Germany (see Chapter 4). The refugees comprised the following proportions of their national populations in 1944: 6 per cent in Estonia, 8 per cent in Latvia and 3 per cent in Lithuania (Misiunas and Taagepera 2006: 127). During the decades of Soviet occupation from 1944 to 1991, the exile communities maintained national calendar traditions, published books in their own languages and kept hoping that one day their homelands would be free again. They also supported their relatives who had stayed behind, sending large amounts of commodities to the Soviet Baltics. However, 50 years of separation and living in vastly dissimilar political regimes proved to be too long. When the former republics regained their independence in 1991, some exiles who came back found that they did not recognize their homelands. Moreover, both those returning from exile and many 'home Balts' felt that they were meeting cultural strangers when they were reunited (Bennich-Björkman 2007).[1] Several Estonian migrants in Sweden have mentioned during biographical interviews that they had lived and continued to live in 'real' Estonia, whereas homeland Estonians were still living in 'Second Estonia' (Laretei 1995; Aarelaid-Tart 2006).

The Baltic states were in the communists' hands from 1944 until the collapse of the Soviet Empire in 1991. During these decades of occupation there were successive periods of terror, repressions, mitigation and even modest liberalization. The years before the death of the feared dictator Josef Stalin in 1953 featured brutal terror, random attacks by the troops of the NKVD, several deportations and the forceful collectivization of agriculture. The woodland guerillas, 'forest brothers', sustained an armed struggle until at least the beginning of the 1950s. They hid in the forests, were the only ones to openly stand up to Soviet sympathizers, police and military and relied on the rural population for food and information (Laar 2002). The most impressive guerilla force was the Lithuanian national resistance against the Soviets, which by the spring of 1945 had approximately 50,000 armed men in military uniform roaming the forests (Kasekamp 2010: 141). The (Soviet Socialist) Baltic republics, deprived of independent statehood and now members of the Soviet Union, stayed completely isolated from direct Western influences up until the 1960s. Even close relatives on different sides of the Iron Curtain were not allowed to contact each other. For decades, the Cold War between the East and the West plagued the European continent, balanced as it was between progressing democracy and stagnating totalitarianism. Economic success was achieved on the eastern side of the Iron Curtain through a restrictive command economy and state redistribution of goods and market economies and welfare states on the western side. The peoples of the Baltic states were forced to live on the eastern side, and their exiled relatives on the western.

In the 1950s, there emerged among Balts in their homelands a conflict between old and new memories, accompanied by a complete separation of public and private spheres. People were obliged to embrace the rhetoric of constructing Socialism, but at the same time, they could forget neither the pre-war events nor the terrible events in the 1940s. This resulted in an ambivalent situation in these societies, which may be treated as a split in national memory. The results manifested as games of ideological hide-and-seek. A peculiar coexistence of 'right' and 'wrong' developed in individuals, a partnership of diametrically opposite poles, of one praising the Soviet mentality while the other simply ignored it. This phenomenon is called 'double mental standards' (Tulviste and Wertsch 1994; Aarelaid-Tart 2003). Blatant anti-state mentality flourished in the shadows of closed underground circles, hidden behind, rather than existing within, the public sphere, which they regarded as a masquerade. Indeed, for practitioners of creative arts, with their discipline intrinsically part of the public sphere, drawing a line between 'right' and 'wrong' was almost impossible (Kiossev 1999). A mutual interdependency of opposite extremes developed, in which the poles were almost inseparable but fed off each other's angst: the stronger the dictates of Moscow, so too increased the strength of the resistance in the Balts' minds. The Soviet experience never, however, completely managed to conquer the Lithuanian, Latvian and Estonian mentalities. The legacy of the inter-war years and the national anti-Soviet sentiments provided a shield behind which individuals could hide from the influence of the occupying power (Šutinienė 2003; Bennich-Björkman 2007: 104).

During the 'golden Sixties', most Balts became used to living under Soviet rule and accepted the prevalent conditions, therefore lifting society's spirits. The fear of repressions had diminished. Many people had learned to employ the informal arrangements of the barter economy and the blat system, and managed to do well in the continual 'chase' after consumer goods that were always in short supply. The Communist Party's style of governing was considered strange, but people became used to the system and learned to manipulate it to their benefit. The Lithuanians were the first to act on the idea of national forces 'silently taking over' the positions of the Kremlin-minded functionaries of the Communist Party. As a result, there were some economic and social improvements and the political climate became significantly more relaxed. Estonians, Latvians and Lithuanians became accustomed to the Russian presence, and Russians restrained from rubbing in their administrative and cultural superiority. The radical Marxists of western and central Europe instigated the idea of 'human-faced' socialism, which became rather popular in the Baltics. The 1960s was the only Soviet decade when people learned to value the inherent security of an isolated system and the benefits of Soviet-type welfare (e.g. low-rent apartments, free healthcare and education, etc.). This decade was followed by the dreary and forlorn 'stagnation' period, which featured the cult of First Secretary (head of state) Brezhnev and enormous shortfalls in the economy.

The political and cultural climate changed dramatically during the last years of the 1980s. The new Soviet leader Mikhail Gorbachev decided to introduce open discussion and grass-roots political participation, the processes called 'glasnost' and 'perestroika' respectively. These processes quickly generated social mobilization, foremost in the Baltic SSRs, which eventually led to the downfall of the entire Soviet Union. Those years saw the formation of national umbrella organizations and popular movements: Rahvarinne (The Popular Front of Estonia), Latvijas Tautas Fronte (The Popular Front of Latvia) and Lietuvos Persitvarkymo Sajūdis (The Reform Movement of Lithuania) (see also Trapāns 1991; Lieven 1993). They worked initially to achieve greater autonomy for their respective SSRs, but aimed for full independence from the Soviet Union later on and became particularly forceful after 1988. The extent of social mobilization was tremendous and came as a total surprise to the Communist authorities who quickly lost the initiative to those popular movements. Since Estonia and Latvia had large minorities of post-war Russian migrants, their mass mobilization also produced several radical nationalist movements. In Estonia, for example, the Citizens' Committees brought together former citizens of the Republic of Estonia (1918–1940) and their descendants. The nationalist movements did not intend to create any new states, but wanted to restore the illegally occupied interwar republics, which is precisely what occurred in Estonia and Latvia following the *de-facto* establishment of independence in 1991. The most apparent consequence of such a course was that the mostly Russian-speaking post-war migrants were not automatically given citizenship, as it was done in Lithuania and other former Soviet republics. Consequently, for almost two decades, Estonia and Latvia have had large groups of non-national residents who have not been granted several key political rights, such as the right to vote and the right to run in parliamentary elections (or municipal elections in the case of Latvia). Therefore, the massive influx of unskilled and poorly educated people from all parts of the Soviet Union that took place in the name of building a vast new Soviet nation broke down the pre-war tolerance of ethnic minorities and created ethnic tensions which remained in the restored Baltic republics.

The majority of our respondents have either lived through or been born in the Soviet time. The oldest people, those born before the war, tend to give a gloomy picture of this period (Chapter 3). The next two generations present themselves as skilful manipulators of the communist system (Chapter 5) and Komsomol functionaries (Chapter 8). The younger generations try, at best, to relate to the Soviet period, since their personal ties with the era tend to be rather limited (Chapters 9 and 10).

Transition years

The life stories presented in our book have been told after the Baltic states' fundamental return from socialism back to capitalism. Representative of the beginning of the 'hot 1990s' was the tremendous enthusiasm with which droves of people undertook the creation of a society of free and active individuals. Freedom was, at the time, a key word in the minds of the Baltic people. Everybody was eager to do something constructive: to establish a local voluntary association or a small enterprise, to gather enough money for their first trip to the West, or to study other languages for more improved communication with foreign partners. One initiative was based on the idea of restoring the continuity of Baltic national memories that were broken through Soviet annexation. There were promotional campaigns that focused on gathering memoirs on the deportations of 1941 and 1949, on Balts' lives in prison camps and Siberian villages (Davoliūtė 2005; Hinrikus 2006a; Stiver-Lie *et al.* 2006). Only a few years after restoration of independence did many social subgroups begin to feel that the rules of the society had changed too much and too fast and that the risks of economic competition now played a decisive role in their lives. For people who had not been accustomed to thinking about themselves as competitors in the labour market or in the public life, the new, uncertain and risky situation was the primary cause for 'transitional cultural shock' (Lauristin 1997). The central characteristic of the cultural atmosphere of post-Soviet Baltic states was the parallel existence of old and new values and symbolic systems.

The 1990s were years of great economic struggles and growing material inequality, as the governments of all three Baltic states implemented policies of both large and small-scale privatization. The transition was painful to most people: GDP fell, the Soviet-type welfare system ceased to function, employment was no longer guaranteed and unemployment rates rose. Even though post-communism conferred political rights that could be exercised in meaningful ways, freedom of expression, open media and allowed one to move freely within the country and even abroad, it raised difficulties for many who had adapted to the Soviet system. People often thought that the immediate 'winners' of the transition, businesspeople who took advantage of privatization, members of the extinct nomenklatura and former directors of state enterprises, had made their profits unfairly. The issues of social justice and equality gained seminal importance in the post-Communist Baltic states, especially in Latvia and neo-liberal Estonia. The young, the city people and the highly educated came out on top, as they could use their acquired skills to prosper in the market economy. They outmaneuvred the middle-aged, less-educated and rural population groups.

The transition from Socialism to Capitalism in the Baltics can be divided into two periods. The first consisted of the early 1990s; a time when entrepreneurs explored capitalism creating an era of small co-operatives, groceries and bazaars. During this period everybody struggled to make ends meet and the first, very limited quantities of Western consumer goods became available to the impoverished populace. The second consisted of the middle 1990s; a period of enthusiastic liberalism, which on the societal level was accompanied by large-scale privatization, the collapse of the kolkhozes and the huge Soviet-type enterprises, the coming of foreign investors and the subsequent rapid economic development based on low wages and significant technological innovation. At the micro-level of the individual, daily living conditions continually improved, but the social and cultural atmosphere remained stressful and uncertain. Unemployment rates went up as high as 20 per cent, birth rates went into a steep decline, social benefits such as the minimum pensions for retired and handicapped people were reduced and health and education services were no longer universal and had to be paid for.

For geopolitical reasons and, as a consequence of having belonged to the Tsarist Russian Empire for more than 200 years, the three Baltic states have never been able to escape Russia's attention. The post-Second World War occupations witnessed an influx of Russian-speaking immigrants into the Baltics, forming novel non-native 'Sovietized communities'. After 1991, these Kremlin-initiated demographic changes became a constant source of extreme tension for Latvia and Estonia in their relations with the Russian Federation, and to a much lesser extent for Lithuania. Ethnic Lithuanians (84 per cent of the population according to the 2009 census), Estonians (68.7 per cent – 2008 census), and Latvians (59.3 per cent – 2009 census) are still the dominant ethnic groups in their respective societies, but the ethnic minorities of Russians and Russian-speakers also form large vital communities, particularly in Latvia (33.9 per cent of the population) and Estonia (28.9 per cent). These particular ethnic minorities are not wholly homogenous as they are composed of the 'almost indigenous' Russians who have resided in the borderlands between Russia and Estonia or Latvia for centuries (Chapter 7), and the post-Second World War immigrants who were relocated due to Soviet settlement policies (Chapter 6). The identities of these migrant populations developed and have continued to evolve through the years and most recently because of the institutional changes that have occurred since 1991. But the same could also be said of the Balts' communities (Vihalemm and Kalmus 2008).

The turbulent and difficult transition period preceded several years of relative economic growth and political stability. In 2004, all three Baltic states became members of the North Atlantic Treaty Organization and the European Union, which marked another turning point in their history of oscillating between sovereignty and dependency. This time, for once, their decisions were made voluntarily. The political leaders of all three states had placed a high priority on becoming members of both Western organizations and unfortunately but predictably, their decisions have caused a quite nervous reaction from their large Eastern neighbour, the Russian Federation. This indicates that the awkwardness of the position of the Baltic region at the historical crossroads between West and East still exists.

The erstwhile youths who started out on their own in Second World War and during the post-war decade had either retired or at least established a stable life by the 1990s. They eagerly welcomed the restoration of the republics, even at great personal cost (Aarelaid-Tart 2011). Those who recall the hardships of the transition period, predominantly belong to the youngest generations of respondents who have yet to find their own way in the renewed uncertain times. Our book includes two chapters referring to the youngest generation, one of which is dedicated to describing the fate of ill-adjusted youths (Chapter 9), while the other treats the completely new vistas of life that opened up to the emerging generations who take an inventive approach to liberal society (Chapter 10).

Manifestation of cultural trauma in life stories

The readily apparent political and economic changes at the institutional level have been accompanied by more tacit cultural traumas. Cultural trauma can be defined as the result of value-aggression when the traditional values of a particular society clash with alien, incongruent, frequently hostile or incomprehensible values. On many occasions, Lithuanians, Latvians and Estonians have experienced the power-holders decreeing how earlier events ought to be remembered in a way that fits their political regimes. During the twentieth century, the peoples of the Baltic nations have consecutively been told to forget their tsarist, republican and socialist pasts. In this book, we want to mirror the complexities of everyday life that our respondents experienced through those times.

Every new political regime has implemented its own redistribution scheme. We have already mentioned how the radical land reforms of the independent republics in the 1920s stripped the mostly Baltic German landowners of their possessions. Later, during the Soviet period, people also lost land and property, or inversely, received the houses and flats of the political prisoners and deportees of the 1940s. The post-Soviet ownership reforms of the 1990s focused on restitution and consequently thousands of people received land and houses that had belonged to their deceased or exiled relatives. There was little economic, social or educational continuity between generations because each new political regime in one way or another implemented its own novel ideas. The land reform of 1920 provided the young volunteers of the War of Independence with their own farmsteads but their agricultural accomplishments were negated in the 1940s when the Soviet regime declared the same men to be kulaks and their lands were collectivized.

Several generations lost their original identities and orientations in the whirlpools of history. For example, the children of the pre-Second World War elite were branded as the 'children of bourgeois nationalists' and consequently had fairly limited education and employment options. Unlike in Russia, the kolkhoz system proved reasonable and prospered in the Baltic region in the 1960–1980 period. The rush of de-Sovietization brought with them (re)privatization, abolished collective ownership and gave lands back to the relatives of pre-war farmers. Once again, many country people in their forties and fifties lost their habitual roots and with rural life becoming uncertain, their children had to look for a better life in the cities. Furthermore, the collapse of the Soviet system catapulted the former Communist Party and Komsomol leaders from power, although they often achieved a soft landing as private businesspeople (Chapter 8). Nevertheless, several of them remained influential in the political arena and became key players in the newly established left-wing or even right-wing parties, rechanneling their ambitions in a democratic setting. As we can see, institutional changes have been swift and drastic, forcing people to realize that discontinuity and disruption are integral parts of their daily lives.

Several specialists of post-Socialist studies have described the mental atmosphere of the transition period as cultural trauma (Sztompka 2000; Aarelaid-Tart and Belobrovtseva 2004; Aarelaid-Tart 2006; Boldane and Snitnikovs 2006; Tota 2006; Abbott 2007). This period of rapid change serves as a background against which biographical stories obtain their meaning. While interviewees invariably, either obliquely or explicitly, highlight the social stress and difficulties in adapting to social change (Grishakova and Kazulja 2008), not everyone talks about these highly unstable periods in quite the same way. Our older respondents preferred to portray their lives in a traumatic manner, emphasizing the loss and betrayals caused by the Soviet occupations of the 1940s.

> The individual narratives try to serve as the normalization of the individual and collective past experience in the light of the present moral and political values and identities. The great degree of collaboration and identification with the Soviet regime is more related to the strategies of 'amnesia' and 'relativization' of the memory of the traumatic Soviet past.
>
> (Šutinienė 2009: 147)

Middle-aged people focus on the disappearance of the former social framing. As one of our respondents, who had emigrated to Estonia as a 33-year-old Russian, succintly explained that 'all that we had been taught was turned upside down'. The younger generations chose to characterize contemporary life as hectic, uncertain and risky. The different generations clearly have their own distinct viewpoints, from which they approach both the current hardships as well as the enormous social and cultural changes of the past. In other words, collective memories of cultural trauma are primarily not specific interpretations of historical facts and events, but ways to capture the more profound insights into changes in contemporary ethnic, social and cultural identities.

Presentation of the book

The scholars whose work appears in this book come from all Baltic states as well as Germany, Finland, Sweden and the United Kingdom. They have conducted valuable fieldwork in Lithuania, Latvia and Estonia and collected life stories in the cultural centres of the Baltic area such as Vilnius, Riga and Tallinn. Their work has also been conducted in geographical peripheries, such as the borderland regions of southern Estonia and northern Latvia. In addition to interviewing respondents who have continuously stayed in their homelands, our researchers have investigated two more communities peculiar to the Baltic area: the exiled Balts and the Baltic Russians. Although respective social groups exist in Lithuania, Latvia and Estonia, their problems are not quite identical in all three countries. We will survey the life courses specific to the Baltic diasporas through the original Second World War Latvian refugees' community in Sweden. The reminiscences of Soviet migrants to the Baltics will be based on a series of life stories of Russian Estonians. The overall fieldwork covers four local languages, Estonian, Latvian, Lithuanian and Russian, treating the biographies in the context of several different cultures.

Usually indigenous scholars have exclusively focused on qualitative research, including analyses of biographical narratives, conducted previously in their own country. In this book, we have instead compiled studies that represent both internal and external perspectives of the three Baltic countries. There are definite advantages and drawbacks related to being an integral part of the society you investigate, but the same generally also applies to cultural outsiders. One aspect is the danger of turning the interviews into a collaborative interaction aimed at reconstructing a shared history. This effect is less present when the researcher comes from the outside. Our enlistment of Finnish, Swedish, German, and British colleagues should guarantee a broad understanding of the local peculiarities of Baltic life stories.

Biographical interviewing is a field focused on individuals, and on how those individuals choose to recreate and present their lived lives and give meaning to them through the narratives they tell. The purpose of this book is not to merely present Baltic life stories. An important objective of the authors, wherever possible, has been to ground empirical studies on a solid theoretical foundation. To interpret the biographical narratives of Lithuanians, Latvians and Estonians, shaped by complex and controversial historical backgrounds, the authors use a variety of concepts and theories. Chief among them are Pierre Bourdieu's concept of social and cultural capitals; ideas on Otherness by the French,

Lithuanian born, philosopher Emmanuel Levinas; the principles of Erving Goffman's framing analysis; Alessandro Portelli's distinction of private and public spheres for analysing life stories and Piotr Sztompka's theory of cultural trauma. The books' analyses of particular biographical narratives are supplemented by brief historical and sociological overviews, which allow the reader to better understand the contexts of these lived lives, and the mental atmosphere in which the interviews were conducted (mainly in the 2000s). We should also note that the body of authors is not only multinational but also has an interdisciplinary background consisting of sociologists, ethnologists, political scientists and an anthropologist.

Vieda Skultans in 'Locating memory within history: Baltic lives in their context' (Chapter 2) combines an analysis of how the development of biographical research can be traced back to the Chicago School of Sociology with a novel and innovative interpretation of famous Estonian and Latvian folk songs and legends as typical life stories at a national level. Contemporary life stories are, as Skultans observes, situated in the historical settings of the twentieth century, thus making the chapter into an insightful reflection as to how life stories are constructed in the Baltic region.

Baiba Bela in 'Everyday life, power, and agency in turbulent Latvia: the story of Otto Irbe' (Chapter 3) portrays and explores Otto Irbe's life story as an expressive example that reveals the characteristics of totalitarianism and its impact on the (inter-war) republican generation in all three Baltic countries. Born in Latvia in 1916, Otto Irbe represents the cohort that in being forcefully thrown into the maelstrom of the Baltic fronts in the Second World War suffered from multiple occupations, which drastically affected its members' life trajectories. For a period of 15 years, Otto Irbe as a young man was coerced into kaleidoscopically changing his positions from initially being a farmer to a Soviet militiaman, a German legionnaire, a deserter, a forest brother, black marketeer with a forged passport, and finally as a prisoner in the Gulag Archipelago.

Maija Runcis in 'The collective strategies of Latvian Second World War refugees adapting to Swedish society' (Chapter 4) explores how the torrent of Baltic refugees arriving in Sweden adapted to Swedish society, and vice versa. Extensive private and state efforts were needed to meet and to give the refugees a place in Swedish society. By the end of the war, approximately 35,000 Baltic refugees, of whom 5000 came from Latvia and 30,000 from Estonia, had reached Sweden. The narratives of the Latvian refugees and their situation immediately after their arrival in Sweden, and the study of their adaption strategies to Swedish society are the focus of this chapter. Of central importance is the refugees' understanding of their own cultural capital (education credits, knowledge of languages) and their social capital (networking and memory communities), and the ways that these capitals changed in the new societal environment and affected the refugees.

Kirsti Jõesalu and Ene Kõresaar's in 'Working through mature socialism: private and public in the life story of an Estonian industry manager' (Chapter 5) constitutes a hermeneutical case reconstruction of a Soviet career story. Heino Vollmann was a mid-level manager in Soviet Estonia and his life story pictures him as a successful intermediary between the official and unofficial social spheres. Vollmann at an early age lost his father and, as such, represents the 'Fatherless generation' of the post-war Stalinist atmosphere, who adopted the superficial features of accomplished Soviet citizens and builders of Communism. When telling the story in 2001, Heino Vollmann is concerned with presenting an unsullied version of himself by constructing the image of a skilled manipulator of the alien system for the benefit of Estonians. However, in the context of mature Socialism Vollman was a typical successful careerist who barely mentions his childhood in the family of a wealthy small-town merchant. During the course of his career, Vollman moves fluidly from one opportunity to another, intentionally building up a wide circle of connections and was extremely successful in using the latter to attain personal prosperity.

Aili Aarelaid-Tart in 'Let me tell me you a sad story: Soviet Russian immigrants in independent Estonia' (Chapter 6), uses Estonia as the basis for providing an overview of the vital issues, which the Soviet-period Russian immigrants who settled in the Baltics have encountered since 1991. At the time of the move to Pribaltika (the collective Soviet name for the Baltic countries) most migrants were in their twenties and belonged to the second (born 1930–1940) or third (born 1950–1960) generations according to the schema. The author's primary goal is to develop a fixed methodological framework for specific empirical material such as life stories. First, the viewpoints in the biographies are sorted out according to the leitmotif method. This collection of leitmotifs clearly shows the Russian migrants' poor cultural adjustment under the circumstances of the restored nation-state. Secondly, the author develops a method of framing analysis that allows comparisons between people's strategic coping abilities to adjust during acute political changes. The chapter uses the comparative treatment of examining side-by-side the biographies of a 'loser' and a 'winner' to show the importance of professional and language skills, as well as family background, for achieving success after the fundamental and historical turning point of the restoration of independence in 1991.

Laura Assmuth in 'Rural belongings: Baltic Russian identities in Estonian and Latvian borderlands' (Chapter 7) describes the multiple identities of Russians living in the rural borderlands of Estonia, Latvia, and Russia. The chapter shows that these Russians, some of whose ancestors came as Old Believers in the seventeenth century, are locally oriented inhabitants of their small villages. Relations between these 'local Russians' and their counterparts in the Russian Federation and with Estonians and Latvians differ from those between the largely urban Russian-speaking communities who immigrated in the post-Second World War years and their counterparts in the Russian federation.

Vaida Obelenė in 'Exit from communism: career decisions of the Lithuanian young communist functionaries' (Chapter 8) conveys the fate of a specific group (born in the late 1950s) within the third generation in the period following the collapse of socialism. The actors are former staff members of the Lithuanian Komsomol Central Committee (Cekomol), who may be described as a social subgroup with a strong administrative and intellectual potential, whose coping with social change proves to be very interesting. The other groups (specialists, craftspeople, intellectuals, etc.) of the same generation did not experience the transition from Soviet system to capitalism quite as strongly, because they lacked direct contact with the machinery of Soviet power. Vaida Obelenė's colorful gallery of characters provides fascinating proof that the Komsomol elite, who all shared a suddenly severed career pattern, did not have either a common or a singular exit-strategy. As Vaida Obolenė reveals there were, however, a multitude of options combined with skilful uses of social resources.

Herwig Reiter in 'Catching up with the West? An insider's perspective from Lithuania' (Chapter 9) analyses the situation that confronted many 20-year-olds of low social status and inadequate educational preparation in the suddenly market-oriented Lithuanian society. The focus, although placed on a specific Lithuanian individual, also provides an aggregate picture of the marginalized and largely unemployed youth group, who had extremely similar analogues in Estonia and Latvia. This jobless group represents the 'losing' members of the fourth generation who in general had been quite successful in the post-socialist years. The formation of identities within this marginalized group was determined by three factors. First, as children of Brezhnev's Stagnation period, they were frustrated with the political climate in the restored states. Second, as a poorly educated group they were unsatisfied with their adverse living conditions and future prospects. Third, as individuals, they lacked strong ties to the current system, since they were not recognized as being personally valuable to the new society.

Raili Nugin and Aida Hachaturyran in 'Mobilizing capitals during transitions: the stories of Toomas and Nikolai' (Chapter 10) focuses on two case studies exploring the life stories of two young men whose paths from childhood to adulthood coincided with the societal transformation from communism to capitalist democracy. Both respondents belong to the fourth generation born in 1970s, having grown up in Estonia in the period of stagnated socialism. The cases differ significantly with one being the life story of a successful businessman and member of the ethnic majority, and the other being a freelancer writer and rock climber, and a member of the largest ethnic minority. Although their life paths are successful, but fundamentally different from their parents', each life path is deeply rooted in their national pasts.

Indrek Tart in 'Background for biographical research: value change in Estonia, Latvia, Lithuania, and Sweden in 1991–2007' (Chapter 11) brings under the same roof biographical research and research into human basic values by using notions of semantic (concept-knowledge-based) and episodic (event-based) memory. With data from 1991–2007, the basic values structure and its change is investigated from the point of view of its episodic-likeliness, finding the shift towards preference of more individualized basic values. Comparing the basic value transformation between three age cohorts in 1991 and 2006 surveys confirms the relocation of basic values, which have become more personal throughout the transition period. Thus a more episodic memory-based motivational environment exists in the Baltic countries, which may be taken into account when analysing life stories of this period.

Note

1 Bennich-Björkman (2007) addresses the topic of how the interwar generation was culturally affected by adult life in separate political contexts: exiles in Sweden and in Canada, and Estonians under Soviet occupation.

References

Aarelaid-Tart, A. (2003) 'Double mental standards in the Baltics during two afterwar decades', in A.M. Kõll (ed.) *The Baltic Countries under Occupation. Soviet and German Rule 1940–1991, Stockholm:* Acta Universitatis Stockholmiensis, Studia Baltica Stockholmiensia, 23, pp. 213–226.

Aarelaid-Tart, A. (2006) *Cultural Trauma and Life Stories*, Helsinki: Kikimora Publishers.

Aarelaid-Tart, A. (2011) 'The Estonian-minded person in Soviet reality: double mental standards in Ailo Ehamaa's life history', in E. Kõresaar (ed.) *Soldiers of Memory: World War II and its Aftermath in Estonia Post-Soviet Life Stories*, Amsterdam and New York: Rodopi.

Aarelaid-Tart, A. and Belobrovtseva, I. (2004) 'The (im)possibilities of Estonian-Russian dialogue in the conditions of cultural trauma', in A.P. Klemeševa (ed.) *Na Perekrestke Kultur: Russkie v Baltiiskom Regione, vol. II*, Kaliningrad: Baltiiskii Mezhregionalnyi Institut Obchcestvennyh Nauk.

Abbott, P. (2007) 'Cultural trauma and social quality in Post-Soviet Moldova and Belarus', *East European Politics & Societies*, 2: 219–258.

Anepaio, T. (2001) 'Trauma ja mälu: mineviku ületamisest represseeritute kogemuses' ('Trauma and memory: repressed Estonians coping with past'), *Kultuur ja mälu (Culture and Memory)*, Studia Etnologica Tartuensia, 4, Tartu: Tartu University Press, pp. 198–214.

Balint, B., Sparschuh, V. and Sterbling, A. (2007) *Karl Mannheim: Leben, Wirkung und Bedeutung für die Osteuropaforschung*, Hamburg: Krämer.

Bennich-Björkman, L. (2007) *Political Culture under Institutional Pressure. How Institutions Transform Early Socialization*, New York: Palgrave Macmillan.

Bertaux, D., Rotkirch, A. and Thompson, P. (eds) (2004) *On Living through Soviet Russia*, London and New York: Routledge.

Bilmanis, A. (1944) 'Grandeur and decline of the German Balts', *The Slavonic and East European Review*, 22(4): 50–58.

Boldane, I. and Snitnikovs, A. (2006) *Is cultural trauma an impediment to society integration?* Available HTTP: www.politika.lv/index.php?id=15655 (accessed 12 January 2011).

Borneman, J. (1995) *Belonging in the Two Berlins*, Cambridge: Cambridge University Press.

Branch, M. (ed.) (1999) *National History and Identity. Approaches to the Writing of National History in the North-East Baltic Region Nineteenth and Twentieth Centuries*, Helsinki: SKS.

Breckner, R., Kalekin-Fishman, D. and Miehte, I. (eds) (2000) *Biographies and the Division of Europe: Experience, Action and Change on the 'Eastern Side'*, Opladen: Leske and Budrich.

Clemens, W.C. (2003) 'Comparative repressions and comparative resistance: what explains survival?', in O. Mertelsmann (ed.) *The Sovietization of the Baltic States, 1940–1956*, Tartu: Kleio.

Crowe, D. (1993) *The Baltic States and the Great Powers: Foreign Relations, 1938–1940*, Boulder: Weatview Press.

Davoliūtė, V. (2005) 'Deportee memoirs and Lithuanian history: the double testimony of Dalia Grinkevičiute', *Journal of Baltic Studies* 36(1): 51–68.

Gerner, K. and Hedlund, S. (1993) *The Baltic States and the End of the Soviet Empire*, London and New York: Routledge.

Grishakova, M. and Kazulja, M. (2008) 'Social risks and challenges of the Post-Socialist transition period in Estonia: analysis of biographical narratives', *Qualitative Sociology Review*, vol. IV(8): 106–125.

Hinrikus, R. (2000) *Eesti rahva elulood, I-II: Sajandi sada elulugu kahes osas* (Life stories of Estonian nation, I-II), Tallinn: Tänapäev.

Hinrikus, R. (2006a) 'Soviet deportations', in S. Stiver-Lie, L. Malik, I. Jõe-Cannon and R. Hinrikus (eds) *Carrying Linda's Stones: an Anthology of Estonian Women's Life Stories*, Tallinn: Tallinn University Press.

Hinrikus, R. (ed.) (2006b) *Sõja ajal kasvanud tüdrukud. Eesti naiste mälestused Saksa okupatsioonist (Girls Who Grew up in Wartime. Estonian Women's Memories of the German Occupation)*, Tartu: Eesti Kirjandusmuuseum ja Tänapäev.

Humphrey, R., Miller, R. and Zdravomyslova, E. (eds) (2003) *Biographical Research in Eastern Europe: Altered lives and broken biographies*, Aldershot and Burlington: Ashgate.

Jackson, H.J. (1940) *The Baltic*, Oxford: Clarendon Press.

Kasekamp, A. (2010) *A History of the Baltic States*, New York: Palgrave Macmillan.

Kelertas, V. (ed.) (2006) *Baltic Postcolonialism*. Amsterdam and New York: Rodopi.

Kiossev, A. (1999) 'Notes on self-colonizing cultures', in B. Pejić and D. Elliott (eds) *After the Wall. Art and Culture in Post-Communist Europe*, Stockholm: Moderna Museet, pp. 114–118.

Kirss, T., Kõresaar, E. and Lauristin, M. (2004) *She Who Remembers, Survives: Interpreting Estonian Women's Post-Soviet Life Stories*, Tartu: Tartu University Press.

Kirss, T. and Hinrikus, R. (eds) (2009) *Estonian Life Stories*, Budapest: Central European University Press.

Kõll, A. (ed.) (2003) *The Baltic Countries under Occupation. Soviet and German Rule 1940–1991, Stockholm:* Acta Universitatis Stockholmiensis, Studia Baltica Stockholmiensia, 23.

Kõresaar, E. (2004) *Memory and History in Estonian Post-Soviet Life Stories: Private and Public, Individual and Collective from the Perspective of Biographical Syncretism*. (Dissertationes Etnologiae Universitatis Tartuensis 1), Tartu: Tartu University Press.

Kõresaar, E. (ed.) (2011) *Soldiers of Memory. World War II and Its Aftermath in Estonian Post-Soviet Life Stories*, Amsterdam and New York: Rodopi.

Kõresaar, E., Lauk, E. and Kuutma, K. (eds) (2009) *The Burden of Remembering: Recollections and Representations of the 20th Century*, Helsinki: SKS.

Kraniauskienė, S. (2004a) 'Identiteto tyrimo metmenys: kartų identiteto paieška XX a. lietuvių autobiografijose' ('Outline for identity research: the search for generation identity in the autobiographies of XX century Lithuanians'), *Sociologija. Mintis ir veiksmas*. Klaipėda: 1: 66–74.

Kraniauskienė, S. (2004b) 'Nepriklausomybės idėja lietuvių autobiografijose' ('The idea of independence in the autobiographies of Lithuanians'). *Inter-studia humanitatis* 1, Šiaulių universitetas: Šiaulių universiteto leidykla, pp. 24–38.

Küng, A. (1980) *A Dream of Freedom: Four Decades of National Survival versus Russian Imperialism in Estonia, Latvia and Lithuania, 1940–1980*, Cardiff: Pitman Press.

Laar, M. (2002) *War in the Woods. Estonia's Struggle for Survival 1944–1956*, Washington, DC: The Compass Press.

Laretei, K. (1995) *Seal kodus, siin võõrsil (At Home There, a Guest Here)*, Tallinn: Kupar.

Lauristin, M. (1997) 'Contexts of transition', in M. Lauristin, P. Vihalemm, K. Rosengren and L. Weibull (eds) *Return to the Western World. Cultural and Political Perspectives on the Estonian Post-Communist Transition*, Tartu: Tartu University Press.

Leinarte, D. (2010) *Adopting and Remembering Soviet Reality. Life Stories of Lithuanian Women, 1945–1970*, Amsterdam and New York: Rodopi.

Lieven, A. (1993) *The Baltic Revolution: Estonia, Latvia Lithuania and the Path to Independence*, New Haven, CT: Yale University Press.

Mertelsmann, O. (ed.) (2003) *The Sovietization of the Baltic States, 1940–1956*, Tartu: Kleio.

Mertelsmann, O. (2008) 'Stalinistlike repressioonide põhjustest' ('The origin of Stalinist repressions'), *Sirp*, 42, November 11.

Misiunas, R. and Taagepera, R. (2006) *The Baltic States: Years of Dependence 1940–1990*, London: Hurst & Company.

Nugin, R. (2008) 'Construction adulthood in a world of uncertainties: some cases of post-Communist Estonia', *Young*, 16(2): 185–207.

Nørgaard, O., Johannsen, L., Skak, M. and Sørensen, R-H. (1999) *The Baltic States after Independence*, Cheltenham: Edward Elgar.

Rauch, G. von (1970) *The Baltic States. The years of Independence. Estonia, Latvia, Lithuania 1917–1940*, London: Hurst & Company.

Raun, T. (2001) *Estonia and Estonians*, Stanford: Hoover Institution Press.

Ruutsoo, R. (2002) *Civil Society and Nation Buildingin Estonia and the Baltic States. Impact of traditions on moblilization and transition 1986–2000 – historical and sociological study*, Acta Universitatis Lapponiensis *49*, Rovaniemi: Lapin Yliopistopaino.

Skultans, V. (1998) *The Testimony of Lives: Narrative and Memory in Post-Soviet Latvia*, London and New York: Routledge.

Smith, D., Pabriks, A., Purs, A. and Lane T. (eds) (2002) *The Baltic States: Estonia, Latvia and Lithuania*, London and New York: Routledge.

Stiver-Lie, S., Malik, L., Jõe-Cannon, I. and Hinrikus, R. (eds) (2006) *Carrying Linda's Stones: an Anthology of Estonian Women's Life Stories*, Tallinn: Tallinn University Press.

Šutinienė, I. (2003) 'Sovietinio laikotarpio atminties bruožai autobiografiniuose pasakojimuose' ('The features of the memory of the Soviet period in the autobiographical narratives'), in I. Šutinienė (ed.) *Socialinė atmintis: minėjimai ir užmarštys (Social Memory: Commemoration and Oblivion)*, *Vilnius*: Socialinių tyrimų institutas (Vilnius: Social Research Institute), pp. 13–66.

Šutinienė, I. (2008) 'Sovietinių represijų atminties reikšmės lietuvių autobiografijose' (The meanings of the memory of the Soviet repression in the autobiographical narratives of Lithuanians), *Genocidas ir rezistencija* (*Genocide and Resistance*), 2(24): 127–134.

Šutinienė, I. (2009) 'Biographical and oral history research in Lithuania', in T. Jaago and E. Kõresaar (eds) The Research of Oral History and Life Stories in Estonia, Latvia, Lithuania and Finland (in Estonian), *Mäetagused*, Tartu: Eesti Kirjandusmuuseum.

Sztompka, P. (2000) 'Cultural trauma. The other face of social change', *European Journal of Social Theory*, 3(4): 449–466.

Tota, A.L. (2006) 'Review essay: public memory and cultural trauma', *Javnost/the Public*, 13(3): 81–94.

Trapāns, J.A. (ed.) (1991) *Towards Independence: The Baltic Popular Movement*, Boulder, CO, San Francisco, CA and Oxford: Westview Press.

Tulviste, P. and Wertsch, J.V. (1994) 'Official and unofficial histories: the case of Estonia', *Narrative and Life History*, 4(4): 311–329.

Vihalemm, T. and Kalmus, V. (2008) Mental structures in transition culture: differentiating patterns of identities and values in Estonia, *East European Politics and Societies*, 22(4): 901–27.

Wulf, M. (2008) Locating Estonia: Perspectives from Exile and the Homeland. Available HTTP: http://papers.ssrn.com/sol3/papers.cfm?abstract_id=1268378 (accessed 12 January 2011).

2 Locating memory within history

Baltic lives in their context

Vieda Skultans

Introduction

The writing of Baltic biographies has been shaped by tensions common to much work in the field of life histories. These tensions relate to the difficulties of reconciling the voice and life experience of informants with the scholarly requirements governing the production of historical data. They are evident from the beginnings of life history research in the nineteenth century and later in the work of the Chicago School of Sociologists. The conflicting demands of voice and history have shaped our writing of Baltic biographies. I will start by considering the Baltic context and then return to consider the commonalities shared with the early work on life histories.

'History is a nightmare from which I am trying to awake'. James Joyce (1922) puts these now famous words into the mouth of Stephen Daedalus. The same words could at different times and with different meanings be uttered by the Baltic peoples. History in the Baltic states is characterized by passionate and intensely personal identifications, of a kind less known in much of Western Europe. We find this both in popular memory (Skultans 1998) and in professional history writing. There is a strong tradition of nationalist history writing that argues that you need to be Latvian to understand the Latvian historical experience (Švābe 1991). This school emerged in opposition to the German Baltic school of historiography, but is clearly linked to the nation-building agenda of the first republic (1918–1940). This tradition has been revived in the post-independence period since 1991 and belongs to what the German historian Eva-Clarita Onken describes as *Geschichtspolitik*: the struggle over different versions of the past in order to forge particular kinds of identity (Onken 2003: 116). Among English speaking scholars this struggle is, following Hacking (1995: 214), referred to as memory politics.

Epics instead of historical memory

In this chapter, I want to consider some of the circumstances that have shaped political struggles over history and memory in the Baltic countries, particularly Latvia. Of the three Baltic states, only Lithuania has a glorious historical past.

The Lithuanian empire was founded in the thirteenth century and lasted until the eighteenth century (Rowell 1994) reaching its apotheosis in the fifteenth century as the largest state in Europe (Bideleux 1998: 122). Perhaps for that reason, and unlike the other two Baltic countries, it had no need of a national epic. Both Estonia and Latvia have epics that have played a key role in the national awakening. Although a recent article points out the differences between the two epics (Kruks 2004), it seems to me that their similar role in nation-building is more important. The Estonian writer F. Reinhold Kreutzwald (1803–1882) wrote *Kalevipoeg* between 1857 and 1861. Kalevipoeg, the hero, is a giant and the epic draws on folkloristic themes and symbols to depict in allegorical form the struggle between the ruling German Balts and the local peasantry. Although brave and strong, Kalevipoeg ends by having his feet cut off. Influenced as it was by the Finnish epic *Kalevala*, the Estonian epic was first published in Kuopio in Finland and came to have a central importance in the moulding of national identity two decades later and in consolidating identity during the period of the first republic.

The Latvian epic *Lacplesis*, written by Andrejs Pumpurs (1842–1902) and published in 1888, draws similarly upon folk legends and myths. It tells the story of Lacplesis, the offspring of a man and a she-bear who possesses superhuman strength and is able to crush bears with his bare hands. He also has bear's ears, which in his iconographic representations are always hidden under a helmet. Although remembered for his strength and fearlessness, Lacplesis, like his Estonian counterpart, meets with an ambiguous end: his ears are chopped off and he tumbles into the dark waters of the river Daugava. Both epics not only draw upon folkloric traditions but also depart from them. While Estonian and Latvian folk songs extol the virtues of diligence, patience and gentleness, Lacplesis and Kalevipoeg are both capable of extreme violence in defence of their fellow countrymen. Each hero is represented as a figure of courageous action, although in their respective epics each is severely mutilated.

Kreuzwald and Pumpurs shared humble backgrounds. Kreuzwald was born in Kadrina in north-eastern Estonia where his parents, recently emancipated from serfdom, eked out a living from a barren land. Turned away from studying in St. Petersburg on account of being a peasant, he eventually succeeded in studying medicine at Tartu. His name was not his own but had been given to him by German Baltic landlords as was the practice throughout Estonia and Latvia. Pumpurs was born in Lielvarde where his parents lived and worked for the manorial estate. He had three years of schooling and thereafter worked first as a carpenter and then as a land surveyor. But much of his adult life was spent in the Tsar's army fighting in the Russian Turkish wars. Pumpurs' military experience no doubt influenced the style of his writing, as would the humiliations experienced by virtue of belonging to a peasant class. Since the first publication of these epics, they have become recurring ingredients of national consciousness. Streets are named after them, statues and images abound that every schoolchild would be able to identify. In Latvia one of the highest military honours 'Lacplesa ordenis' is named after the epic.

Family memory and history

How have these literary figures with superhuman powers acquired a reality and hold in people's minds? More precisely, how have these epics shaped the history of individual memories? One answer lies in the closeness of serfdom and the 'corvée' to the present time and the intergenerational transmission of memory. Let me give two examples from my own family history. During my childhood, both my mother and grandmother gave accounts of my great-great-grandfather's experience of obligatory peasant labour. My grandmother's grandfather Reinis was born in 1835. Although serfdom had been abolished in 1817 in what was then the province of Kurzeme, the position of the peasantry was in no way improved. Their rights to use of the land became more tenuous and were linked to a system of corvée or statute labour for the German Baltic barons (landowners). Failure to put in the necessary days of work on the baron's land resulted in public physical beatings. Family memory has it that when Reinis was in line for a beating, being industrious and disciplined, he asked to jump the queue and to be beaten first, so that he could get on with his other work. He provides an example of a stern work ethic being taken to its extreme.

Let me give you another portrait from family history. After the Soviet occupation of Latvia my great uncle Ernests ended up in Germersheim, in Germany, where we visited regularly throughout my childhood. He was a professor of Russian Studies in the nearby University of Mainz but he owed his education and his academic position to the benevolence of a German baron. My great uncle was born in 1890 on the estate where his mother, as a cook, and father, as the head gardener, worked. The Baron of the Mežotnes estate had noticed that his head gardener's son appeared to be a particularly bright boy and offered to pay for his schooling in Liepaja. This kind of arrangement was not infrequent at the time, but it was arbitrary and promoted an atmosphere of servitude. I mention this example because it underlines the recentness of this kind of feudal patronage.

Both fragments from family memory suggest why an epic about a warrior superman might have so readily formed a building block in national identity. I would suggest that the epics were not only about literary equality, but also about resistance to feudal structures and about nation-building.

From 'dainas' to autobiographies

'The attempt to establish a beginning refers back inexorably to a pattern of social memories' (Connerton 1989: 13). This movement from past to present is evident in the folk songs collected by Barons. The historical and collective shape of lives is visible in the *dainas* or oral folk songs collected and arranged by Krišjānis Barons (1835–1923). Published in six volumes between 1894 and 1915 they were organized so as to both reflect and direct the life history of the ordinary peasant. In this sense, the 'dainas' could be thought of as constituting a national or collective life history. As Andrups and Kalve have written

> The 'I' in the Latvian folk-song embodies the feelings of a whole community; it is a member of a community and therefore gives voice to words that could equally well be spoken by hundreds of thousands of other members of the community.
>
> (Andrups and Kalve 1954: 28)

Since these songs were not written down but were transmitted orally, only those parts which spoke to later generations were remembered. The particular was discarded and in this way a communal voice emerged. These songs describe the ritual demarcations of the life course, as well as common experiences of serfdom, early death, and separation through long years of military service, excessive drinking and loss of love, a girl's dilemmas on marriage, as well as a celebration of the joys of physical love.

However, the emergence of a Baltic tradition of autobiographical writing in a more conventional sense coincides with the emergence of national consciousness towards the end of the nineteenth century. Much of this writing combines the particularities of an individual's life with the self-conscious moulding of national values and identity. Indeed, the first genuine piece of Baltic life writing by an Estonian countryman, Mart Mitt, which appeared in the 1880s was entitled Mart Mitt's *Life Story Recounted in a Manner Connected with History*. Many well-known Latvian poets and novelists also chose to write autobiographical accounts of their childhood. These were invariably set in a rural highly poeticized farmstead where the agricultural seasons were described in idealized and lyrical language. For example, Anna Brigadere (1861–1933) the poet and children's playwright published the first volume of her autobiography *Dievs, Daba, Darbs* (*God, Nature and Work*) in 1926. Although her account is not sentimentalized, her joyous recollection of a rural childhood is in sharp contrast to the uncomfortable constrictions of urban life described in the second volume *Akmens Sprodze* (*In a Stone Vice*) published in 1933. Janis Jaunsudrabins (1877–1933) also chose to focus on his childhood, providing both the text and the illustrations in his autobiography *Balta Gramata* (*The White Book*) serialized between 1914 and 1921. Although both writers had long since moved to Riga, their preoccupation with, and idealization of, their rural roots and the dissemination of their writing through school textbooks helped to shape a national identity that was proud of its peasant heritage. Jaunsudrabins subsequently rewrote his memories from his position as a refugee in a camp in Germany and this time they appeared under the title *Zala Gramata* (*The Green Book*). The independence period between 1918 and 1938 witnessed a flowering of autobiographical writing, but this came to a halt with the Soviet occupation, when life writing was largely confined to communist hagiographies.

However, among the 200,000 Latvian refugees who fled to the West in the closing stages of the Second World War, the need for autobiographical writing that could find a link between a lost identity and world and the disconnected present assumed a greater urgency. The ruptures of war and migration highlighted the need for personal continuity. The historian Arveds Švābe's autobiography (1947) written in exile in Sweden concentrates on reconstructing a lost world. The publishing house Gramatu Draugs brought out a three-volume series, *Sejas un Proze* (*Faces and Prose*). The second volume entitled *Paspor-treti: Autori Stasta par Sevi* (*Self-portraits: Authors Speak about Themselves*) (1965) gives brief autobiographical accounts of some 124 writers in exile. The continuity of Latvian identity was an important impetus to the writing of lives in exile. *A Woman in Amber* (1995) is an autobiography by Agate Nesaule, a Latvian–American academic, written originally in English and translated into Latvian. It opens in the autumn of 1944 and charts her memories as a six-year-old child fleeing the family's country vicarage in western Latvia in the face of the advancing Soviet army, their move to refugee camps in Germany and the eventual transfer of the family to America. By contrast a contemporaneous autobiography *Bille* (1992) by the acclaimed national poet Vizma Belsevica describes an impoverished and unloved urban childhood on the outskirts of Riga with painful realism.

However, the largest outpouring of autobiographical writing in the post-Soviet period is composed of the numerous anthologies whose editors have invited personal accounts from forest partisans, deportees and those sentenced to labour camps. One of the first of this rapidly growing genre was *Via Dolorosa*, edited by the poet Anda Lice and published in 1990. An English translation appeared in 1999 under the title *We Sang through Tears: Stories of Survival in Siberia*. Other collections have since appeared very much in the spirit of testimonies to the national history of Latvians. There are also a number of book-length individual accounts of deportations and imprisonment. Those available in English include Silva Darrel's *Sparrow in the Snow* (1974), Ruta Upite's *Dear God, I Wanted to Live* (1974), Helena Celmina's *Women in Soviet Prisons* (1986) and more recently Sandra Kalniete's *With Dance Shoes in Siberian Snow* (2006). Juris Rozitis published doctoral dissertation deals with Latvian exile literature much of it of a biographical nature (2005). Estonian life history literature includes the volume entitled *She Who Remembers Survives* edited by Tiina Kirss and others (2004) and the life history research of Ene Kõresaar (2004).

The lyricism of marginality

More generally life history studies have a long lineage within the human sciences which stretch back to the mid-nineteenth century. These studies deal with the neglected and marginal elements of society and the dilemmas of this kind of work are present from the outset. They are already to be found in the work of the nineteenth-century social researcher, journalist and advocate Henry Mayhew. His 'street biographies' of the destitute and outcast in London first appeared in book form in 1851. These are written from a position of passion and rage; they are rhetorical and persuasive in intent, challenging stereotypes of the poor and inviting empathy and identification with the lives of the poor. They are played out against a background of rapid social change and urbanization which shapes their plot and thus invites a delineation of character. Thus, these biographies combine drama with a human and social perspective. There is in Mayhew's writing, particularly when talking with the little watercress girl, something of what Foucault described as 'the lyricism of marginality' which has remained a feature of oral history writing to this day (1977: 301).

Life history research has played a significant role in the development of sociology as an academic discipline. The first systematic use of life history as a research tool is to be found with the Chicago School of Sociology. In particular, these sociologists were interested in exploring the impact of urban disorganization on individual lives. Thomas and Znaniecki's (1927) *The Polish Peasant in Europe and America* was a landmark study in five volumes that was first published between 1918 and 1920. It was based on personal documents such as letters and diaries and included an extended life history of a Polish peasant called Wladek. The aim of the life history was to further scientific generalization by offering a representative case or social type rather than simply facilitating an understanding of the subjectivity and life experience of a Polish immigrant. Indeed, the life history approach was seen as having a role similar to that of the microscope in the biological sciences (Bulmer 1984: 106). The approach yielded a number of rich ethnographic studies that have since become classics. By and large they were studies of the underside of urban life: delinquency, thieving, organized crime and homelessness were viewed through the prism of individual lives (Anderson 1923; Sutherland [1937] 1956; Shaw [1930] 1966; Landesco [1929] 1968). The life history studies aimed to 'tell-it-like-it-is' and also to make deviant behaviour intelligible in relation to its social context. This genre of work is ably summarized by James Bennett (1984). Thus, for example, organized crime was seen as having its roots in the difficulties of urban living rather than in the negative qualities of individuals or groups. Aiming for scientific respectability, these life history studies lacked the moral passion that fired Mayhew's writing.

However, these early participant observation studies also carried within them clues to the ways later biographical work developed. For example, although Clifford Shaw came from a traditional farming background and Stanley the 'jack-roller' was a city boy of immigrant Polish parents, Gelsthorpe has unearthed many points of similarity in their seemingly contrasting early lives (2007). Gelsthorpe concludes: 'The interviewer [of] Shaw's story is [the] interviewee [of] "Stanley's" story, "Stanley's" story is Shaw's story, and all of it a social science story' (Gelsthorpe 2007: 538). Nels Anderson's study *The Hobo: The Sociology of the Homeless Man*, which was first published in 1923, draws both upon his own earlier experiences of being homeless and upon the advantages this background gives in opening up the lives of homeless men. John Landesco, the author of *Organized Crime in Chicago* (1929), was born in Rumania and came to the United States at the age of ten in 1900. His own early experience of inner-city immigrant living facilitated his research among Sicilian criminal gangs in a way that could not be substituted by any amount of theoretical understanding. What these early biographical studies reveal is that in telling the story of another person, the researcher inevitably shapes that story by drawing upon their own experience.

They refute the assessment of personal documents as merely useful in formulating and verifying a scientific hypothesis (Gottschalk *et al.* 1945: 180–1). By the late 1930s the heyday of biographical research had passed, perhaps because its aspirations to generalize law-like findings could not be met.

For a radically different experience of working with life stories, we can look to the writings of Sidney Mintz and his study of the life of Don Taso, a Puerto Rican cane-worker. Mintz is generous in his acknowledgement of his emotional indebtedness to Don Taso. Mintz writes:

> But what I regard as the bigger things I learned are hard for me to describe. In my growing friendship with Don Taso, and probably for the first time in my life, I learned to look down the corridor of time through which a man had walked. I found myself deeply stirred by what I could dimly understand. Taso, though only a few years older than I, had lived so differently, so hard, had suffered so much more, even in terms of the fundamentals of life, that knowing him and feeling his liking for me made me humble.
>
> (Mintz 1960: 4)

Through his friendship with Taso, Mintz becomes aware of the privileged nature of his own life compared to Taso's: 'And yet these human beings are not so thwarted as they might seem. They make do with what they have, and at times they can manifest a nobility and courage that I am awed by' (Mintz 1960: 11). Acknowledgement of the moral qualities of one's informants means that one can no longer treat them as exemplars of a general law, or as case studies.

> Taso is such a person. He is not an 'average' anything – neither an average man, nor an average Puerto Rican, nor an average Puerto Rican lower class sugar cane worker. He has lived just one life, and not all of that. He doesn't think of himself as representative of anything and he is right.
>
> (Mintz 1960: 11)

This is very different from the tone of the Chicago sociologists who think in terms of illustrations, exemplifications and case studies. The term 'quarrying' has been used for this type of life history research. In the Puerto Rican study, by contrast, life stories remind us of the fragility of human existence and the vulnerability and unrepeatability of lives.

Baltic exception: life stories within the grand narratives of history

Baltic life history writing, from its first appearance in the mid-nineteenth century, has had a different focus from that of the English-speaking world. Rather than salvaging the voices of the individual oppressed, Baltic life histories have tried to position individual lives within the grand narratives of history. It is as though people from this part of the world have felt that history writing could not be left to the historians. Many Baltic accounts of lives start by situating their experiences at the very heart of twentieth-century history. My stepfather's earliest memory is of sitting on his mother's shoulders watching soldiers marching in front of the Winter Palace in St. Petersburg. His mother said to him, 'Your father is one of those soldiers.' It was the summer of 1918 and my step-father must have been around 18 months old. Whether this is a real or re-constructed memory does not matter. The point is the way in which my stepfather situates his earliest memory at the heart of the most momentous historical events of the twentieth century. In a similar vein, a country woman from the remote south-eastern province of Latvia summed up her relationship to history by sighing and saying: 'So many important events in such an unimportant life'. This situation is unlike the one described by Alastair MacIntyre, in which a person may have thought that they were playing a major role in another's life only to discover that they had been assigned a mere bit part.

> We enter upon a stage which we did not design and we find ourselves part of an action that was not of our making. Each of us being a main character in our own drama plays subordinate parts in the dramas of others, and each drama constrains the others.
>
> (MacIntyre 1985: 213)

The point of my example is, precisely, that this woman had a modest view of her own importance and yet she claimed a role in history: she was insisting on a walk-on part in the unfolding of world history. Such claims add a whole new dimension to life history research in the Baltic states.

These examples encourage a radically different approach to the study of life histories. These are not marginal lives in the Anglo-American tradition of life history research since so many Baltic life historians place their account at the very heart of world events. They are not a response to the oral history mission of filling in the small or large gaps left by the macro historians. Neither is it possible to squeeze these lives into instantiations of sociological categories and generalizations in the way that the Chicago sociologists hoped. Rather, we are called upon to bear witness to the unique trajectory of individual lives and to give respect to their verbal expression with all the pleasure and discomforting questions that this may involve. We have a certain amount of choice in how we represent these encounters with individual lives: whether we do so as answers to our socio-historical questions or whether we treat them as narrative identity constructions (Bruner 1986: 18; Shotter 1993: 20). But whatever may be our decisions over the style of writing of life histories, all our writing has to pay respect to and leave space for the prior human encounter and to the effort and dedication that narrators have already put into transforming their past experiences into words. Lives are recounted in the spirit of witnessing, with all the religious and legal connotations that such terms carry with them. But the use of witnessing in literature or life history writing is not simply about a private life. Rather it is, 'a point of conflation between text and life, a textual testimony which can penetrate us like an actual life' (Felman 1992: 2). Many of my respondents claimed that they had never recounted their stories to anyone else, and I think that in very many cases this was true. But it was also clear to me that these stories had been privately rehearsed, meticulously searching and matching words to the events experienced. For such reasons these texts reach our hearts like homing pigeons. Our responses are both visceral and awesome.

Thinking about, and with, life stories

This leads into a discussion of Arthur Frank's work and his distinction between thinking not only about stories (although this too is important), but also about thinking with stories (Frank 1995). As Frank reminds us, we lose a great deal if we confine ourselves to thinking only about stories (2004: 209). Namely, we fail to recognize that other peoples' narratives are not merely the literary expression of their lived experience, but also that these narratives are the phenomenological embodiment and extension of their identity. Witnessing is morally transformative both for the witness and the witnessed. Sidney Mintz (1960) experienced this transformation in getting to know Don Taso's life.

In practice, we find that thinking with and about stories are intertwined. We may start by thinking with stories and then find that we are compelled to think about them. To ask of someone who they are very often collapses into an answer about what they are (Cavarero 2000: 63). Alternatively, we may find ourselves in a moral dialogue with the story and then notice that there are historical and social details that demand to be recorded. The ability to move between these two registers is the mark of a skilled oral historian, but also, as we all know, of an empathetic friend. The Italian philosopher Adriana Cavarero expresses these aspects of life history research as a 'confrontation between two discursive registers which manifest opposite characteristics.... The first asks "what is Man?" The second asks of someone "who he or she is"' (2000: 13). Arendt has written 'Who somebody is or was we can know only by knowing the story of which he himself is the hero – his biography in other words' (1958: 186). However, 'who' questions often collapse into 'what' questions and 'what' questions may leave us feeling that we still do not know the person with whom we have spoken. However 'what' questions are easier to ask and to answer. They require less emotional involvement and less self-revelation. Only questions in the 'who' register are able to elicit the kind of textual witnessing, which I have been describing.

These two dimensions of life history research can also be delineated by the terms 'characterization' and 'narrative'. Understanding human beings requires both narrative and characterization. Peter Goldie gives the example of what is involved when an actor prepares for a part (2000: 198). The actor not only needs to study the script but also to learn about the background details for the part. Although the characterization does not form part of the narrative unless the narrator is self-consciously reviewing his characteristics, say his social class origins or his deprived childhood, it nevertheless contributes to an understanding of the narrative or script. In order to do justice to the totality of the individual we need both the narrative life plot and social characterization and generalization. Thus skilful life history research must encompass both social history and narrative methodology.

This approach diverges from those who opt for either a socio-historical or a narrative approach. For example, Alessandro Portelli in recounting the reactions of workers to the closure of a steel plant in Terni claimed that he chose not to enter the steel plant himself because he did not want his understanding of the narrative accounts to be contaminated by his personal experience of the steel works. In so doing, he prioritized the experience and literary expression of his narrators over the social and contextual information that he might have gained by entering the steelworks himself. The extreme version of this approach would be to shut one's eyes while listening to a story thus eliminating any visual and non-verbal cues. However, not all researchers would want to do this, thereby denying or destroying the performative and corporeal dimensions of storytelling. Nevertheless, it is true that one reason why we attach so much importance to contexts is that stories have a habit of breaking free of their contexts as Bauman and Briggs (1990) point out. Their question is, 'What factors loosen the ties between performed discourse and its context?' (Bauman and Briggs 1990: 73). My answer would be that the matching of experience and memory to words and story constitute the act of textual witnessing and that it is the resultant literary precision that grants stories the power to break loose of their contextual moorings.

Studying life histories requires what Aristotle in the *Nichomachean Ethics* called 'phronesis' or practical wisdom; namely the ability to discern the right thing to do in particular situations or contexts. We may be helped by certain rules and guidelines but when confronted by the life of another we need to call upon our phronetic resources or practical wisdom. My own research in Latvia from the early 1990s onwards demanded these kinds of phronetic decisions of me.

Implementation of the theoretical part into my own experience in Latvia in the early 1990s

I had planned a fairly conventional research project in medical anthropology and was hoping to learn about illness ideas and practices. I anticipated neither the need people had to describe the Soviet past as well as the damage it had done to their health, nor the literary and rhetorical force of the narratives. The narratives I collected reminded me of Geertz's claim that individuals give meaning to the accidents and violence of their lives not only through religion but also through art (see Geertz 1973). For these Latvians, it was important to aestheticize their experience. Let me give you three examples: Mara, Milda and Anna. The first, Mara, is a woman of roughly my age. She frames her childhood memories of arrest and deportation by emphasizing the age of their farmhouse and the huge size of the orchards:

> I was born in the farm house that my great grandfather built more than hundred years ago. There were large lime and apple orchards around. And my childhood came to an end there on 25th. March 1949, in the morning half-light, in the dawn. On waking I saw soldiers in the room with daggers. My grandmother dressed me and then I remember that father took me in his arms and carried me out into the courtyard … I was six, it was my seventh year. My seventh birthday took place in Siberia in the region of Tomsk.

This is not simply a literal account of what happened. The descriptions of solidity and age are carefully judged and set against the sudden reversal of fortune. I do not wish to over analyse Mara's words: their literary quality speaks for itself.

The second is Milda, an 80-year-old describing her return from a prison camp in Siberia:

> It was exactly 1950. The ticket was free. I had some money too. We spoke Latvian, being all Latvians together. I couldn't speak Russian. Now the camp gates are open and I'm shown 'Go there'. I go to one place and my ticket isn't accepted. I go to a second, it isn't accepted. At last, it's accepted in a third place. I sit down and I think madness, how do I know where to go. The train moves a bit and then stops. Moves a bit and then stops. I am on my own. Everyone else was given at least ten years. Nobody had as short a time as me. I was the first to be set free. Because nobody proved my guilt … I didn't know the language. And then I thought 'Dear God, give me some companion who would take me to Moscow, to Riga.' Once I got to Riga I would know from there on. I must have looked terrible. Two young people come in the carriage. Russians, of course, and they give me such a look. I was sitting there alone. It wasn't a cattle wagon, it was a carriage for humans. I look, they are coming back, they sit down opposite me and start to speak to me. I tell them I don't understand, but they don't give up. One of them has been in Riga during the German time and he knows a few words of Latvian. And they were on an official trip to Moscow. And so he spoke one word Latvian, one word Russian and so in two weeks we got to Moscow. And that time we were travelling forty days and nights to Komsomolsk and we got back to Moscow in twelve days. They brought me back to Moscow and showed me the Moscow Riga train. God has listened to all my prayers.

This narrative is full of biblical resonance. The figures 3, 12 and 40 are not accidental. The repetition of phrases adds to the literary quality of the narrative.

The third is Anna, a psychiatrist and now a friend, talking about her own damaged nerves and neurasthenia.

> I don't for one moment consider that I am the only one who hasn't succeeded or something like that. I have always told myself that I am not the only one like that. The whole Latvian nation is like that. I think that every

> other family has all sorts of problems. You could call it destiny, or the situation or this communist epoch. I don't know how to put it more precisely: there is nowhere where this mystical epoch hasn't interfered and hasn't transformed life. My destiny isn't anything special. There are many more tragic destinies than mine.

Here again the narrator is situating herself in history and offering her story as representative of many others.

Conclusion

It has been suggested that the personal witness is the paradigmatic genre of historical writing in the twentieth century. The point about witnessing, as a literary genre, is not only that the account stems from experience but that the witness speaks on behalf of a social group. The experience of the witness represents or is the mouthpiece for the community. For this reason, the representation and interpretation of witnessed material is always beset with problems. Unlike the traditional historian, social anthropologists and oral historians do both the living and the recording. The late Oxford anthropologist Edwin Ardener used some apt metaphors to convey these differences. He wrote: 'The ethnography is a kind of slaughter of the experience and a dissection of the corpse ... the exact point at which the opportunity for such an understanding both exists and vanishes – the exact moment of the slaughter' (Ardener 1989: 94). These are harsh words but they convey some of the difficulties experienced in transcribing and translating experiences of extreme suffering. I have argued that turning a difficult life into a compelling story gives meaning, moral authority and dignity to the teller as lives are turned into literature. Leona Toker introduced the term 'the Lenten mode' of literature, in contrast to Bakhtin's carnavalesque mode (Bakhtin 1941) and as an example she writes, 'Gulag prisoners do not starve voluntarily, they are denied sufficient food, yet Gulag literature repeatedly suggests that the answer to hunger is fasting' (Toker 2000: 94). It is a paradoxical way of retaining moral agency or authority: of turning something contingent into something willed.

Literal accounts of violence, dispossession and dislocation do not naturally translate into good stories. In order to succeed they must draw upon all the literary resources inherent in language and to which the narrator can find access. And yet there is always the lingering doubt that, as Toker writes, 'foregrounding the artistic merits of concentration camp literature may, but should not, obliterate its admonitory aims' (2000: 10). Of course, as she also argues 'there are worse things than turning into statistics – and one of them is dropping out of statistics' (Toker 2000: 5), but it is so much better to locate past experience and memory within a story and within history. So acknowledgement of the literary qualities of a life history is not an irrelevance. Contrary to the philosopher Max Black's example of praise for the beautiful handwriting of a logician as a way of belittling rather than enhancing their reputation (Black 1962: 25), it is rather to acknowledge the life-enhancing properties of literary language. One way of safeguarding the personal story and protecting its fragility is to attach it to another larger story. Thus, as agents, our freedom may be curtailed or taken away but as authors we can take charge of our story and reclaim a measure of dignity.

References

Anderson, N. (1923) *The Hobo: The Sociology of the Homeless Man*, Chicago and London: The University of Chicago Press.

Andrups, J. and Kalve, V. (1954) *Latvian Literature: Essays*, Stockholm: Goppers.

Ardener, E. (1989), *The Voice of Prophecy and Other Essays*, edited by Malcolm Chapman, Oxford: Basil Blackwell.

Arendt, H. (1958) *The Human Condition*, Chicago: Chicago University Press.

Bakhtin, M.M. (1941, 2nd edn. 1965) *Rabelais and His World*, trans. Hélène Iswolsky (1993) Bloomington, IN: Indiana University Press.

Bauman, R. and Briggs, C. (1990) 'Poetics and performance as critical perspectives on language and social life', *American Review of Anthropology*, 19: 59–88.

Bennett, J. (1984) *Oral History and Delinquency: The Rhetoric of Criminology*, Chicago and London: The University of Chicago Press.

Bideleux, R. (1998) *A History of Eastern Europe: Crisis and Change*, New York and London: Routledge.

Black, M. (1962) *Models and Metaphors: Studies in Language and Philosophy*, Ithaca: Cornell University Press.

Bruner, J. (1986) *Actual Minds, Possible Worlds*, Cambridge, Mass: Harvard University Press.

Bulmer, M. (1984) *The Chicago School of Sociology. Institutionalization, Diversity and the Rise of Sociological Research*, Chicago and London: The University of Chicago Press.

Cavarero, A. (2000) *Relating Narratives: Storytelling and Selfhood*, London and New York: Routledge.

Celmina, H. (1985) *Women in Soviet Prisons*, New York: Paragon.

Connerton, P. (1989) *How Societies Remember*, Cambridge: Cambridge University Press.

Darrel, S. (1974) *Sparrow in the Snow*, London: Souvenir Press.

Felman, S. (1992) 'Education and crisis', in S. Felman and D. Laub (eds) *Testimony of Lives Crises of Witnessing in Literature, Psychoanalysis, and History*, New York and London: Routledge.

Foucault, M. (1977) *Discipline and Punish: The Birth of the Prison*, London: Allen Lane.

Frank, A.W. (1995) *The Wounded Storyteller: Body, Illness, and Ethics*, Chicago and London: The University of Chicago Press.

Frank, A.W. (2004) 'Asking the Right Question about pain: Narrative and Phronesis', *Literature and Medicine*, 23(2): 209–225.

Geertz, C. (1973) *The Interpretation of Cultures: Selected essays*, New York: Basic Books.

Gelsthorpe, L. (2007) 'The Jack-Roller: telling a story?' *Theoretical Criminology*, 11(4): 515–542.

Goldie, P. (2000) *The Emotions: A Philosophical Exploration*, Oxford: Oxford University Press.

Gottschalk, L., Kluckhohn, C. and Angell, R. (1945) *The use of personal documents in history, anthropology and sociology*, Social Science Research Council Bulletin, No. 53, New York, Social Science Research Council.

Hacking, I. (1995) *Re-Writing the Soul*, Princeton: Princeton University Press.

Joyce, J. (1922, 2nd edn.) *Ulysses*, Harmondsworth: Penguin.

Kalniete, S. (2006) *With Dance Shoes in Siberian Snow*, Riga: Museum of Occupation.

Kirss, T., Kõresaar, E. and Lauristin, M. (eds) (2004) *She Who Remembers Survives: Interpreting Estonian Women's Post-Soviet Life Stories*, Tartu: Tartu University Press.

Kõresaar, E. (2004) *Memory and History in Estonian Post-Soviet Life Stories: Private and Public, Individual and Collective from the Perspective of Biographical Syncretism*, Dissertationes Etnologiae Universitatis Tartuensis 1, Tartu: Tartu University Press.

Kruks, S. (2004) 'The Latvian epic *Lacplesis*: passe-partout ideology, traumatic imagination of community', *Journal of Folklore Research*, 41(1): 1–32.

Landesco, J. (1929, 2nd edn. 1968) *Organized Crime in Chicago*, Chicago and London: The University of Chicago Press.

MacIntyre, A. (1985) *After Virtue: A Study in Moral Theory*, London: Duckworth.

Mayhew, H. (1851, 2nd edn. 1985) *London Labour and the London Poor*, [Selections and introduction by Victor Neuburg], London: Penguin.

Mintz, S.W. (1960, 2nd edn. 1974) *Worker in the Cane: A Puerto Rican Life History* New, York: Norton Press.

Onken, E-C. (2003) *Demokratisierung der Geschichte in Lettland Staatsburgerliches Bewusstsein und Geschichtspolitik im ersten Jahrzehnt der Unabhangigkeit*, Hamburg: Kramer.

Rowell, S.C. (1994) *Lithuania Ascending: A Pagan Empire within East-central Europe 1295–1345*. Cambridge: Cambridge University Press.

Rozitis, J. (2005) *Displaced Literature Images of Time and Space in Latvian Novels Depicting the First Years of the LatvianPpost-war Exile*, University dissertation from Stockholm: Acta Universitatis Stockholmiensis.

Shaw, C. (1930) (Paperback edn. 1966) *The Jack-Roller. A Delinquent Boy's Own Story*, Chicago and London: The University of Chicago Press.

Shotter, J. (1993) *Conversational Realities: Constructing Life through Language*, London: Sage.

Skultans, V. (1998) *The Testimony of Lives: Narrative and Memory in post-Soviet Latvia*, London: Routledge.

Sutherland, E. (1937: Phoenix edn. 1956, Midway Reprint edn. 1989) *The Professional Thief*, Chicago and London: The University of Chicago Press.

Švābe, A. (1991) *Latvijas vēsture 1800–1914 (History of Latvia. 1800–1914)*. vol. 1. 3rd edn., Rīga: Avots.

Thomas, W.I. and Znaniecki, F. (1927) *The Polish Peasant in Europe and America*, New York: Knopf.

Toker, L. (2000) *Return from the Archipelago: Narratives of Gulag Survivors*, Bloominngton: Indiana University Press.

Upite, R. (1981) *Dear God, I Wanted to Live*, Riga: Grãmatu Draugs.

3 Everyday life, power, and agency in turbulent Latvia

The story of Otto Irbe

Baiba Bela

Introduction

Everyday life has become a significant area of study in modern sociology, possibly due to all essential decisions being made and played out in everyday life, instead of at a special stage or in a specific time. An understanding of the differing models of everyday life enables us to have an external, broader perspective into our own lives and, consequently, our society and times. We can only directly experience our own everyday life, and by default, the lives of other people, especially of other generations and times, are accessible to us only indirectly: through history, literature, or the stories of people about their own experiences.

By using the approach of oral history, I wish to offer an insight into a time and space that has been a turning point in twentieth-century Latvian history and has had a deep and long-term impact on the daily lives of the population. The paper focuses on a complicated and dramatic period in Latvia's history: the 1940s when Latvia experienced one Nazi German and two Soviet occupations, and the 1950s. The relationship of power and agency is discussed on the basis of the life story by Otto Irbe (1916–1998), who represents the generation that grew up when Latvia gained independence in 1918. The Soviet occupation of Latvia on 17 June 1940, dashed the dreams and plans of this generation and forced not only Irbe, but almost two million citizens of Latvia to take on new roles and directions for the rest of their lives. Like many other Latvians in the 1940s and 1950s, Otto Irbe was flung about in the machinations of the two conflicting powers. But unlike many others, Irbe found himself at times on the same side as the authorities in power, and other times in opposition to them. Irbe has been a farmer, a militiaman, a legionnaire, a deserter, a partisan (forest brother), a black-marketer, and finally a prisoner. However, his story is not that of a victim, but rather that of a capable and able person, because in every situation he aspired to retain control over his own life.

The chapter first addresses the research context of the study, and the Latvian collection of life stories. The chapter then examines the relationship between political power and individual agency, based on the personal viewpoint of the period as reflected in Otto Irbe's life story.

Life story research in Latvia

The life story of Otto Irbe is one of approximately 3000 life stories in the Latvian National Oral History (LNOH) collection, which requires a brief explanation.

The movement for the renewal of Latvia's independence in the late 1980s was based largely on the historical memory of the first period of Latvia's independence (1918–1940) and of the crimes against the people of Latvia carried out by the totalitarian Soviet regime (1940, 1944–1991). Life stories have held an important role in the nation's social life after the renewal of Latvian independence in 1991. They formed a new resource for the formation of identity (Tisenkopfs 1993: 4), and were important also in the context of official history of the early 1990s, which was silent about events during the Soviet period (Ķīlis 1998: 124). Life stories were a source of information about historically significant events, such as deportations, resistance movements and dissidents, which had scant documentation and had been the focus of even less research. Likewise, for the first time after the Soviet occupation, people were now able to freely form opinions about life in Latvia during the 1920s and 1930s, repressions in Soviet period and also to talk about the experience of Latvians in exile. The LNOH was established within the Institute of Philosophy and Sociology in Latvia in the early 1990s and took into account the intensive circulation of life stories in the social environment and the necessity to shape an interpretation of recent history that would be attuned to people's experience of those events.

The primary goal of the LNOH project is to document as many accounts and testimonies of the everyday life lives of the inhabitants of Latvia during the complex and contradictory twentieth century, thereby recording events from the points of view of the participants. Second, the project aims to preserve life stories both as a cultural heritage and as a source of study for researchers from various disciplines making use of testimonies of oral history. Third, the project aims to perform life story research. Fourth, one of the essential tasks assigned to the LNOH project is the integration of the nation, thereby facilitating the unification of the experience of the Latvian nation, which was divided by the Second World War and the Soviet occupation. Over the past 15 years a considerable archive of life stories has been created. In addition, research studies have been performed, the results of which are reflected in more than 70 scientific publications in Latvia and abroad. The LNOH archives consist of thematic collections, such as the project 'House', which includes life story interviews with the inhabitants of a single tenement block in Riga, interviews recorded by LNOH project researchers and trained volunteers throughout Latvia and collections of memoirs submitted by Latvian scholars. The life stories have been recorded in all regions of Latvia, as well as in the exiled Latvian communities of America, England, Canada, Germany, Sweden, Norway, Brazil and Russia (Bela 2008: 88–91).

The life story of Otto Irbe was recorded in Riga in 1996 and preserved in the LNOH archive (as LNOH 327) in the form of handwritten memories (two notebooks, recompiled as 79 pages of computer printout), as well as an oral narrative (approximately six hours of recordings). Irbe's oral memories covering his entire life story are more spontaneous and more detailed than the written, but are less structured and use simpler language. Irbe's written memories ending with the experience of imprisonment in the Gulag are, by contrast, well-structured and more frequently contain patriotic evaluations of events, and the language is more poetic. This paper uses the written version of Irbe's memories.

Irbe's life story expressively reveals history in the making, particularly the characteristics of totalitarianism and its impact on an individual's life. The analysis of Irbe's life story concentrates on such aspects of totalitarian power as the mechanisms of involvement, control of inhabitants, types of limits on personal freedoms and various methods of state aggression. Particular attention is paid to individual endeavours to retain personal freedom by using various forms of resistance, as revealed by the story. The analysis reviews several aspects of the guerrilla movement of the forest brothers: survival strategies, forms of resistance and forms of support.

Oral history and relationship with the other

Everyday life, power, and agency will be explored from the oral history perspective. Oral history has contributed to broadening and democratizing the scope of history research. From a discipline focused on power and politics, history is turning into a discipline concerned with ordinary people and their day-to-day lives in changing communities. Oral history is a form of history in which ordinary people, who have often been denied the right to speak by the dominant discourse, regain their voices. Oral history also, as Thompson explains, enables researchers to take a close look at people's lives, views and actions (2000: 3, 117).

But oral history is more than reconstruction of past experiences or creation of new, alternative sources for research. Oral history is a space of dialogue between people or a space of understanding that builds bridges of understanding between generations or between different ethnic, cultural or social groups.

First, oral history brings to light the understanding of the past. Oral history establishes relations between the lived experience of people of other times or places, and today's researchers and readers. Life stories can therefore help to reconstruct the lived, non-repeatable experience and bring a narrative understanding to the field of historical or societal knowledge. As American oral historian Ronald Grele explains 'oral history has a unique role to play in revealing in detail the ways in which the processes of that world impinge upon everyday lives upon those caught up in those changes' (2007: 20).

Second, a life story is a dialogue between two human beings: the speaker and the listener. We must listen to narratives not only because of the authenticity of experience, but simply because the narrator is a human being (Skultans 2007: 34). There is an important ethical dimension in the telling of a life story. I will use the term 'ethical' in the sense of the philosophy of Emmanuel Levinas, whose central theme is the relationship with the Other. We are responsible for the Other and this responsibility is prior to epistemology, ontology or philosophy; there is no 'why' regarding this responsibility, as the responsibility is neither intellectual nor intelligible. Ethical attitude and responsibility towards the Other is connected to the relationship with the Other as a relationship to the face. 'Face' in Levinas' sense is not what we can see, a nose, eyes, lips, but rather 'the face in its nudity is the weakness of a unique being exposed to death, but at the same time an enunciation of an imperative which obliges me not to let it alone' (Levinas 2001: 236, cited in Lapinska 2007: 52). We can consider a life story as either or both a face of a narrator and as a manifestation of the Other. A life story can introduce an ethical attitude towards the Other in our everyday life as it allows us to have a close look at the vulnerability of another human being and to establish the relations of proximity with their otherness.

Third, the question of dialogue and relationship between I and the Other has yet more dimensions. Human existence is always coexistent and relationships between I and Other can be developed either as dialogue or conflict. Levinas notes that European consciousness is oriented towards the unity of the One that disturbs all alterity. The being 'drunk with being in himself and for himself' attitude towards Other as an object or stranger results in exploitation of the human being, world wars, cruelty of fascism, Stalinism, as well as unemployment and poverty (Levinas 1999: 5, 132, 136). Dialogue is possible only when you recognize equality of the different Other. Oral history in this sense introduces dialogue on the stage of history. Others, ordinary people, minority groups, children, family etc., regain their faces and voices. Simultaneously, an examination of particular life stories discovers dialogues and conflicts between I and Other of different times and spaces. Irbe's story clearly shows this disturbing consciousness, mentioned by Levinas; an orientation towards one's own ideal truth, and the relationship to the Other as a stranger. Contradictions between certain projects of politics open up contradictions and violence between human beings.

A change in Irbe's life path; the Soviet occupation of 1940

Otto Irbe was born in 1916 in the small rural district of Birzgale, central Latvia. He finished his army service in 1939, aged 23. In 1940 he planned to take over the management of the farm bestowed on him by his grandfather and to take out a large loan to purchase farm equipment and pure-bred livestock. However, the events of 17 June 1940 ruined these intentions when the Soviet army occupied Latvia, causing Irbe to postpone borrowing the money. The 'cell' of local Communist Party activists took over the governance of the district. This was the year that Otto Irbe's life path began the roller-coaster ride of twists and turns towards the labour camp in the Gulag Archipelago. The power relationship between totalitarianism and an individual is clearly revealed in the episode in which the Communist Party 'cell' votes Otto Irbe into the ancillary service without Irbe's knowledge. The duty of assisting in the maintenance of public order and safety had previously been performed by the Latvian paramilitary organization, Aizsargi, which the Soviets had dissolved on 18 June 1940. The next stage of Irbe's life path was the communists' proposal that he become a people's militia-man, to which Irbe consented after a long exhortation. The challenge of power is at the same time a challenge to the conscience of morals. Irbe only consented to the position after a long exhortation by the communists and Irbe remembers his mother's consequent cry of distress: 'Oh, son, now you've become a servant of murderers and executioners' (LNOH 327). Otto Irbe's mother clearly remembered the behaviour of communist activists during the short-lived Latvijas Sociālistiskā Padomju Republika (Latvian Soviet Socialist Republic, 1918–1920). She did not harbour any illusions that this time the Soviet rule would be different or any less violent.

Otto Irbe became a member of the people's militia in the municipality of Jumprava and later in Skrīveri. His narrative about this period reflects a highly complex relationship with power. First, Otto Irbe uses the authority bestowed on him by his position to turn upon those members of the people's militia who persecuted former members of the *Aizsargi* and the *budži*. Many of the people's militia treated the protection of public order not so much as combating crime, but prosecuting individuals of the 'incorrect' (i.e. non or anti-communist) political persuasion. Second, using the information, to which Irbe's post allowed access, sometimes served as an early warning system for those people who had unfortunately come to the attention of the MGB (Ministry for State Security). For instance, as the militia was involved in raiding the homes and work places of potentially suspicious people, Irbe could warn them about impending visits. Despite this activity, Irbe notes he did not, at the time, understand the MGB's mechanisms of power. Third, Irbe acquires a form of meaningful power through a friendly relationship with a policeman from the time of Ulmanis' authoritarian regime. Irbe absorbs this policeman's knowledge and experience, which enables him to combat crime in the municipality with success.

The events of 14 June 1941 marked a new turn in Irbe's relationship with power when more than 15,000 people were deported to Siberia and his relations with communist activists became strained. During the second week of June, Irbe went to visit his parents and upon his return he heard that arrests were going on and the arrested people were being placed aboard freight trains used for transportation of cattle at the railway station. Subsequent events, revolving around his inability to gain access to the cattle wagons, proved the insignificance of Irbe authority. A particularly significant episode occurred when Irbe took an arrested acquaintance's spectacles to them, which had been left behind. Although Irbe was a respected and influential militiaman, he had great difficulty in persuading one of the guards to hand the spectacles to the person in the cattle wagon. Furthermore, the locals associated Irbe, as a member of the militia, with Soviet authority and, therefore, to the organizers of the deportations. In Irbe's own words:

> From all that, only then did I realize how small and powerless I am from some greater power. I could not sleep at night, was totally shattered. On the following day, when I met the [communist] party secretary, I asked why and what had happened here. First of all I got cursed at, where had I disappeared to? She thought I must have gone with them! [The Party secretary told me] 'All that needs to be like that and you need not to worry about it'. The days went on heavy and difficult. I went out in the street as little as possible, so as not to meet people. When I had to go out, meeting the passers-by, it seemed they looked at me with contempt. Formerly kind greetings now seemed heavy, coming from dour faces. Did they really think of me as a servant of this awful power? But what else could they think?

After a period of gloomy reflection, Irbe went to Riga to hand in his resignation, but the authorities could no longer be reached.

The German occupation of 1941–1944

The change of power in 1941 consequent to Hitler's Operation Barbarossa and the German armies' invasion of Soviet territories marked the beginning of the Second World War in the Baltic region. Many Latvians, particularly the families and friends of arrested, deported and missing people, initially viewed the Germany occupying forces as liberators. But it soon became quite evident that the German regime, like any totalitarian regime, existed on the principle 'either with us, or against us'. As a former Soviet militiaman, Irbe was taken to Riga Prefecture, where people whom he had helped during his militia service produced positive testimonials, and he was acquitted. Irbe's decision in 1942 to voluntarily enlist in the Latvian Legion and the Latvian School of Aviation, thereby accepting the authority of the occupying power, was a matter of survival rather than support of Nazism.

The formation of ethnic Latvian units within the Waffen-SS remains to this day a hotly debated topic. At the time, many Latvians considered the move was an illegal and politically short-sighted one that would eventually be interpreted at the international level as collaboration with the Nazi regime. However, just as many others saw the move as an opportunity not only to take revenge for those the Soviets had killed or deported, but also for preventing the Soviet Union from occupying Latvia again. Furthermore, there was also the naïve belief in a repeat of 1918, when Latvia gained independence in the midst of a war between Russia and Germany. The legionnaires shared this belief, as reflected in the popular legionnaires' song with the lyrics 'We'll bash the reds and then the blue-grays' and the word-play of the shouted salute of 'Lej litrā' (Latvian for 'pour in a litre') instead of 'Heil Hitler'. But irrespective of whether the legionnaires were fighting for a Nazi victory or the independence of Latvia, Irbe was primarily interested in survival:

> In 1942 the German army suffered heavy losses in the east. In order to fill those losses, a call up, or the drafting of volunteers, into the Legion began. As

> a friend to a friend, Kārkliņš [a police chief] suggested joining the legion. It's possible that there might be more arrests, and you can't be sure how the locals will look at you; you might be pulled along. He would wish to save me, but by then it might be too late. I understood what that meant! I went to Riga and got permission from the Legion to join the Latvian School of Aviation.

In 1944, Irbe was shot down on his first flying mission, flying in the direction of Koenigsberg, and although parachuting to the ground he was injured on landing. Partly restored to health by the local Germans, Irbe left for Latvia and several months later returned to his parents' home. In July 1944, Soviet army formations invaded Latvia, at which point Irbe decided, as the Germans had clearly lost the war, there was no point in fighting. But there was still sense in living and Irbe decided that the war would go on without him and became a deserter hiding at his parents' home. Perhaps Irbe was not valiant, but at least he was alive and not starving in a military camp.

Life in the forest brotherhood: 1944–1952

Irbe remained in hiding in his parent's house until May 1945, because the Soviets would have sent him to the labour camps as a former legionnaire. Hiding in his parent's house quickly became too dangerous and Irbe joined the partisans ('forest brothers') in the forests until 1952. This period of his life marks a resistance to the political power of the occupiers, as well as an enforcement of power over himself (control over his own life). For the next seven years Irbe led a clandestine way of living, characterized by secretive communications with supporters and confederates in other forests, and hiding from the official power. Irbe's story reveals the routine of the resistance movement within the totalitarian environment and the gradual changes in Latvia as the Soviet power used increasingly aggressive methods to assert their control over Latvia and the consequent strategies of survival and resistance of Latvian people. The most divisive method in the Soviet's assertion of control were the activities of the 'destruction battalions' in combination with those of the MGB, the people's militia and Communist Party activists. By contrast, the most unifying movement for the Latvian populace was the armed resistance of the partisans. While most of the populace of an invaded country suffers the yoke of occupation in silence, only the bravest and most arduous resist. The concept 'resistance movement' denotes disobedience to an occupying regime, its institutions, and public, political and religious organizations (Strods 2001: 592). Resistance can be divided into armed and unarmed and active and passive forms. Strods (1996) argues a national partisan war is military combat for national independence organized by a small nation against an overwhelming aggressor. Irbe's account is therefore both a testimony of individual experience, as well as an insight into the relationship between an occupying power and a resistance movement, which affected the post-war everyday life of thousands of Latvians. The only untypical aspect of Irbe's story is that he spent seven years in the forest, whereas the average life span of a forest brother was approximately two years due to injuries, disease and return to civilian life (Misiunas and Taagapera 1993: 86). In 1952, Irbe managed to successfully return to civilian life using forged documents, which was a typical survival strategy for forest brothers in all three Baltic states (Misiunas and Taagapera 1993: 93).

The Soviet occupation of Latvia was based on the concept of an internal and external enemy (Strods 2001: 592). The search for the internal enemy (of anti-communist elements) and the control of the people began immediately after the territory had been liberated from Nazi powers. Initially Irbe attempted to retain his freedom by hiding in the house of his parents who constructed a bunker for Irbe to hide in when Communist Party activists and members of the destruction battalions arranged visits to search for anyone who did not have a registered place of residence. Registered residents, like Irbe's parents, had to certify that no strangers were staying in their living space. These searches became too dangerous and Irbe eventually joined those who had already sought freedom in the forests. Irbe characterizes the mood and situation of these people soon after the capitulation in 1945:

> But then at the end of May or the beginning of June, depending on the region, the news spread that armed men had appeared in the forests, who had not surrendered to Russian captivity. Women, old men and children cheered, they will be our saviors! They began to fish out guns, grenades, cartridges, mines and various other weapons. Here and there the newcomers themselves appeared, the 'forest brothers'. Women ran in joy from neighbor to neighbor, sang and waved fists in the air, now these devils are finally finished, now we are saved—hurrah! [...] The American 'Free Voice' also confirmed it all. [...] We were amply supported and bestowed with presents. (LNOH 327)

The forest brothers were well armed, as a document by Colonel Polyikarpov (Fourth Department of the State Security Committee of the Latvian SSR's Council of Ministers) notes when between 1944 and 1956 5 mortars, 738 machine guns, 3287 automatic guns, 11,863 guns, 3193 pistols, 8835 hand grenades, 1306 cartridges, 5177 mortar bombs and almost 4 tons of explosives were confiscated from 'bandits, outlaws, and inhabitants' (Strods 1999: 587, 588).

Irbe describes the negative attitude people had against Soviet occupying power manifesting in the support and help provided by local people to the partisans, the hopes the partisans would defeat the occupiers, as well as in the mechanisms used by the MGB that served to create fear among the populace and to cut the partisans' support within a few years. The Soviet regime's keys to success were the methods of fear creation, which Irbe's story recounts.

First, he mentions various forms of control over the inhabitants: the unexpected searches and inspections of the residential register books and residences of suspected supporters; document and luggage inspections at trains and stations and the placement of sentries for extended surveillance in potentially suspicious houses.

Second, Irbe's story reveals the aggressively divisive methods of the totalitarian regime: raids on work places and homes, arrests (Irbe's parents were also arrested and severely beaten), torture, searching the forests and combat operations. Irbe notes four operations against the partisans in which the KGB, local employees of the Ministry of the Interior and the army participated. A list of Soviet army combat operations, compiled in 1955, gives 60 combat operations in the district of Riga (this district includes the forests in which Irbe's group hid) during the period from 1944 until 1951 (Strods 1999: 617, 618). Irbe also talks about the persecution of particular groups of inhabitants (farmers who had owned large farms, members of the *Aizsargi*, legionnaires, partisans, their relatives and supporters) as well as social demagogy (tactics of inducement, such as offers of amnesty to the partisans). Particular tactics of demonstration and intimidation used by the Soviet power were the exhibition of dead partisans for public viewing and acts of outrage performed on the dead.

Irbe's story illustrates the resistance to the state's aggression. His story focuses on active forms of resistance: the armed resistance, as well as various forms of support given to the forest brothers. Irbe reveals the survival strategy of the partisans and their temporal and seasonal dynamics. The partisans initially lived in large groups, sheltering in bunkers in the summer but hiding at the homes of relatives or acquaintances during the winter. Later, when finding food for large numbers became difficult, they started to live in smaller groups. At this stage they were using tents and lean-tos in summer and bunkers in winter, as by then hiding with acquaintances had become too dangerous. Winter was the most fraught season for the forest brothers, because it was difficult to hide tracks in the snow and there were certain movements vital to the welfare of the partisans, such as the exchange of information or the transfer of fighters from one group to another for a number of various reasons (food supply difficulties, skirmishes, changes of resting places, treason, etc.). The partisans were self-sufficient: they wove baskets and hoops for sowing, which the farmers exchanged for food; in places where they were not recognized as partisans, they did odd jobs for cash payments and they also forged documents. Irbe's story depicts four operations against the representatives of Soviet power: two related to stealing the party candidates' food reserves; one against three members of the destruction battalion in Vidzeme who terrorized the locals (however, Irbe tells us nothing of their fate); and during the fourth operation the partisans disarmed a female postal carrier from Jumprava (the motivation being that Irbe's father lacked a proper gun). Irbe notes also several fights involving the use of arms, but they all occurred in defence of Soviet attacks.

The narrative marks out the diverse relationship between the partisans and the local people, encompassing both support and treason. The supporters were mostly close relatives, friends and acquaintances. Irbe mentions various forms of support: food, clothing, provision of shelter for the night, tools, materials and medical aid. The story also shows how the locals' support for partisans decreased with the increasing control by the state and the repressions committed by the MGB and officials of the Ministry of the Interior. Irbe relates that by 1948 almost all of the most courageous supporters had been convicted or deported and the remainder had become uncommunicative. This is the probable reason for Irbe omitting any mention of the deportations on 25, March 1949, when approximately 42,000 people, mainly peasants, where deported. This event is considered as genocide of the Latvian peasants (Bleiere 2001: 579). Only after the deportations was the idea of collective farming widely accepted. At the beginning of 1949, only 8 per cent of Latvian farms had been collectivized, but by April the proportion had risen to 50 per cent and by the end of the year, 93 per cent of farms had been 'voluntarily' collectivized (Misiunas and Taagapere 1993: 102).

The section of Irbe's story concerning the 'forest brothers' comprises more than 50 of the 79 printout pages. It is difficult to choose an excerpt that illustrates typical daily life for the partisans. The narrated events flow into one another and often include references to previously narrated events or those yet to come in the story. However, Irbe does relate the experiences of a trek through the forests, which demonstrates many aspects of the partisans' daily lives such as the reciprocal networks, the depravity of Soviet functionaries and the attitude towards the Soviet regime.

> I crossed the Daugava [river] towards the forests of Vidzeme in order to visit the forest brothers living there. They have united into a larger group. Siliņš and Liepiņš, who have both been seen in previous years, have joined them. There was also news about Grosbergs, Kalniņš (Bārdiņš) and Alis, who was with us in Birzgale in 1946. Somewhere in the area of Koknese or Bebri all of these guys became victims of treason and were burned in a hay barn. No more details are available. Kārkliņš invited us to go to Taurupe; he had relatives or some good acquaintances living there. I was not familiar with that area, but Kārkliņš had topographical military maps, so we followed those and took off on a trek through the forests. We made a small camp of tents in a large forest. We were tired and soaked through; we dried out and drank tea (water with no sugar). The house that was our destination was probably still five or more kilometers away. The next day around noon we drew straws to see who would have to leave and who was to stay in camp. Vēzītis, Skujiņš, Siliņš, Leitis, me and, of course, Kārkliņš. Liepiņš and Krēgers stayed. In general the forests of Vidzeme were lush, swampy, with lots of grass and overgrown firebreaks. Kārkliņš led the way and suddenly gave a sign to stop and be silent. He swung his gun up to his shoulder and a shot rang out! When we walked up to it, we saw a buck lying on the ground. Shot right in the head, dead on the spot. He was a great marksman.
>
> (LNOH 327)

Here we can see many aspects of life in the forests, migration as a survival strategy, the death of comrades, size of partisan group, everyday life in the forest including getting soaked through and drying out, decision making (drawing lots), some idea of their nutrition (herb teas, the lack of sugar, wild venison).

> My assignment was to go scouting, to 'sniff the air'. Not far away was a house, surrounded by forest and with a stream flowing around it. A woman came out of the house and looked towards the forest. I assumed that she had probably heard the shot. I looked and listened, there was nothing suspicious, so I approached her. I gave her Kārkliņš's greeting and asked for permission to come inside. She said that everything was OK, nothing suspicious had been noticed, and to come on in. I told her that there would be more of us, Kārkliņš too. Fine, fine, she said. In the meantime the boys had already processed the deer, and we went. The housekeeper cried out of joy, as if she had welcomed very dear guests and saviors. She ran to two nearby houses to tell about the visitors. Two other women and their children came. They began to prepare dinner. I had got chilled on the journey and did not feel very well. They told me to lie down in the warm area by the stove and brought me a home-brewed 'čarka' to drive away the sickness. It had been years since I had had such a warm rest, and I fell asleep. Around midnight they woke me up for dinner. The room smelled like a roast and the table was set. It was obvious that they had once been very good cooks and homemakers. The other men have also each got a 'čarka' and have become more helpful, more supple, more talkative and are telling jokes.
>
> (LNOH 327)

This episode is quite exceptional, because Irbe seldom mentions groups of partisans entering supporters' homes. This excerpt repeats the motif, mentioned earlier of the communication of neighbour housewives and their very positive attitude towards the forest brothers. The excerpt also illuminates the contrast between home (female domain) and the forest (male domain), which Vieda Skultans identifies, in that forest give shelter to dangerous men, but homes give shelter to women and children (2007: 47).

> The husbands of these wives have been arrested and deported. They are not afraid of hard work, but it's the attitude of the local Communists that is unbearable. When they go from house to house, supposedly searching, they break open cupboards and drawers, as if there were weapons hidden in them … and rings and jewelry go missing. They call locals in for questioning and keep them until late at night, but during that time others go to break open their granaries and cellars and steal things. They smash whatever they don't take, put manure in the milk cans, etc. Tears and more tears, curses and laments; the things these women and children have been forced to endure. It brings to mind somber memories of my own mother, who was beaten black-and-blue by the Chekists and then thrown out onto the street in the middle of the night. Kicked, fingers and arms broken, called a bandit whore, and all so that she would confess and tell them where her son was hiding. She, poor thing, crawled and pulled herself to the train station in order to warm herself a little and recover a bit. I was distraught and shocked. That night when I listened to those women, I relived all of those emotions in an inexpressible

hate. A person who has not experienced it himself and has not felt such things about his dearest people will never understand and will never feel such pain.

(LNOH 327)

This episode characterizes the worst part of everyday life under the Stalinist era of Soviet regime: the vulnerability of any individual associated as an enemy of the Soviet regime; the threatening impunity of officials and the total helplessness of ordinary people. Irbe also depicts feelings as the important driving force of life.

Life with forged documents

In 1952, the status and life of Irbe changed significantly after an attack in which his forest bunker was destroyed and some of his fellows killed or arrested. The following excerpt illustrates Irbe's search for security after the attack and informs about the fate of one supporter of forest brothers (Jānis Vēzītis) and at least two members of the group (Lideris and Lukstiņš):

> I was left alone after my father was arrested. The activity of the Cheka is felt all around. Our benefactors and supporters have also cooled and become reserved. Everyone has lost faith in a different, better future. I want to meet some of those who are wandering around after the attack on March 28. But I don't succeed, everything is a risk. There are rumors that Jānis Vēzītis and his whole family have been arrested at the headquarters in Krape. And Augusts Lideris has become entangled with some Chekist spies and is now missing. (There are also spies truly roaming about, not just rumors of it!) The woman living on the 'Kalna Žagari' farmstead has betrayed Lukstiņš. There was nothing known about the others. It was as if a dark, impassable swamp lay between me and life … But one can't give up so easily; I searched for old acquaintances. I remembered one with whom I had worked together in the motorists' group during the construction of the Ķegums power plant. It was Viktors Sloka in Laubere (or maybe Zādzene). I didn't know anything about him. Maybe he had turned red or was a Chekist? I looked him up. He lived in his own home and he hadn't been affected by the regime, but he cursed these times and the Communists. But neither have forest brothers been noticed in this area, and it's possible that that's the reason the Cheka hasn't paid more attention here. He had a broken, lame leg and said that I could come in handy with the field work. But I couldn't stay there for long, either, because the neighbors had started to take an interest in the unfamiliar young man. Viktor's brother drove a taxi in Riga, but nothing sensible came out of that for me, either. So then I wandered back to Skrīveri and Zinaīda. She had been dismissed from her job as the executive committee secretary and was now living in an empty room at the post office. But it was not safe to stay there, either.

Otto Irbe searched for other means of survival and with his girlfriend Zinaīda began a semi-legal life in the eastern part of Latvia, Latgale, under a different name. He had acquired the skills of document-forging and produced the necessary documents: a passport, a military service certificate and work certificates. Officially Otto Irbe was Arnolds Auziķis, an engineer at a republican local-level road administration, but in reality he earned his living with various activities that qualified as speculation at the time. He bought wool that was subsequently spun into yarn. Together with his girlfriend (she worked at a Soviet farm) he dyed it and knitted sweaters and cardigans for sale in Riga's 'black market'.

Unfortunately, Otto Irbe was taken into custody in Riga in 1956 and was compelled to succumb to the repressive mechanisms of the regime. He lost control over his own life and spent several years in penitentiary institutions.

Short note on life in prison, and after return to Latvia

Despite the death of Stalin in 1953 and the amnesties of 1955 and 1956, Irbe was still considered to be an enemy of the Soviet state and experienced interrogation by the KGB, a court trial, prison and labour camp No. ŻX-385/7 in Mordovia. Irbe's parents, who had been sent to labour camps in 1952, had returned and were able to give moral support to Irbe at his trial in May 1956. The penalty for being a partisan of '10 + 5' (10 years in strong regime camp and 5 years without rights) was more lenient than the death penalty or '25 + 5' sentences of previous years.

Irbe spent nine years in the Mordovia labour camp. The time of his arrival to camp coincides with the releases of those who had been convicted of 'stealing of bread and support of forest brothers' (LNOH 327). Each day more than 20 people went home. Irbe did not work for a while and spent his time playing music, then he worked in the camp library and attended courses for electric welding, lathe operating and driving. Irbe experiences upheaval and a strike in his camp in 1957. According to his story, all the strike demands were promised to be upheld to satisfy the inmates, but immediately afterwards the army occupied the camp and arrested the leaders and most active participants of the strike. Soon after the strike, Irbe was invited to work in the camp's power station (Latvians and Estonians were highly esteemed in the camp because of their work skills and accuracy) as a lathe operator and quality inspector. Irbe's story shows the working and daily life in the camp, including relationships between inmates and the conflicts, the suicides, and attempts to escape the camp.

Here the written story ends, but continues with the oral interview. After returning to Latvia, Irbe stayed with his parents in Birzgale, but there was nothing to do. The work conditions and salary on the *sovkhoz* were even worse than in the labour camp. Irbe decided to go to Riga to look for a bride. In 1966 he married and in 1969 had a daughter. Irbe continued to work as welder, but also as a locksmith. His work at the large and renowned State Factory for Electrotechnics was acquired through his wife's connections, but it was a long way from his home and soon he left to find a job within walking distance. Until he retired, Irbe worked at an institute for blind people, doing all the necessary metal work. He also continued his school years' hobby by playing in the blind people's orchestra. In the 1980s in Skrīveri, Irbe's photograph and name were exhibited on the desk of honour, naming him one of the best militiamen in Skrīveri history (it was a common practice in the Soviet period that the best workers were honoured by a public display of their photos and names on special desks in their workplaces or communities). Unfortunately, the officials found out that Irbe had not only guarded the safety of the Soviet people, but had also endangered it as a 'bandit' (the official name for forest brothers in the Soviet period) and removed his photograph from the desk.

End note – the times and the story

The life story of Otto Irbe takes us into a different world and introduces us to everyday life in a totalitarian environment, the three occupations of the Second World War and the early post-war years of the Soviet regime in Latvia. The story shows us the influence of a malign ideology, of a framework of power and of the relationship between the populace and a regime's political activists that can have an affect on our everyday lives when personal freedoms and personal choice have become severely restricted.

In addition to being a portrait of an era, Irbe's story can also show us aspects important in the life of any person. For example, issues of power and fairness, or of good versus bad. It is difficult in everyday life to always clearly disassociate binary oppositions. An individual can find themselves alternating from one binary opposite to the other, depending on the perspective of the ruling power. Invariably, in the circumstances of multiple occupations by totalitarian regimes, Irbe's choice of roles was beneficial to one regime but detrimental to the next or vice versa (see Table 3.1). Irbe's story clearly shows us that the extremes of binary opposites are relative and that each person determines the moral parameters for their own life by drawing their own personal dividing line between the opposites.

Irbe's story also reveals complicated and often conflicting relationships between I and the Other. There are a great many Others ranging from named individuals and societal groups to the relatively anonymous umbrella organizations of the two key overarching structures influencing Irbe's life story, the Soviet and Nazi regimes. Irbe's Others are friendly and some are not. Some are portrayed with empathy and with responsibility regarding their lives and destinies. Some are portrayed neutrally, but some, the alien, hostile strangers, with no particular face, against whom shooting and warring is necessary, anger and hate are the dominant emotions. The same can be said regarding the reaction towards Irbe, some see him as the Other with a face, some as a faceless stranger and a representative of a hostile power. We can see it is easier to be hostile if you do not see the face of the Other, if the latter remains just some faceless representative of an abstract concept, especially an ideologically interpreted social group.

Essentially, every life story is a dialogue, which expresses the narrator's face and Otherness. A life story is a dialogue with oneself; with the listener or reader; with a particular period of time, in either or both the present and the past. We

Table 3.1 Binary opposite perspectives on Irbe's choice of roles and the choices of partisan supporters

Irbe's roles	*Latvian republican*	*Communist Soviet occupier*	*Nazi German occupier*
Farmer (pre-1940)	(+)		
People's Militia 1940	(–)	(+)	
People's Militia post-1940	(–)		(–)
Legionnaire 1944	(+)	(–)	(+)
Deserter			(–)
Ex-Legionnaire 1945		(–)	
Partisan	(+)	(–)	
Black Marketer		(–)	
Prisoner (Gulag)		(+)	
Others' roles			
Partisan supporter	(+)	(–)	
Partisan supporter turned traitor	(–)	(+)	

Note
Perspectives (+) = positive/beneficial (–) = negative/detrimental.

can look at a life story as a historical testimony or as a resource for analysis, but I wish to remind the reader that a life story is always also a testimony about the narrator. A life story is about the fragility and tenacity of a person's existence and the necessity of sharing one's experience and to form a conversation, in order to be understood and to understand the Other.

References

Bela, B. (2008) 'Dzīvesstāsti kā resurss sabiedrības izpētē: Nacionālās mutvārdu vēstures projekts' ('Life stories in the research of society: National Oral History Project'), *Scientific Papers University of Latvia, 736. Sociology*, Riga: University of Latvia.

Bleiere, D. (2001) 'Represijas pret zemniecību Latvijā 1944–1953.' ('Repressions against farmers in Latvia in 1944–1953'), *Latvijas vēsturnieku komisijas raksti. 3. sēj. Totalitārie režīmi un to represijas Latvijā 1940.–1956. gadā*, Rīga: Latvijas Vēstures institūta apgāds.

Ezergailis, A. (ed.) (1997) *The Latvian Legion: Heroes, Nazis or Victims? A collection of documents from OSS war-crimes investigation files. 1945–1950*, Riga: Historical Institute of Latvia.

Grele, Ronald J. (2007) 'Reflections on the practice of Oral History', *Suomen Anthropologi. Journal of the Finnish Antropological Society*, 4: 11–23.

Otto, H. (2000) 'How the Germans conscripted "volunteers" for the Latvian Legion', in *Symposium of the Commission of the Historians of Latvia, vol. 1. Latvia in World War II*, Riga: Historical Institute of Latvia.

Ķīlis, R. (1998) *Sociālā atmiņa un nacionālā identitāte Latvijā* (*Social Memory and National Identity in Latvia*), Rīga: N.I.M.S.

Lapinska, I. (2007) 'Relationship with the Other as grounds for value system', in M. Kūle *et al.* (eds) *Dilemmas of Values and Contemporary life-World*, Riga: LU FSI.

Levinas, E. (1999) *Alterity and Transcendence*, New York: Columbia University Press.

—— (2001) 'On the usefulness of insomnia', in J. Robbins (ed.) *Is It Righteous to Be? Interviews with Emmanuel Levinas*, Stanford: Stanford University Press.

Misiunas, R. and Taagapera, R. (1993) *The Baltic States. Years of Dependence 1940–1990*, London: Hurst & Company.

Skultāns, V. (2007) 'Mutvārdu vēstures pētīšanas nozīmīgums Latvijā' ('The significance of oral history research in Latvia'), in M. Zirnīte (ed.) *Dzīvesstāsti: vēsture, kultūra, sabiedrība*, Rīga: LU FSI.

Strods, H. (1996) *Nacionālo partizānu karš* (*The National Guerilla Warfare*), Rīga: Preses nams.

—— (1999) *Latvijas nacionālo partizāņu karš Dokumenti un materiāli 1944–1956 (The Latvian National Guerilla Warfare. Documents and materials 1944–1956*, Rīga: Preses nams.

—— (2001) 'Latvijas skolu jaunatnes nacionālā pretošanās kustība, 1944. gads—50' ('The national resistance movement of Latvian school youth, 1944—mid-1950s'). *Latvijas vēsturnieku komisijas raksti. 3. sēj. Totalitārie režīmi un to represijas Latvijā 1940.–1956. gadā*, Rīga: Latvijas Vēstures institūta apgāds.

Tisenkopfs, T. (1993) 'Dzīve un teksts' ('Life and text'), *LZA Vēsti*, 5(93): 1–8.

Thompson, P. (2000) *The Voices of the Past*, London: Oxford University Press.

4 The collective strategies of Latvian Second World War refugees adapting to Swedish society

Maija Runcis

Introduction

Throughout history people have migrated across the Baltic Sea for a variety reasons. War, revolution, famine, as well as expectations of a better future on another shore, have caused people to leave their homes and look for new dwelling places, temporary or permanent. In 1945, Sweden hosted about 35,000 Baltic refugees who in most cases sought a safe refuge from the German–Russian war front. About 5000 Latvian and 30,000 Estonian refugees were assembled in various refugee camps in Sweden (for a general view concerning the numbers of Second World War refugees in Sweden see chapter 2 of Olsson 1997). They had, having avoided the Red Army's relentless invasion from the east, managed to flee across the Baltic Sea during the cold and dark nights of autumn 1944 and the winter of 1944–1945. As refugees, they were naturally extremely anxious about their immediate future. Should they return home, or remain in Sweden, or would they be compelled to flee further westward to escape feared Soviet communist reprisals in Sweden? Many refugee testimonies witness the personal convictions that everyone would return home as soon as the war was over. One example is the former president of Latvia, Vaira Viķe-Freiberga, who relates in her life story how her mother cleaned the house and hung new curtains at the window so it would be nice to return home when the war was over (Cimdiņa 2003). Indeed, many refugees during the first years of exile never even unpacked their suitcases in the hope that it would be possible to return home. The Balts had a strong belief that the Western allies would not leave the Baltic states within the Soviet Union, but they were wrong (Stiver-Lie *et al.* 2007). Quite soon after the war, Latvian and Estonian refugees started to create a new life in Sweden by learning a new language, starting new families, getting an education, and by working. They also started to organize new cultural institutions and transnational committees to maintain contacts with fellow Balts in other host countries. The Latvians in exile formed ethnic communities in their places of settlement, often in or near major cities: Toronto, New York, Chicago, San Francisco, Sydney, Melbourne, London, Stockholm, and Hamburg.

In this article I focus on the Latvians in Sweden and their efforts to create a new life in exile (see Šūpulis and Bormane 2007). As source material I use some life stories recorded in 1996 by participants of the Latvian National Oral History (LNOH) project. In this project, 24 interviews were collected in 1996 with Latvian-born Swedes and a further 20 in 2006. The majority were conducted with people who left Latvia by boat from Kurland (the west coast of Latvia) and a small number with people coming from Germany. For a more detailed presentation of the LNOH project, see Chapter 3.

One intention of this chapter is to explore the specificity of life stories as source material and the conceptual and theoretical implications of the way this source is to be treated. However, as a scholar of history, I also want to comment on the recorded life stories and their limitations in respect of my research. In Latvia, life stories have taken an important space and place in 'the nation's social life after the renewal of Latvian independence' (Beļa, ch. 3, p. 38). In Sweden, most people and researchers trust the Swedish state and state archives, which is not always the situation in the former Soviet Baltic republics. During the Soviet era people never completely trusted any Soviet institutions and, conversely, the regime did not trust the people and the archives were closed to ordinary people (Kirss and Hinrikus 2010). But nowadays, after the Baltic states regained their independence, people still do not trust the officials and the official history writing. The problem is that history and historical symbols, such as the Bronze Soldier in Tallinn, have often been used as political accusations between former national enemies and new governments. The fact that history is still being used as a political weapon in the former Soviet republics is exactly the issue that has led the citizens of these countries to lose faith in state history writing. During the entire Soviet era, history writing had more to do with ideology than with science. Partly in order to deal with this issue, historians' commissions were established in the three Baltic states and given the task of investigating communist crimes against humanity.

Another way of dealing with the citizens' deep-rooted distrust of public history writing has been to let people relate their own history. After the fall of communism, the collection and preservation of biographies from the Soviet era has served to compensate for the deficiencies of public history writing. Events that people had been forbidden to talk about could now be recorded for posterity.

The Swedish state and the archival environment, as well as the long experience of democracy and peace, are different from those in the Baltic states. The divergence in trust is noticeable in some of the life stories told by the Latvian narrators in Sweden. They do not want to talk about matters already documented in books, even if they were involved in the events! A typical example consists of the life stories of Sergejs Ozoliņš, Jānis Zalcmanis, and Valdis Bigestāns. All three refer to history books and to the Latvian historian Uldis Ģermanis, who also fled to Sweden and took his doctoral degree in history at Stockholm University. I am not quite sure, but this could be an explanation for the unwillingness among the Latvian refugees in Sweden to talk about important events in history, which by extension means that educated Latvian Swedes seem to have adopted the Swedish sense of trust and way of thinking. For my research and interpretation of the refugees' life stories, the unwillingness to talk about well-known facts could be a limitation particularly in respect to my efforts to get more information about the dramatic escape over the Baltic Sea. On the other hand, the limitation could also give me new possibilities of interpreting the different cultural approaches between the native Latvian interviewer and the Latvian Swedish narrator, as the different cultural contexts and their relationship are located at the centre of the interpretation.

Swedish historians do not habitually use oral history as a method in their research. Using source criticism as a method, historians try to come as close as possible to 'the truth' in history research and in this respect oral historians differ from historians. The Estonian professor Tiina Kirss explains the differences succinctly: 'Undoubtedly a life story is a narrative about the past, but history is not the summa of life stories, of remembered "great lives"' (Kirss and Hinrikus 2010: 1). The past presented in oral memories consists of stories with many layers told from the bottom-up individual point of view in direct contrast to the state level's top-down version of real history, such as political decisions, social structures, and so on. Oral history has more to do with communication than with the documentary description of historic events, which can also be another limitation to my research, because I did not personally conduct the interviews. I have to interpret and try to understand the communication between the interviewer and the interviewee, but sometimes the communication is hidden to me because of internal understandings. In some cases, as the interviewer I would have asked other questions. I have also noticed some interesting diversities in the understanding of the context between the interviewer and the narrator, but I will return to this relationship later in this chapter.

Narratives are not remains of history, they are rooted in 'culturally defined modes of communication and closely tied with culturally available narratives and dominating discourses in the community' (Bela-Krūmiņa 2003: 11), which is the key difference between the recorded life stories, lives lived and lives remembered, and the lives documented in literature and archival documents. In historical research, source criticism is, as already mentioned above, the main guide and method but when interpreting life stories, other tools must be used and other questions must be asked. Oral historians do not examine historical sources in the traditional meaning of 'scrutinize'. The evidence provided by the narrators reveals previously unknown details in relation to well-known events, allowing us to view the development of historical events through the individual experience and everyday life which are based on memory, consciousness, the situation, and rules of communication and knowledge of societal processes (Hansson and Thor 2003).

Research on migration

In Sweden, oral history gained a brief uplift in popularity during the 1970s when the leftist movement opposed the official top-down version of history. From the leftist perspective, the time had come to rewrite history and to start from the bottom-up, i.e. from the industrial workers' position. History writing from the bottom-up elucidates history from the perspective of the individuals who are experiencing and creating history (Lindqvist 1978). During this period of rewriting history from the bottom-up, minority groups and migrants were, however, excluded.

Swedish immigration research has mainly focused on the attitudes of the Swedish populace and the state (legislation and actions of state authorities) towards refugees and migrants. Swedish historians have, however, studied the arrival of refugees to Sweden and the attention given them during their post-arrival period. The focus of this research is mostly on the immediate welfare requirements and the efforts of the state and trade unions to find a position for the refugees in the labour market (Olsson 1997). Baltic refugees have not been of special interest and have only been treated in a few studies, such as Carl Göran Andrae's analysis (2004) of the political organization of the Estonian refugee traffic across the Baltic Sea and the reception of Baltic refugees in Sweden.

Important contributions to the oral history research on Baltic refugees in Sweden have been made by Baiba Bela, who has used the Latvian National Oral History (LNOH) collection of the Swedish Latvian narrators (Bela 2007). The editor of this book, Aili Aarelaid-Tart, has also written several articles about Estonians in Sweden, one of which is 'The Estonians' adaption to new cultural realities: lesson from history' (Aarelaid-Tart 2002) is of special interest for my research. In this article Aarelaid-Tart identifies three types of failings in the narratives of Estonians. The first and the second involve the overestimation of the hardships the Estonians faced when they arrived in Sweden and the mystifying of the reasons why they left their homeland. The third relates to various 'white lies' to show that their lives had been worse off in the new country of residence than they really were (Aarelaid-Tart 2002). This result is very interesting, primarily when compared with the results from the Swedish immigration researchers, who contend the Balts to be one of the most integrated migrant groups in Sweden, who succeeded in integrating successfully into Swedish society as well as maintaining their own cultural identity. I was interested in examining the Latvian narratives for similarities with those of their Estonian counterparts to see how they describe their reception and their new lives in Sweden.

Latvian refugees creating an identity

For this article I had access to 15 of the life stories collated by the LNOH project, which form part of the 1996 Collection held by Latvian Oral History Centre. I selected life stories narrated by three Latvian men of similar age living in, or nearby, Stockholm. I made the choice without any scientific reasons, just out of curiosity wanting to know more about them. Out of the 15 life stories from the LNOH collection, the majority of the narrators consisted of well-known people who were personally known to me. The Latvian community in Stockholm is rather small and everybody knows everybody else.

The chosen biographies are seen as narrative constructions and life stories about self-realization processes and identity formation. They are representations reflecting on the narrators' understandings of the experiences of real life and how they found meaning with their lives in Latvia and later as refugees in Sweden. My prime interest is to analyse the three narratives, which concern the period around the 1940s, before and soon after their escape to Sweden. The aim is to encapsulate their traumatic war experiences and their final decisions to leave Latvia. Other issues concern the refugees' agency in meeting the challenges of living in a new country, and how they experienced and understood the societal changes affecting their lives. I also explore how (and if) the Latvian national culture and ethnicity could be maintained by refugees living in exile.

The first narrative NMV 454 (52 pages) is told by Sergejs, a Latvian born in Tallinn in 1914, the second NMV 458 (24 pages) is told by Jānis, born in Riga in 1919; and the third NMV 445 (16 pages) is told by Valdis, born in Moscow in 1919. The narratives will be analysed and interpreted within a social and political context, and for communication between sender and recipient. The context is important when interpreting narratives, but it cannot be decisive to the meaning. The context will just help us to decide the frames of plausible interpretations. The narratives will be presented in a thematic order.

The experience of war

Latvia gained her independence in 1918. Politically the years after the declaration of independence were quite turbulent and the parliament with many political factions was unstable. In 1934, the Farmers Union leader, Prime Minister Kārlis Ulmanis, ostensibly fearing a coup by right-wing extremists, the *Lāčplēša kara ordeņa kavalieru un brīvības cīnītāju biedrība* 'Leģions' (The Legion) conducted his own political *coup d'état*. Ulmanis outlawed all political parties, including the Farmers Union, and particularly the politically extreme right-wing parties such as The Legion and the fascist Pērkonkrusts (Thunder Cross). Latvia's independence ended when the Red Army invaded Latvia for the first time in June 1940. This occupation lasted until the German invasion in July 1941. The dominant Latvian discourse refers to the Soviet occupation of 1940–1941 as the 'terrible year of horror', while the period of independence before the war is associated with good recollections in people's memories (Šupulis and Bormane 2007). The Nazi German occupation of 1941–1944 is more troublesome to interpret in the Latvian discourse because of the warm welcome that the Latvians gave to the Germans in the belief that they would be liberated from terror and horror and that Latvia would regain its independence. The friendly relationship of 1941–1944 with Nazi Germany is nowadays a disadvantage and historical burden, since the post-socialist Russian discourse views Latvians as fascists and perpetrators of Nazi crimes and not as victims in the Soviet–Nazi conflict. Another element of this troublesome discourse is that many Latvians refer to the Jews as members of the Soviet communist party and are consequently viewed first as enemies and second as victims of the Holocaust.

Sergejs, born in Tallinn in 1914, is a very happy person and tells his life story in a positive mode. His memories of his childhood are exceedingly bright, and indeed comprise 20 per cent of the transcript. In Tallinn, he and his family lived very well during the First World War:

> And our conditions of living were at that time very good, considering the circumstances. We had an old German lady, who cooked and bought our food. The children were cared for by a young French girl, she was about seventeen, eighteen years old … We children, and especially me, had lovely days, and lovely years. My memory from my childhood is very, very bright.
>
> (Sergejs NMV 454)

After the independence of Latvia, Sergejs and his family moved to Riga in 1920. His father had been injured during the First World War and life became harder for Sergejs and his family in Latvia.

Sergejs got married in 1937 when he was only 23 years old. He had difficulties finishing his engineering studies at university because he was working in a printing house at the same time. He did military service as a radio-telegraphist from 1939 until September 1940, by which time the Red Army had invaded Latvia. He tells about these events in an easygoing way, but is very upset when talking about Ulmanis' passivity when the 'Russians' invaded Riga:

> You see, these Russians with their small berets (on their heads) drove by in their small tanks. There weren't any big tanks. We counted them to two hundred and forty. It was really humiliating, that we were not allowed to do anything. … And, my opinion in this case, I say, it was a crime not to allow us. We should (have done something) … after some days, maybe two or three we would have capitulated all of us. We would have stopped the action temporarily and we would have shown our standpoint, and this is one thing I can't forgive Ulmanis that he said 'Stay where you are, I stay where I am!' Silliness it was!
>
> (Sergejs NMV 454)

The laws and decrees proclaimed by the Ulmanis government in 1940 caused enormous discontent and confusion among the Latvians and especially among the Latvian youth, who had grown up in a social environment of freedom and patriotism. A strong sense of national identity had developed and therefore they were very disillusioned and disappointed with Ulmanis' passive standpoint and submission towards the Russians (Siliņš 2004) and Sergejs shows his disappointment. After this brief burst of anger in the narrative about Ulmanis, Sergejs makes a quick about-turn:

> And then the Russians absolutely wanted to make sports, and we created a sports group, as a matter of fact, our military group was one of the keenest groups on sports, so we played volley ball with the Russians.… This is the

> only time when I had something to do with the Russians. We lost the game [by a fine] margin ... it was only a game and nothing serious.
>
> (Sergejs NMV 454)

When Sergejs relates the assaults and injustices perpetrated by the Red Army, he often refers to official historians and documents or renowned historical events, as for example, the deportations to Siberia: 'My best friend disappeared. My wife's school-friend disappeared, she worked at the French embassy, she was a doctor, she disappeared. One by one, they disappeared. But that is nothing to talk about, that is a well-known fact' (NMV 454: 19). One reason why Sergejs does not want to talk lot about renowned historical events could be that he was not personally involved in these events (i.e. the deportations). They are not a part of the self-construction of his life story.

Janis, born in Riga 1919, tells his life story in a very serious way, quite the opposite to Sergejs. He does not want to speak about his childhood and starts his narrative talking about the gymnasium and the year 1937 when he was 18 years old and his political consciousness had started to grow. When he finished school he immediately continued his education with university studies. Jānis's narrative of his war experiences contains a lot of disappointments, anger and conscious resistance. He stayed at the university until 1940:

> In the year 1940, in the summer, then everything ended. In moved, into our country, the Red Army, 'liberated' us, so to say, from everything. ... with that, life turned onto absolutely new tracks. And in July, when the demonstrations were taking place on Brīvības Street, the shouting and the waving of red flags – I can't forget, it was a lot of Jews who participated in the demonstrations – a good friend of mine invited me to enroll in the resistance movement. And I entered into the movement as a block leader until the Germans came and I was 21 years old. ... So, and then followed the 'terrible year of horror' as we said: people disappeared, no doubt, I thought about my own security. We must count on that, that some from our organization could be captured and under torture inform the Russians. We waited for the Germans with warm feelings, you could say, we believed in war and that the Germans should give us our independence back. ... So, we waited for the Germans with ... really with warmth. In Riga they were welcomed on the streets with flowers. They marched through Riga ... as a parade. But after a few month we understood, there was no difference, only different uniforms, different colors and different language.
>
> (Jānis NMV 454: 2)

When Jānis looks back at the war events and the invasion of the Red Army, he is aware of the contemporary troublesome discourse and accusations of Latvian war crimes. It seems to me that Jānis tries to defend his own political standpoint by emphasizing the participation of Jews in the demonstrations in Brīvības Street. But how could he know that they really were Jews? What identified them as Jews or was this the work of his imagination?

It is interesting to notice the different approaches that Sergejs and Jānis take when talking about 'the terrible year of horror'. On the one hand their life stories can be seen as examples of the narrative creating the individual and the identity process. On the other hand, it is important to problematize the way these stories are embedded in, and relate to, the larger cultural and social contexts. Jānis is very aware of the political situation in Latvia, and his story is part of the collective hegemonic Latvian discourse. Jānis's story has all the ingredients of world war trauma and the feeling of humiliation we usually hear when discussing the events of June 1940 to July 1941. His memories of the German invasion are also partly a collective memory, which he rationalizes when it becomes impossible to talk about the Germans and the Second World War because of the hegemonic post-war narrative of the Holocaust. Between 1941 and 1945, Jānis was working as a war correspondent and reported for different Latvian and German newspapers. In the interview he refers sometimes to the articles that he has written as an *aide-memoire*. The narrative of Sergejs is partly quite the opposite to that of Jānis. Sergejs is a very easygoing narrator because he refers to the 'bad' year with the aside of 'by the way' and he dares to talk about sports and humorous events with Russians. This aspect is a total exception from the main hegemonic narrative of the 'terrible year of horror'. Sergejs' memories from the German occupation of Latvia are told in the same easygoing way. He talks about all the fun activities he has done together with the Germans and nothing about the war crimes, which also is an exception from the hegemonic post-war narrative of the Nazi German occupation. The political dimension in his life story is not visible!

The third narrative is told by Valdis in a very calm and distanced mode. He was born in Moscow 1919, but his family settled in the Latvian countryside in 1920. Valdis was a hard-working student during the war. When he finished secondary school and the gymnasium he moved to Riga to continue studying 1939 at the Technical University. He graduated as an engineer in 1944, when the Red Army moved into Riga for the second time. Until 1944 his life story was without any dramatic elements. He talks about his family and the life he lived in the countryside in Latvia before he went to the university.

The narrative of Valdis makes sense in an academic context and in the identity formation process belonging to the 'intelligentsia'. His life story could really be seen as narrative constructions in a self-realization process. Valdis does not say much at all about the Red Army and the invasion of 1940 during the second year of his studies at the Technical University in Riga. He seemed to be a serious student with very conscious academic goals. The war experiences Valdis had in 1944, when he graduated from the Technical University, occurred when the Red Army was on its way to occupy Latvia for the second time. By that time, he already had met his fiancé and when he wanted to travel to meet her in Liepaja from Riga, he realized that the war front had come close and the Red Army had cut off the land routes to Liepaja. The only way to go there was by boat with a special permit, which he got from the Germans. In Liepaja, he applied for work at the sugar refinery plant and took the job so that he could earn enough money for his wedding. Valdis got married in August 1944 just before he decided to leave Latvia. Prior to that decision Valdis had never contemplated leaving Latvia and he did not have any plans to do so. He was convinced that he would stay in Latvia after the war. The idea to escape to Sweden came from some university friends in autumn 1944, and by that time, in October 1944, the Russians had already entered Riga.

Over the sea – 'the dark autumn nights'

The number of Second World War refugees in Sweden reached a peak during the winter of 1944–5, by which time about 170,000–180,000 foreigners resided in Sweden. The largest groups came from the neighbouring Nordic countries, particularly Finland and Norway. At the end of the war some survivors of Nazi labour and concentration camps were also transferred to Sweden. The number of Latvian refugees in Sweden was, at the beginning of 1945, initially about 5000, but the decision of the Swedish government to repatriate 146 Latvian legionnaires back to the Soviet Union caused many refugees to choose to leave Sweden and escape further afield to America and Australia and other distant countries. Nowadays, the Latvian minority, closely integrated into Swedish society, consists of slightly more than 3000 concentrated mainly Stockholm, Gothenburg, and Malmö.

The wave of refugees from Estonia and Latvia began in 1943 and ended in the autumn of 1945, during which time a variety of sea-going craft, fishing boats, tugboats, barges, yachts and even rowing-boats, crossed the Baltic Sea to Sweden. The sea evacuation from Latvia was organized partly by the Latvian Central Council (LCC) and the American War Refugee Board (AWRB), supported by the Swedish security police and military police (Siliņš 2004: 72). This support of help from America and Sweden was not simply a humanitarian activity. Organizations within both America and Sweden were interested in getting first-hand information from the eastern front, which was the reason for the selection by the LCC and AWRB of the 'intelligentsia' to comprise the majority of the Latvian refugees. After the war, the Swedish government was anxious not to provoke Stalin and the Soviet Union, and consequently returned all the Latvian and Estonian boats to Soviet territory (Andrae 2004; Siliņš 2004).

The twin aims of the LCC were to organize a Latvian resistance group and to help the Latvian 'intelligentsia' to escape from the Red Army. The majority of the Latvian refugees in Sweden were 'intelligentsia', about which the narrators were well aware. This awareness also has an impact on the narratives, such as Valdis referring to the Latvian 'brain drain' during the Stalin era:

> What happened? [...] All the [Latvian refugees, we were somehow ... compared to the whole Latvian nation ... we are somehow the wrong division. Because we are not the average, who came to Sweden. We, about four thousand refugees who were in Sweden from the beginning, we are somehow selected. We are not the average, except those soldiers who were here, and except those who came after May 8 [WWII ended in Europe on May 8 1945

> – MR]. But all these persons who came the autumn before, they were more of, as we say in Sweden, the intelligentsia, the intellectuals. They were all politicians, authors, artists, poets, painters and engineers. A bit ... somehow of a higher cultural standard. We could say, the intelligentsia was the majority, they who came to Sweden, they were not workers, not factory workers. The ordinary Latvian people who left Latvia, the majority of them went mostly to Germany.
>
> (NMV 458: 23)

Valdis tells about the escape to Sweden with excitement, but without mentioning the LCC and the organized evacuation of the 'intelligentsia', because it was Valdis's friends who took the initiative in planning the escape, not the LCC. A relative of Valdis provided a boat. There were 27 people on the boat and Valdis had to fix the engine, which was in quite a bad condition. Each time the engine 'died', Valdis repaired it and they got away from the Latvian coast, arriving at Gotland in February 1945. The reception by the Swedes was very welcoming and they were immediately moved to a nice hotel in Visby and Valdis immediately got a job in the chemical industry.

Jānis does not talk about the LCC. As a forest brother (the pan-Baltic name for the partisan resistance movements), Jānis planned his escape together with other members of his partisan group. The way he talks about this event during the interview, particularly his unwillingness, is interesting:

JĀNIS: The plan was created ... how to get a boat. And I will not tell about this, because you have an article available in Svenska Dagbladet [a Swedish daily newspaper MR]. In this paper everything is described.

LATVIAN INTERVIEWER: Maybe you could tell something briefly, because the article is in Swedish...

JANIS: Na but, that woman can help you. She can read it to you. It isn't any problem.

LATVIAN INTERVIEWER: But please, maybe you could tell...

Then Jānis starts to tell his story in a highly detailed way about the 17 men who arrived in Gotland in autumn 1944 and were interrogated by the Swedish Security Service:

> [A]nd that I have mentioned in that article, but I will tell you shortly. The Security Service had a lady with them, a Swedish teacher, because the Security Service police surely couldn't speak German, but she ... good enough ... When we walked to the interrogation, this happened ... I was chosen as spokesman for our group. She took my hand and she said: 'Please tell what you want but not that you have fought against the Russians, in that case they will extradite you'. After we got this information ... it was about November 4–5, that we were not very welcome, I don't know how to say ... we who had fought on the German side.... Then we decided quickly in Latvian

> language, for our own sake, that the other sixteen ones couldn't talk any other language than Russian, excluding me. So I translated to German what my friends told me in Latvian, and the teacher translated it to Swedish. This was absolutely necessary, because some of the men started to talk about the battles and the struggles in Latvia, but this I kept to myself ... What more do you want to know?
>
> (Jānis NMV 445)

Jānis and his friends stayed in the refugee camp until January 1946. In February 1946 (when the Swedish government extradited the Latvian legionnaires to the Soviet Union), Jānis moved from Gotland to a refugee camp in the middle part of Sweden, where he got a job in a factory. In Jānis's case (compared to the two other narratives) the Swedish authorities seemed to be very suspicious of Jānis and his friends.

Unlike Valdis and Jānis, Sergejs did receive help from the LCC. Sergejs recounts a lot of details from the escape, when he and his family waited in a village on the western coast of Latvia for a boat. From his story it is clear that they fled together with many distinguished Latvian families. He recalls that among those who waited with him were highly prominent people – famous poets and writers, one composer, and some relatives of the first Latvian president. Sergejs emphasizes the presence of the 'intelligentsia' in his story and counts all the persons by their family names. There were 104 people aboard the boat 'Centība', who arrived at Gotland on 9 November 1944 (NMV 454: 28). After only a few days in Gotland they were moved to a refugee camp outside Stockholm. Some month later Sergejs got a job 'digging earth' in a rose garden.

Soon after their arrival, all refugees in Sweden had to do their share of the national production and were initially given low-paid manual labour assignments within sectors that had significant but unfulfilled demands for labour. Refugees were not allowed to do any other work, for which they may have been suited or qualified, before they had completed any of these initial assignments for at least four to six months (Svanberg 2007). Sergejs, Jānis, and Valdis were not exceptions.

Creating a new home

The events of the Second World War and particularly the final act of their escape from the Red Army caused a break in the continuity of kinship ties, both of family and adult relationships, for the refugees. Nevertheless, the act of immigration opened up new horizons. What consequences did this break have in a social, political and cultural context to the narrators? Patterns of integration into a new society can differ depending on personal life stories and levels of contacts with the new society. How well did Sergejs, Jānis, and Valdis integrate into the Swedish society? How did they preserve the Latvian national culture in exile? In this section of the chapter I try to answer these questions and elucidate their life in exile.

Aili Aarelaid-Tart emphasizes the deep changes in identities and re-estimations of values of migrants. 'Extensive and quick migrations (escaping one's homeland, deportation, invading armies marching in, a massive introduction of foreign labour etc.) are usually accompanied by a value aggression directed to the local population' (Aarelaid-Tart 2005). Swedish historians of migration have maintained that the Balts were often met with open arms but expressions of xenophobia were not uncommon when competition in the labour market was experienced. At many work places, the trade unions expressed a fear that unorganized refugees would disrupt the established order between employers and employed and lead to a reduction in wages (Horgby 1996; Byström 2006). Politically based suspicion and antagonism, especially expressed by the Swedish communist press, pictured the refugees as 'Baltic fascists' claiming they had entered Sweden to escape justice. In order to meet these accusations and international demands for clarity, Swedish police questioned refugees (Deland 2007).

Underlying these claims were that the Latvian and Estonian refugees, due to their war experiences, were anti-socialist and therefore refused to accept the organizational aspect of trade unions, and consequently were unwilling to adapt to the model of the Swedish labour market. The political activities of the Baltic exile community in Sweden with their forceful repudiation of Soviet Communism went against the essence of the Swedish culture. This was particularly true in the Baltic exiles' criticism of the post-war responses of the Swedish social democrats to Soviet activities regarding Sweden, such as Khrustchev's visits in 1959 and 1964 and the Soviet Russian 'parliamentarians' visit in 1966. There was also a constant degree of politicized tension between the Swedes and the Balts, especially in the late 1960s and the 1970s when the leftist movement was strong in Sweden. Among the Baltic exile communities the distrust was clear, and they got used to being called 'fascists'.

The distrust of the exiles for Swedish intellectuals is visible in the narrative of Valdis when he talks about his relations to Swedes:

> But one thing is really disturbing me all the time, and that is the Swedish lack of interest in the Latvian circumstances, the circumstances in the Baltic countries. Indifference. What really disturbs me, is that they shows interest in assaults and injustices in Nicaragua, South Africa and some islands in Polynesia or Tonga islands, or somewhere else where they could be together with Negroes.... They defend the Negroes much more, and talks about how suppressed they are. Because in Sweden all the newspapers and the press, all the official propaganda didn't say a word about the Baltic countries during the post-war period. But I, of course, told everyone as soon as I got a chance.
>
> (Valdis, NMV 458: 17)

Valdis continued to work and study in Sweden and defended his doctoral thesis in 1953 at the Royal Institute of Technology in Stockholm. He had six children, all of whom have assimilated into Swedish society and none of them are fluent in Latvian. He and his oldest daughter were the only ones who sang in the Latvian exiles' choir. During his active period of work and having his family, Valdis did not have many contacts within the Latvian community in Sweden. He was satisfied with his life in Sweden, but was worried about his relatives in Latvia because he could not get any information from them after the war.

The Latvian exiles in Sweden were not such a homogenous group as might be believed when they are talking about their identity as 'intelligentsia'. The exiles had, naturally, brought with them from Latvia their existing diverse opinions and political views. Consequently, despite the need to maintain homogeneity as a small group of outsiders in Swedish society, there existed many tensions and serious discussions between Latvian exile organizations and cultural institutions. But there were also tensions between the exiles and their political groups. The Latvian exiles had, soon after their arrival in Sweden, restored, as an 'exile organization', the *Latvijas Sociāldemokrātiskā Strādnieku Partija* (Latvian Social Democrats Workers Party), which Ulmanis had outlawed in 1934. However, many of the Latvian exiles were politically against centre-left parties of any origin, Latvian or Swedish.

Jānis never accepted the Swedish Social Democrats and continued his resistance against the Russians in his own way. In his narrative he tells how he contacted the Russians in Sweden for some 'inside' information about the USSR, which he passed on to the Chinese embassy. He is very proud about his secret meetings with the KGB agents in Sweden and maintains that he has them under control and is cheating them (NMV 445: 10). He continues to publish a few articles in the Swedish newspapers about the forest brethren in Latvia. The political dimension is very strong in his narrative. During his first few years in Sweden, Jānis says that he was waiting for the Second World War, when the Americans and British would liberate the Baltic countries. He had this naïve thought for several years, he says, but nothing happened, there was no Third World War. During the 1950s he began to study history at the University of Uppsala, got married and they had a daughter, Ieva. He was very active in the Latvian exile community and he taught history and the Latvian language to children of the Latvian exiles. Later on, Jānis worked as a history teacher in a Swedish school until he retired, and unwittingly provides us with the supreme irony of history-telling because Jānis is very proud that he could teach the children the 'real history' (the top-down version) and especially about the Second World War.

Jānis never returned to Latvia after the second independence in 1990, because he detested the Russians and what they have done to his homeland. At this juncture in the interview, Jānis mentions, as an aside, a surprising earlier marriage. He married prior to leaving Latvia and they had two daughters, one of whom is married to a left-winger, which Jānis could not stand at all. Jānis is creating his new identity as a conscious teacher who has taught children, both Swedish and the Latvian exile community, a lot of good things, which they would not have learned without his past experiences. The most surprising aspect of his story is his admission, at the end of the interview, that he already had a family and children in Latvia. It seems as if he wanted this aspect of life secret from his younger children.

Sergejs, who was not at all interested in politics, defended former president Kārlis Ulmanis as a symbol for the Latvian national identity: 'if Ulmanis' time would not have happened, then Latvians would not have fought for Latvia, because it was him and his surrounding who roused people's confidence'. But he was still angry that Ulmanis had not objected to the Russians entering Latvia in 1940. Sergejs spent all his active life within the Latvian exile community in Stockholm. He was a very involved member of different Latvian organizations in exile, which gave him the opportunity to travel around the world to meet other Latvians in the Diaspora. Sergejs seems to be very happy and satisfied with his life in Sweden. He has a good job and he has travelled around the world. Sergejs' story of his life in Sweden is full of detailed humorous family occasions and events, and brings his children and grandchildren into focus.

Conclusions

Life stories as source material gives us new insights into of the everyday life during unusual circumstances and hardships, which is impossible to find in official documents. The life stories of these three Latvian men show the differences in their experiences and their self-interpretations despite a shared relationship to being Latvian 'intelligentsia'. I agree with Aili Aarelaid that their narratives' reasons for leaving their homeland are mysterious and their escapes to Sweden seem to have been as a result of mere chance and pure coincidence. The narrative of Jānis could be seen as a political declaration of his own struggle for Latvian independence. His self-confidence is strong in his relation to the interviewer and he emphasizes the different cultural approaches between the native Latvian interviewer and the Latvian exile narrator. Jānis wants to teach the interviewer and shows distrust towards the interviewer who lives in Latvia alongside many Russians. A common element of the narrators is that they want to put their own narrative in a broader context or in a hegemonic discourse, which could explain why they often refer to well-known historians and renowned Latvian authorities when talking about well-known historical facts and events.

We can also discern from the three contrasting life stories that the narrators are aware of their identity as belonging to a group of highly educated people. This is visible when they talk about the Latvians in Sweden with pride and refer to themselves as the most intellectual exile society compared to other exile Latvian societies, for instance, in Germany. This kind of positive perception and collective consciousness is nourishing their own self-confidence. Thus the collective consciousness could also be seen as formed in an intersection of positions, where class relation, social, and political belonging is of importance in their life stories.

References

Aarelaid-Tart, A. (2002) 'The Estonians' adaptation to new cultural realities. Lesson from history', paper presented at the Fourth Nordic Conference on the Anthropology of Post-Socialism, April, Available: www.AnthroBase.com (accessed 8 March 2011).

—— (2005) 'Migration and cultural trauma', paper presented at the Baltic Migration Workshop, Sigtuna, February.

Andræ, C.G. (2004) *Sverige och den stora flykten från Estland 1943–1944* (*Sweden and the Great Escape from Estonia 1943–1944*), Uppsala: Swedish Science Press.

Bela, B. (2007) 'Stāsta dzīve valodā: naratīvās stratēģijas Latvijas un trimdas dzīvesstāstos' ('The language in life stories: Strategies in life stories of Latvians and diasporas'), *Spogulis*, Riga: The Latvian Academy of Science, Letonica.

Bela-Krūmiņa, B. (2003) 'Relationships between personal and social strategies of everyday life in the process of radical social changes', *Pro Ethnologia 16, Studies on Socialist and Post-socialist Everyday Life*, Tartu: Eesti Rahva Muuseum, pp. 9–19.

Byström, M. (2006) *En broder, gäst och parasit: uppfattningar och föreställningar om utläningar, flyktingar och flyktingpolitik i svensk offentlig debatt 1942–1947* (*Brother, guest and parasite: Foreigners, refugees, and refugee policy in the Swedish public debate, 1942–1947*), Stockholm: Acta Universitatis Stockholmiensis, Stockholm Studies in History, No 85.

Cimdiņa, A. (2003) *In the Name of Freedom. A biography of the President of Latvia Vaira Vike-Freiberga*, Rīga: Jumava.

Deland, M. (2007) 'Polisen och krigsförbrytarna' ('The Police and the war criminals'), in M.L. Andersson and M. Tydén (eds) *Sverige och Nazityskland, skuldfrågor och moraldebatt* (*Sweden and Nazi Germany, questions of guilt and debate of ethics*), Stockholm: Dialogos.

Hansson, L. and Thor, M (eds) (2003) *Oral History 1, Teoretiska perspektiv på individuella och kollektiva möten (Oral History 1, Theoretical Perspectives on Individual and Collective Meetings)*, Växjö: Växjö University.

Horgby, B. (2006) *Dom där. Främlingsfientlighet och arbetarkultur i Norrköping 1890–1960* (*The Others. Xenophobia and Workers' Culture in Norrköping*), Stockholm: Carlsson.

Kirss, T. and Hinrikus, R (2010) 'Preface', in *Estonian Life Stories.* On the Collection of Estonian Life stories, Budapest: Central European University Press.

Lindqvist, S. (1978) *Gräv där du står* (*Dig where you are*), Stockholm: Bonnier.

Olsson, L. (1997) *On the Threshold of the People's Home of Sweden*, New York: N.Y. Center for Migration Studies (CMS).

Siliņš, L. (2004) *Östersjön. Vägen till Frihet* (*The Baltic Sea. The Way to Freedom*), Tidtryck Uppsala.

Stiver-Lie, S., Malik, L., Jõe-Cannon, I. and Hinrikus, R. (eds) (2007) *Carrying Linda's Stones. An Anthology of Estonian Women's Life Stories*, Tallinn: Tallinn University Press.

Šūpulis, E. and Bormane, D (2007) 'The Latvian community in exile biographies: distinct experiences from Germany and Sweden', paper presented at the panel 'Doing Biographical Research in the Baltics', 7th ESA Conference, Glasgow, September.

Svanberg, J. (2007) *Arbetets etniska dimensioner. Flyktingar och arbetskraftsmigranter från Estland vid Svenska Stålpressnings AB i Olofström 1945–1952* (Labour Relations and Ethnic Dimensions of Work. The Swedish Engineering Employers' Association, the Swedish Metalworkers' Union and the Estonians at Svenska Stålpressnings AB in Olfoström 1945–1952), Göteborg: Linneaeus University Dissertations No. 9/2010.

5 Working through mature socialism

Private and public in the life story of an Estonian industry manager

Kirsti Jõesalu and Ene Kõresaar

Introduction: workplace as everyday practice

The domain of everyday life is the foundation of tacit practical knowledge and pre-reflective levels of articulation (Giddens 1984: 336–337). Everyday behaviour manifests the characteristic features of an era and those features help us understand the norms and strategies which are valid during a certain period of time. Ethnologists' and anthropologists' studies of Soviet everyday culture have mainly concentrated on how people have organized their daily life and made it meaningful (e.g. Wedel 1992; Nagengast 1991; Lampland 1995; Grimm and Roth 1999; Giordano *et al.* 2000). Other researchers have focused on adaptation to new societal structures and how traditional living practices are used to adjust to new circumstances (e.g. Benovska-Săbkova 1993, 1997; Giordano and Kostova 2002; Pine 2002). There has also been some interest in the parallels between certain structures in socialist and post-socialist transition societies (Kideckel 1995). In all those cases it is essential to clarify the relationship between the public and private spheres, in-depth research of which is still only in its initial stages (Miethe 2000: 331). The distinction between public and private is one of the most fundamental ordering principles of social life, yet one of the most unstable. In day-to-day life the distinction operates as common sense and a basic reference point but as Bailey (2002: 15) suggests is, at the analytical level, a useful tool for describing social change.

We have chosen to study Soviet everyday culture from the oral historical point of view using Alessandro Portelli's concept of history-telling, which differentiates between institutional, social, and personal levels in narration. The analysis will focus on how life history narratives manifest the day-to-day complexity of the Soviet era, when tension between the public and private spheres was pivotal. We will work with the era, which spanned the end of the period of 'high totalitarianism' in the 1950s to the period of late socialism, which lasted from the 1960s to the 1980s. Yurchak characterizes the latter period as a 'performative' shift of authoritative discourse and the subsequent normalization of that discourse; the post-Stalinist period between the mid-1950s and mid-1980s became thought of as a particular period with shared characteristics (Yurchak 2005: 31). As far as Estonian biographical material is concerned, late socialism effectively lasted until the second half of the 1980s. The Russian sociologist Oleg Kharkhordin describes mature socialism as the period of 'mature soviet society' (Kharkhordin 1999: 279) and contends that during this time many alternative, more or less autonomous spheres of life sprouted beneath the monolithic surface. On the one hand, official terminology took root in people's cognition of life, while on the other hand, there developed spaces of discourse that were inconceivable in the institutional sphere (Kharkhordin 1999: 280).

On the public–private scale, working life in the late Soviet period may be considered to lie between the two spheres. Working life was, at the formal level, regulated by the rules of central planning and official ideology, which regarded the working collective as a model of Soviet society but at the informal level, it functioned as a hotbed of 'pervasive clientelism and unregulated particularism' (Garcelon 1997; see also Zdravomyslova and Voronkov 2002). Since an individual depended on the state, the workplace was transformed into a central resource for satisfying both public and private needs. In this process, close relationships, both utilitarian and personal, existed between colleagues (Jõesalu 2004, 2006). Theoretical studies have mainly considered the impact of public, state-sanctioned control on working life and the working collective (e.g. Shlapentokh 1989; Kharkhordin 1999). Biographies provide the researcher with an actor's perspective, a powerful tool for complex analyses of the opposing spheres.

We are interested in whether and how the previously discussed complex interactions of the opposing spheres of life manifest in the narrated experiences of Soviet working life. Therefore our research properly belongs to socialism studies, a recently established sub-field of European ethnology (Roth 2004, 2006). The Soviet workplace was a 'total' institution, which took care of far more than just professional relationships, such as providing the registration of workers' place of residence, certain medical services, a sanitarium, tourist passes, leisure and day care facilities, and transportation, etc. Researchers underline that working life was subordinate to the norms of official ideology and the working collective was seen as part of a meta-community that was to form the basis of the entire Soviet society (Kharkhordin 1999: 280, 282). The autobiographical narratives tend to bring out those everyday practices that did not function exactly in accordance with ideological norms' regulations. We use a hermeneutical case reconstruction of a Soviet career biography to illustrate the meanings of public and private in Soviet working life.

Is socialism worth remembering in Estonia?

The following analysis is based on a life story sent to the Estonian Cultural History Archives (ECHA) in response to the life story writing contest 'My life and the life of my family in the Estonian SSR and the Republic of Estonia'. The competition was announced in 2000 and people contributed a total of 330 stories (Life Story Competition Appeal 2000). In the life stories that had been sent to the archive up until then, everyday life during the late Soviet period had seen little attention. The narratives had concentrated on war-related events, and the pre and post-war years. The focusing of attention on certain historical periods was caused by the prevailing public discourse that described the Soviet period as an occupation and 'a time unlived', which in turn also influenced the submissions to the previous contests. The frameworks for openly remembering the maturity of Soviet society did not exist. Written life stories – sent to a museum, a manifestly public institution – are inherently more open texts than biographical interviews, as authors may become affected by the discourses that are dominant in the society. The majority of the autobiographers of the 1990s have concentrated on how the public sphere has interfered with their personal lives during the Soviet period.

The campaign of 2000 was productive, and one reason could have been the changed attitude towards the Soviet period. A similar tendency had already been noted in earlier biographical interviews (e.g. the thematic biographical interviews of 1997–1998, conducted for a research project by the Department of Ethnology of the University of Tartu, 'Memory as a cultural factor') and in the public space one could also observe a (gradual) comeback of topics related to the Soviet period.

In the preface to a compilation of selected life stories from the campaign, sociologist Marju Lauristin explains why it is worth while to collect life stories about the Soviet period. She writes:

> The dispute that has just become topical in the Estonian society about how to evaluate the older and middle-aged generation compromising with their conscience in the period of the ESSR refers to the need to restore to memory the circumstances and human relationships in that society in as much detail as possible. It is not possible to restore the complete experience of life at that time in the memoirs of any single person, in any novel or film. It is only the collective memory that can capture the elusive picture of the daily struggle of a million Estonians for their physical and moral survival.
>
> (Lauristin 2003: 7)

In her introduction, Lauristin talks about making compromises: how people have conciliated the official stance with their private values and experiences of the Soviet period. The title of Lauristin's introduction, 'The man and the system', could also be interpreted as a reference to the opposition between the public and private in Soviet society – an assumption that the autobiographers themselves do not always make.

The campaign neither focused on the conflict between the different spheres of life nor attempted to judge the past. Yet the short analysis Lauristin makes after reading and analysing the stories still differs from the discourse of resistance and dissent, which was dominant in the society.

The 2000 campaign included a request to concentrate on describing daily life first and foremost. Considering the importance of work in Soviet society and daily life, it is not surprising that the focus of most of the received stories was on working life in the Soviet period.

Becoming an intermediary: the case of Heino Vollmann

In this chapter we take a closer look at the life of a Soviet-period Estonian mid-level manager. We chose the life story based on the author's description of the relationship between the public and private spheres in the 1960s to the 1980s. Our selection represents the challenges common to many people in similar milieux in socialist countries. Considering that a life story is narrated through a personal prism, we were interested in biographies where the tension between public and private can be easily followed. In the analysis of a specific story we can rely on the experience gained from reading the whole corpus of texts submitted to the contest. The author of the chosen biography was born in 1928, which places him in the republican generation who were also familiar with the Stalinist era that preceded mature socialism. While the previous periods are not our main interest, it does make it possible to follow individual experiences of the changes in the relations between public and private.

Heino Vollmann sent his life story to the Estonian Cultural History Archives in 2001. His story was published in the anthology of the competition, *Estonian Life Histories III: Life in the Estonian SSR* (Hinrikus 2003: 168–174). In our analysis we will use the original, unedited version of the text (see Vollman 2001).

For the greater part of his working life, Heino Vollmann worked in Tallinn as a manager for state industrial enterprises. He was well integrated into Soviet society and because of his position functioned as an intermediary between the official public and the informal spheres, which makes his story quite appropriate for our setting. Anthropologist Katherine Verdery writes about the importance of managers in the Socialist planned economy:

> Because planning could never foresee all contingencies, these managers had considerable discretionary power. Expected to achieve Party directives with inadequate wage funds and to exceed their plan targets with inadequate raw materials, they bore responsibility far greater the means allotted them for fulfilling it. Therefore, they strove constantly to expand their local power base and their effective capacities. In so doing, they posed a threat to their superiors, who thus were motivated to encourage subordinates' loyalty with favours and patronage.
>
> (Verdery 2004: 4)

Heino Vollmann began studying finance at Leningrad University in 1949. He graduated in 1953 and thereafter started to work in the Estonian higher and special secondary education system, quickly moving up the career ladder. From an ordinary vocational school teacher, he rose to the position of acting director for the newly founded Tallinn Economic School in 1960. He left that position in 1963 and became the chief accountant of a construction materials plant in Tallinn due to the patronage of the chairman of the Council of National Economy. From 1968 onwards, he worked as a manager of the small industrial plant 'Estonian Dolomite' that had split off from his former employer a year earlier. There, he was in charge of economics, finances and salary management of the factory. A change of management at 'Estonian Dolomite' caused Vollmann to change jobs and become a chief engineer in the Ministry of Construction Materials Industry. In the typical Soviet manner of distributing positions among senior officials and the nomenklatura, Vollmann was transferred to a seemingly better central government post, which however did not match his education and skills. He exclaims in his life story that 'they gave me the [job of] chief construction engineer for a higher salary!?' Although the remuneration was better, he was no longer provided with such extensive freedom of action as in his previous management job. Vollmann reached retirement age at the end of the 1980s and but returned to 'Estonian Dolomite' as a senior supervisor until the position became redundant in 1992.[1] Since then, he has been living in his renovated summerhouse, doing odd jobs and occasional gardening to earn a little extra to supplement his pension. He was also involved, as was common in the 1990s, in small-time illegal activity, in his case moonshining. According to Vollmann's own words, he was aware of the gradual economic decline in the Soviet Union throughout his career because of the positions he held. Additionally, during the process of restoring the independence of Estonia, he actively participated in the national movement and related activities, he helped resurrect the Defence League and was a member of the national political party 'Pro Patriae'.[2]

'Reading glasses': public and private in history-telling

Our analysis will rely upon Alessandro Portelli's classic treatment of the narrative modes of history-telling (Portelli 1992, 1997a, 1997b). Portelli's concept has proved to be fruitful in research on the experience of the Soviet period from the adaptation aspect: the possibilities this method offers in a complementary comparison of autobiographical texts and archive materials from different periods (Jaago and Kõresaar 2008). Portelli views the personal narrative as a structurally complex text, in which variations in language use and grammatical tense mark changes in experience. Other significant factors include the characters, the extent of the space of activity and grammar alterations, depending on the story-teller's standpoint. Proceeding from this, Portelli differentiates between institutional, communal, and personal layers, which manifest in the narrative as tendencies and, which are never entirely separate but quite the opposite, as the meaning of history in the text emerges in a combination of those layers. More specifically, Portelli describes the narrative layers of history-telling as follows: (i) the institutional mode of the narrative using the third-person plural is impersonal and relates to activities going on at the national level (politics and ideology, what the government did, what the parties or trade unions thought, and what they set out to do, etc.); (ii) the communal mode, mainly using the first-person plural, extends closer to environmental surroundings, community (city, neighbours) and working life; (iii) the personal mode, using the first-person singular focuses on the home or family and events in private life (births, deaths, employment, children), but also has links to the two previous modes (Portelli 1997b: 27). The narrative layers (modes) form the primary aspect that references the narrative's point of view, i.e. institutional ('they'), communal ('we'), or personal ('I').

As Garcelon argues (1997: 317), the private–public sphere typology used in analysing Western countries may be rather misleading, limited as it is to the state, political and civil society, and personal life. This raises the issue of how, and under which conditions, Portelli's concept can be adapted to the context of Soviet Estonia. In our treatment the institutional mode of history-telling corresponds to the occupation regime's voice of self-legitimization, signified by the use of self-descriptive political phraseology and fragments from official history. This includes both the state-approved view of the workplace and its operating principles, and the rules of conduct and integration in Soviet collectives. On the personal level, a story-teller draws upon first or second-hand memories and talks about personal life and family members. The political dimension is added only when someone comes into contact with state institutions, e.g. when the family comes to the interest, or under the supervision, of the authorities. The personal level can also occur when the narrator's best judgement conflicts with ideological requirements. The communal level is the most complex, as it may simultaneously involve a village or neighbourhood and work colleagues, but also an ethnic community if it is distinct from the institutional level from the perspective of historical awareness. In certain cases the personal and communal levels may coincide by default, e.g. if everyday, or political, problems are classified as belonging to a certain group. In Estonians' post-Soviet life story writings, the ethnic dimension typically overlaps with the personal and the communal levels, as the social integration of the Soviet and post-Socialist periods had a strong ethnic character (Kõresaar 2005: 37–110; Jaago and Kõresaar 2008). But the personal and communal levels may also intersect when the narrative touches upon instrumental practices, i.e. when the use of material and social resources of the workplace is represented as widespread, common behaviour (e.g. 'everybody does that'). In narrating Soviet everyday life, it is frequently possible for the institutional and the communal levels of history-telling to coincide, especially when someone reminisces about working in the conditions of a centrally planned economy. Often the different levels cannot be clearly distinguished in the narrative. However, it is important to add that both institutional and communal levels manifest in biographies through the personal point of view (Jaago and Kõresaar 2008).

Portelli showed that when telling about critical or conflict situations, the three narrative layers come to the fore more clearly and intensively. Conflict is the node of the narrative, in which all three modes concentrate and support each other (Portelli 1997b: 33–34). The conflict may lie in a past experience (Portelli focuses on this aspect), but the storyteller can also find a contradiction between personal experience of an event and its interpretation in the society at the time of recollection, i.e. which frames of remembering are enabled in the public discourse.

As we see in the following section, this factor plays an important part in memories of the late socialist period in Estonia. In the following section, we use Portelli's three modes of history-telling to analyse Heino Vollmann's (own) biographical recollections of working life. The focus of our attention will be primarily on how his life story opens up the interplay of the different narrative layers, which we consider to more or less correspond to the (different) spheres of Soviet society. While we do follow Portelli and predominantly investigate conflict as the most evident manifestation of the narrative modes, we do not assume that an individual experience necessarily has to exhibit disagreement between the different levels of society.

'To outsmart the Russian state': taking advantage of experiences of the conflict between private and public

In his life story, Heino Vollmann primarily concentrates on his working life and those people who meant something for him in that sphere. He does not mention his wife and family, because he finds that his work and personal life (which he equates to being a husband and a father) have not affected each other[3]:

> The visible life of a person consists of events, meeting people, common activities with them, and opportunities arising, making or not making use of the latter, potential positive or negative results. In the following description of my life story I will proceed only from these aspects, leaving out the hidden personal and family life with all its joys and problems, because it has had no impact on my public activities or position.
>
> (Vollmann 2001: 1)

The decision not to write about his private life applies only to his own family and not to his childhood and youth. Here the conflict between the public sphere and the private sphere becomes evident: the Soviet authorities forcefully limit both his personal space and his family's chance to keep their social status. Vollmann was born into the family of a wealthy small-town merchant and lost his father at an early age.

> The first change that affected my future life happened in 1940 when all our property was nationalized; we had to do without the housemaid and move into a more modest apartment. Mother had to start earning her living with her own hands (mainly by doing underpaid sewing jobs).
>
> (Vollmann 2001: 1)

At the age of 13 years, Vollmann had to support the family and became a farm-hand. The experience of doing hard work from an early age and being deprived of his earlier life shaped principles that would last his whole life:

> At that time my character also started to develop: stubbornness and pride developed, also the habit to work and a love of working, which resulted in my creed of life: I am able to, I can and I simply must cope with everything.

> [–] Stubbornly following this principle pushed me into several conflicts later in life, both with the established order and with people and unfortunately also with the ethical standards cultivated at home (mainly the principles of honesty).
>
> (Vollmann 2001: 2)

The well-to-do status of his family in the pre-Soviet period hampered Vollmann in making and implementing his study plans, especially in the choice of a university major. Having been expelled from the Tallinn Polytechnic Institute for telling 'anti-government jokes', he intended to go to Leningrad to study finance. He took advantage of a campaign at the end of the 1940s, which was aimed at steering young Estonians to the universities in Leningrad and Moscow. Vollmann convincingly describes the background of the campaign with the insights of an insider, as if his later experiences in positions close to the decision-makers had retroactively given him a 'third eye' to adequately assess the situation. He actually credits himself with being in the circle of authority,[4] a narrative strategy that coincides with his creed of life. This strategy also involves calling influential persons in his life by name and title, contrary to how he uses a less definite approach in denoting officialdom in unfamiliar situations that he lacks control over, e.g. 'was appointed', 'they', or 'the authorities'.

Vollmann only partially resolved his conflict with the (official) public sphere. Although his social status became more appropriate for his studies and future career after correcting the personal details, all information on his parents' social status during the pre-Soviet period was also consistently retained as far as Vollmann knew. This affected him both financially and in getting a job immediately after graduating:

> But when I started to fill in the form [of the university entry application], it appeared that my social background was not acceptable. But the plan [of the campaign] had to be fulfilled and this is why the personnel manager E. Pappel decided to basically correct my social origins. From that day until the end of Soviet rule my social origin as entered in the forms was 'craftsman'. In autumn '49 I went to Leningrad as a 'right man', but with very poor Russian language. [—] But to the credit of the authorities, it should be mentioned that they did not lose their watchfulness of me and already at the end of the same year I received a notice from the Ministry of Education that because of my actual social origins I was not entitled to special benefits and no more scholarship from the republic's funds would be paid to me (the scholarship from the institute remained, naturally). It should be said, however, that the Ministry of Finance did not disown me and Minister A. Tihane positively reacted to each of my requests for help.
>
> (Vollmann 2001: 4)

Another line in Vollmann's life story that conflicts with the (official) public sphere was his anti-Sovietism, the roots of which, according to his story, also lie in the childhood. Vollmann justifies it as revenge for the expropriation of his family and the ensuing hardships in his life. Examples of that include the post-war smuggling of ammunition stolen from Red Army soldiers and later on the forging of official statistics in order to improve the performance (figures) of the company that employed him. The latter took place when he working during the second half of the 1960s and 'everyone was satisfied. Me too, of course, because I was able to outsmart the Russian state' (Vollmann 2001: 9). His anti-Soviet attitude is related to the issue of membership in the Communist Party, which is a topic that Vollmann returns to again and again, when talking about the different stages of his working life. In the post-Soviet life stories of older-generation Estonians, the narrator's relationship with Soviet mass organizations in general is a central theme that requires some explanation. This applies to Komsomol, but especially to the Communist Party. The conflict between party membership and Estonianness has usually been perceived in very strong terms, but membership in Komsomol and national awareness were not contrasted as sharply (Siemer 2002: 129; Kõresaar 2005: 94). Vollmann also thought about joining Komsomol for practical purposes, and did so because membership guaranteed him the diploma that enabled him to teach at a vocational school. However, he did not make a similar decision about joining the Communist Party, although succeeding on the career ladder definitely was part of Vollmann's idea of a successful working life. He attributes all his unused career opportunities both as an education official and an industry manager to the fact that he had managed to keep himself from falling into the 'party's trap':

> ...in 1955 I was transferred to the Vocational School of Finance. There, I took the first steps on my career ladder: during the following five years I was a teacher of special subjects, director of the correspondence courses department, director of the all-USSR studies and consultation centre after the school was closed in 1958, then a branch manager, from 1960 acting director of the recently established Tallinn Economic School. My last promotion took place thanks to the then chairman of the Committee of Higher and Secondary Vocational Education M. Pesti, an honest person with liberal views [–]. The subordinate senior officials did not approve of this decision (I was not a party member) and even made efforts to get rid of me, so-to-say, fairly. I remained in the position of an acting director until I retired of my own accord in 1963, because the City Committee of the Party did not authorize me to take the office.
>
> (Vollmann 2001: 7)

> Looking back, at least in the sphere of working life there were opportunities that remained unused: later it was said behind the scenes in the ministry that had I been a member of the Party, I could have even run for the position of deputy minister at the end of the 1970s. But it seems that my working life at the middle level was much more interesting and maybe even more profitable for me.
>
> (Vollmann 2001: 10)

On the other hand, Vollmann knew how to make good use of the opportunities offered by the official system. He was skilled at finding influential supporters among the elite of the Estonian SSR, making himself useful by offering favours in return. As an education official, he used his influence when certain top executives who were failing in their correspondence courses asked him to, and fictitiously improved their study records.

> In a few cases it was possible for some not-so-assiduous and (un)-talented senior executives to graduate from the School of Finance via correspondence courses, based on the applications of top executives and using my unprincipled (inter)mediation.
>
> (Vollmann 2001: 7)

As an industry manager, he could make (unauthorized) changes to the official statistics of his manufacturing plant's economic plan, allowing the enterprise (and consequently the ministry) to 'achieve' better results. He could skilfully make use of the weaknesses of the system, which derived from the fact that the domains necessary for the legitimization of a party state, such as (constant) welfare growth and the socialist character of work, (cf. Garcelon 1997: 313f) had to be demonstrated to be in good order at all costs:

> In 1968 I went to work for [director] Kivisson in the mini-factory Estonian Dolomite. His instructions were the following: you'll start running the economics, finance and salary management independently. I promised Veimer [chairman of the Council of National Economy] that I would take the factory among the top ones in the system in its qualitative performance figures. [He said:] 'How you are going to achieve it is your business, I won't interfere, and I will endorse everything.' We got the position among the first, in some indicators we even were the first, but it was not possible to achieve this absolutely honestly. The first step in the following chain of lies and forgeries was to entice a meritorious employee of the ministry's planning department to work for us – naturally, by offering a significantly higher salary. Guaranteed by that person's reliability plus flowers, cakes, chocolate, cognac; our periodical reports were not inspected thoroughly. This made it possible that the so-called omissions which were very important for us went undetected. For example, the distorted representation of productivity and average salary figures created a more favorable basis for the factory in the following planning period. The game also included bribing an auditor of the ministry, illegal substitutions of certain parts of the plant's plan and secretly making changes into these in the ministry. The factory had a good reputation, everyone received bonuses and everybody was satisfied. Myself included, of course, because I was able to outsmart the Russian state. It should be kept in mind that this illusion of a beautiful life was created and supported almost everywhere. I remember an incident where the minister made the auditor simply

> clear the negative facts from the auditor's report on a factory which had won a Socialist competition.
>
> (Vollmann 2001: 8–9)

Patronage and favouritism in the workplace during the Soviet period had both official, public qualities and some that were more informal and remained outside that sphere, as shown by Garcelon (1997). As a departure from Portelli's concept, here we can see the institutional, communal, and personal level intersecting strongly, which in our opinion is the characteristic feature of the world of the Soviet manager. In the following section we examine the double standards of working life in the 'informal public' sphere (Zdravomyslova and Voronkov 2002). Due to Vollmann's position as an industry manager, it can primarily be represented in terms of instrumental personal ties (Benovska 2004) and their implementation in both the public and private spheres.

'Favours were received and given': formal and informal in a Soviet factory

In his life story, Vollmann shows himself to be skilled in making use of the resources of the Soviet workplace and economies, directing them from the 'official' (public) economy towards the 'informal' (private) economy (Verdery 1996: 27). Moreover, he presents himself as a progressive, studious person who in every new position learns how to act in the official sphere (in which the workplace belonged) to gain advantages in the informal and personal sphere. Volmann began shifting the borders between official and private economies, when as favours for useful executives in the Vocational School of Finance he marked up their study results. Next, while working in the factory 'Silicate' that produced construction materials, he had the opportunity to redirect the building supplies at his disposal to the informal economy and thereby do favours for his friends, picturing himself as a helper and an intermediary rather than a beneficiary. Yet, such intermediating activity can be interpreted as an investment for the future (Ledeneva 1998). Alena Ledeneva points out that although *blat*, the economy of favours, already existed in Stalinist Russia, it gradually expanded and became widespread during the Brezhnev era or the period of mature socialism, during which Vollmann spent most of his working years.

> I also acquired a very important experience – although production was limited and strictly allocated, it was possible to sell anything to good [read: useful, KJ&EK] friends, often even at half price [–] This way, I also made an acquaintance whom I needed very much: the director of the Raeapteek pharmacy in Tallinn, pharmacist Liias, who was in charge of the so-called Käbin's cabinet, that is, the drug fund of the ministry. Pharmaceuticals that were not freely available were exceptionally easy to get from him, even without a prescription. I remember when my good friend's daughter took ill with leukemia and her life could only be saved with a certain patented

> medicine produced in Switzerland. My friend called me from Saaremaa in the morning and gave me the name of the medicine, and by the evening the medicine was in his hands [–]. Of course, with my intermediation, Liias got the necessary building materials both for himself and his friends until his death.
>
> (Vollmann 2001: 7)

In addition to the above-mentioned high-level supporters, from the mid-1960s onward Vollmann also began to extend his network through travelling abroad. It appears that during the period of mature socialism even his 'unfavourable' origin did not prevent him from journeying together with the elite of the Estonian SSR. His applications for participating in long cruises seem to have been satisfied; at least the life story does not show any conflict with the public sphere. Thus we see him enter into 'high society' with the aid of informal relationships. A former colleague helped him in this context.

> The year 1965 became significant for me. The ESSR Trade Union Committee formed a tourist group for a tour of Northern and Central European countries. I submitted an application, but did not have much confidence in my chances, as there was only one vacant place. But my backing was helpful, because my onetime good colleague was there as the chairman of the committee. Unbelievably, I succeeded in getting out of the USSR for a whole month in a really higher society, who did not disdain me at all.
>
> (Vollmann 2001: 7)

So he went on three longer trips, which in his own words provided him with 'useful relationships for the future'. In 1967, he managed to visit the Montreal EXPO in a group formed by the ESSR government. Once again there was only one vacancy and again Vollmann 'got' to go on the trip:

> There were 50 candidates, including myself. Again I was chosen, the only non-party-member (behind the scenes it was said that this was in the interests of Soviet democracy, but some claimed that Vollmann was just a high-caliber spy).
>
> (Vollmann 2001: 9)

Having a '[c]lose and friendly and easy communication with the elite of ESSR' made it possible for him to invest in informal networks. For example, he describes how he got a phone connection installed at his home, which was rare at the time. On the other hand, this description also demonstrates that the network of favours was of a limited nature – favours were offered between certain people, their extension to 'friends of friends' tended to be a rare practice:

> I recall a few cases, when I had got telephones for myself and a couple of my colleagues from the chief engineer of the Ministry of Communications

> (later a Minister and Prime Minister) B. Saul, and quite shamelessly I went to ask for a telephone for another good colleague, he hesitantly-kindly said to me, 'Heino, your friends might not be my friends; let this be the last time, now.'
>
> (Vollmann 2001: 8)

At the same time that network of personal (informal), instrumental personal relationships could be used to benefit non-personal (formal) networks. Managers could apply the former to perform their work duties. So it was Vollmann specifically whom his superior sent to the Minister to get a company car. We may thus say that the success of a good intermediary depended on his extensive networks of relationships. As Katherine Verdery says when describing the Soviet planned economy in comparison with Western business practices: 'In socialism, the locus of competition was elsewhere: your competitor was other buyers, other procurers; and to outcompete them you needed to befriend those higher up who supplied you' (Verdery 1996: 22).

In the episode about building his summer-house, Vollmann refers to his 'own guys', a network of relationships, which evidently served both the official economy (by fulfilling the five-year plan of the factory 'Estonian Dolomite') and the informal economy (by building a summer house out of materials from state factories):

> Material had to be procured from neighboring factories as well. And everything one needed was available, some at half the price, some completely free of charge, because there were 'own guys' in the lead everywhere. And nobody ever asked what I was going to give in return. The principle was that today I help you, and the next time you will try to help me. No accounting was kept over favors received or provided.
>
> (Vollmann 2001: 9)

In the life story, Vollmann does not discuss how the network of his 'own guys' came into being. Unlike relationships with his patrons or the elite, we get to know nothing specific about his personal networks. But as we already mentioned, the focus of his working life story is specifically about discussing the public and institutional levels, which are closely intertwined in the narrative.

Conclusion

The central question of the chapter was how post-Soviet autobiographers position themselves with regard to the peculiarities of Soviet everyday life. As the characteristic features of the system, we primarily considered the complex differentiation between public and private and the proliferation of the informal sphere. Our focus was on a specific little life world (Honer 1993), as exemplified by the life story of a middle-level manager. The author of that biography, Heino

Vollmann, comes from the middle class of the pre-Second World War republic of Estonia, and therefore his social roots are already at odds with the Soviet order. Therefore people like him had to convince the new regime of them being 'suitable' to be considered as full members of the new society. In his early teens, 10–15 years of age, he experienced the forcefulness and brutality of the Soviet regime. That experience made him ready to assert himself in a society he did not fully respect. A typical characteristic of Vollmann and many others of his generation is a certain aversion of the Soviet system, which does not, however, preclude him from learning how to skilfully manipulate the system while outwardly demonstrating complete loyalty. In Vollmann's case, his retirement and the rebirth of the republic of Estonia coincided, and thus we are not able to continue observing his career story: adapting to the new, sovereign Estonia is more of a question of personal coping, not so much an issue of (re)building up a working life in rapidly changing conditions.

Heino Vollmann's life story clearly showed the dissimilarity in an individual's perception of the relationship between the Soviet (official) public sphere and the private realm in the 1940s–1950s[5] and the 1960s–1980s. The earlier, totalitarian Stalinist era is always menacingly present in the recollections; its invasion of the private (sphere) and impact on (individual) life were total and inescapable (see Kõresaar 2004: 307–308). However, the narrative experience of the 1960s–1980s rather implies the possibility of a detached private sphere existing parallel to the official public realm. This phenomenon was clearly evident in the analysed life story as the total dismissal of any adult private life from the narrative – a fact that is obviously idiomatic of Soviet society, but (in our case) also has strongly individual and gender-specific features. The role of the workplace as a mediator between the (official) public and private spheres can also be observed in the story, although Heino Vollmann does not recognize it as such. The change in the workplace encouraged the evolution of the (personal) private sphere, simultaneously bringing about a variety of informal practices.

In Vollmann's recollections of the different periods in his (working) life, there were two basic representations of the official public realm that were expressed quite distinctly in everyday life: the ideological norms and rituals that cemented the legitimacy of the regime, and the regulations of central planning. According to Vollsmann's story, the main rules in everyday life were to utilize existing free spaces, including those which the Soviet system involuntarily created by legitimizing itself, through vertical and horizontal networking. At the same time, it was clear how skilful Vollmann was in operating efficiently within both official and informal public realms, respecting the invisible boundary between them and not confusing the different rules regulating behaviour in either sphere (Zdravomyslova and Voronkov 2002: 61; Aarelaid-Tart 2003: 213). As Garcelon (1997) has shown, an individual in Soviet society tended to form relatively disparate ways for self-representation in different spheres. Vollmann's life story is exemplary in demonstrating how an individual in Soviet society could simultaneously epitomize both loyalty to the norms of the party state and the 'bargaining persona oriented to particularistic patronage relationships, second-economy activities, and barter exchange' (Garcelon 1997: 325). In Vollmann's case, we were dealing with a success story in the form of a career biography. Therefore, he was not motivated to include certain aspects of Soviet work life in his story such as pastime activities which have been represented in connection with working life in many other life stories written at the same time (Jõesalu 2006).

Vollmann's text quite untypically lacks also any references to either Soviet ritual calendar or his role as patron in the informal relationships that occurred at the workplace. Apparently the reason for this lies in his individualistic manner (of writing) that is centred on his success story and possibly also in his one-time lifestyle (the aforementioned estimations of his salary, responsibility, and relative freedom to act). Due to this or some other causes, the working collective was not in his focus either in its institutional or communal sense (Jõesalu 2004). Nevertheless, Vollmann's life story represents some wider trends in the relationships between the official and the private in Soviet working life, including the interests and practices that consolidated that specific social milieu.

Acknowledgement

At various stages, research pertaining to this article has been supported by the Estonian Science Foundation (Grant No. 8190), the State Targeted Project SF0180157s08, and by the European Union through its European Regional Development Fund (Centre of Excellence in Cultural Theory).

Notes

1 This is an example of a widely used pre-retirement strategy – before retiring, people called upon their acquaintances to find a well-paying job that would guarantee maximum pension.

2 Vollmann's life confirms Garcelon's observation that post-Communist social movements largely relied on the 'middle strata' of Soviet administration who possessed the necessary organizational skills and networks of solidarity (Garcelon 1997: 328).

3 At the same time, Vollmann does not consider his job change due to getting married and settling down a situation in which family life affected career-related decisions. Such gender-specific experience and use of different spheres of life remains outside the scope of this article (cf. the woman's perspective e.g. Miethe 2000; Heinen 1997; another male perspective in Kukhterin 2000).

4 At the time of applying for enrolment at Leningrad University, Vollmann was an expelled college student and was employed as a manager of a local housing office in a suburb of Tallinn, therefore he could not have possessed any significant information about the decisions. However, in the narrative he leaves an impression of himself as an enterprising person who does not mind mastering the 'chains of command' and communicating with people necessary to meeting his needs. In a later context he described this pattern of behaviour as follows: I kept my eyes and ears open and learned a lot of things necessary for the future (Vollmann 2001: 6).

5 The 1941–1944 German occupation of Estonia is not taken into consideration in this analysis and was also left out of the life story.

Unpublished sources

Life stories from the collection of the Estonian Cultural History Archives ECHA f350: 1129.

Vollmann 2001 refers to the original life story of Heino Vollmann stored at the Estonian Literary Museum'Estonian Cultural History Archives as ECHA 350.

References

Aarelaid-Tart, A. (2003) 'Double mental standards in the Baltics during two afterwar decades in Baltics', in A.M. Kõll (ed.) *The Baltic Countries under Occupation. Soviet and German rule 1940–1991*, Acta Universitatis Stockholmiensis, Studia Baltica Stockholmiensia 23, Stockholm: Stockholm University, Department of History, pp. 215–228.

Bailey, J. (2002) 'From public to private: the development of the concept of private', *Social Research*, 69(1): 15–31.

Benovska, M. (2004) 'Social networks, coalitions and clientelism at the workplace in Bulgaria', in K. Roth (ed.) *Arbeitswelt-Lebenswelt: Facetten einer spannungsreichen Beziehung im östlichen Europa*, Münster: Lit-Verlag, pp. 109–128.

Benovska-Săbkova, M. (1993) 'Arhaichni kulturni modeli i totalitarisăm', *Bălgarski folklor*, 4: 3–15.

Benovska-Săbkova, M. (1997) 'Tradition as a means of survival under the conditions of economic crisis in Bulgaria', *Ethnologia Balkanica*, 1: 113–123.

Garcelon, M. (1997) 'The shadow of the Leviathan: public and private in communist and post-communist society', in J. Weintraub and K. Kumar (eds) *Public and Private in Thought and Practice: Perspectives on a Grand Dichotomy*, Chicago, IL: The University of Chicago Press, pp. 303–332.

Giddens, A. (1984) *The Constitution of Society: Outline of the Theory of Structuration*, Cambridge: Polity Press.

Giordano, Ch., Kostova, D. and Lohmann, E. (eds) (2000) *Bulgaria. Social and Cultural Landscapes, Studia Ethnographica Fribourgensia*, vol. 24, Fribourg, Switzerland: University Press Fribourg.

Giordano, Ch. and Kostova, D. (2002) 'Die soziale Produktion von Misstrauen', in C. Hann (ed.) *Postsozialismus: Transformationsprozesse in Europa und Asien aus ethnologischer Perspektive*, Frankfurt and New York: Campus Verlag, pp. 117–141.

Grimm, Fr. D. and Roth K. (eds) (1997) Das Dorf in Südosteuropa zwischen Tradition und Umbruch, *Südosteuropa aktuell*, 25, München: Südosteuropa Gesellschaft.

Heinen, J. (1997) 'Public/private: gender – social and political citizenship in eastern Europe', *Theory and Society*, 26(4): 577–597.

Hinrikus, R. (ed.) (2003) Eesti *rahva elulood III: Elu Eesti NSV-s* (*Estonian Life Stories III: Life in the ESSR*), Tallinn: Tänapäev.

Honer, A. (1993) *Lebensweltliche Ethnographie: Ein explorativ-interpretativer Forschungsansatz am Beispiel von Heimwerker-Wissen*, Wiesbaden: Deutscher Universitätsverlag.

Jaago, T. and Kõresaar, E. (2008) 'Complementarity of sources in studying adaptation: an oral history viewpoint', *Folklore: Electronic Journal of Folklore*, 39: 17–38. Available: www.folklore.ee/folklore/vol. 39/jaago_koresaar.pdf (accessed 4 March 2011).

Jõesalu, K. (2004) 'Das informelle Kollektiv in Behörden der Estnischen SSR. Praktiken und Strategien in einem sozialen Netz', in K. Roth (ed.) *Arbeit im Sozialismus – Arbeit im Postsozialismus. Erkundungen zum Arbeitsleben im östlichen Europa*, Münster: Lit-Verlag, pp. 129–145.

Jõesalu, K. (2006) 'Nischenbeschäftigung – ein Überschneidungsbereich von privat und offiziell in der Lebenswelt. Das Beispiel des sowjetischen Estland (ESSR)', in K. Roth (ed.) *Arbeitswelt-Lebenswelt. Facetten einer spannungsreichen Beziehung im östlichen Europa*, Münster: Lit-Verlag, pp. 63–82.

Kharkhordin, O. (1999) *The Collective and The Individual in Russia: A Study of Practices*, Berkeley, CA: University of California Press.

Kideckel, D. (ed.) (1995) *East European Communities: The Struggle for Balance in Turbulent Times*, Boulder, CO; Westview.

Kõresaar, E. (2004) 'Towards a social memory of work: politics and being a good teacher in Soviet teachers' biographies', in K. Roth (ed.) *Arbeit im Sozialismus: Arbeit im Postsozialismus. Erkundungen zum Arbeitsleben im östlichen Europa*, Münster: Lit-Verlag, pp. 291–310.

Kõresaar, E. (2005) *Elu ideoloogiad: kollektiivne mälu ja autobiograafiline minevikutõlgendus eestlaste elulugudes (Ideologies of Life: Collective Memory and Autobiographical Meaning-Making of the Past in Estonian Life Stories)*, Tartu: Eesti Rahva Muuseum.

Kukhterin, S. (2000) 'Fathers and patriarchs in communist and post-communist Russia', in S. Ashwin (ed.) *Gender, State and Society in Soviet and Post-Soviet Russia*, London and New York: Routledge, pp. 71–89.

Lampland, M. (1995) *The Object of Labor: Commodification in Socialist Hungary*, Chicago: Chicago University Press.

Lauristin, M. (2003) 'Inimene ja süsteem' ('The man and the system'), in R. Hinrikus (ed.) *Eesti rahva elulood III: Elu Eesti NSV-s* (Estonian Life Stories III. Life in the ESSR). Tallinn: Tänapäev, pp. 7–9.

Ledeneva, A. (1998) *Russia's Economy of Favours: Blat, Networking and Informal exchange*, Cambridge Russian, Soviet and Post-Soviet Studies, Cambridge and New York: Cambridge University Press.

Life Story Competition Appeal 2000, Available: www2.kirmus.ee/elulood/uleskutsed.html (accessed 23 November 2008).

Miethe, I. (2000) 'Changes in the spaces of political activism: transforming East Germany', in R. Breckner, D. Kalekin-Fishman and I. Miehte (eds) *Biographies and the Division of Europe: Experience, Action and Change on the 'Eastern Side'*, Opladen: Leske and Budrich, pp. 315–333.

Nagengast, C. (1991) *Reluctant Socialist, Rural Entrepreneurs: Class, Culture, and the Polish State*, Bolder, CO: Westview Press.

Pine, Fr. (2002) 'Rückzug in den Haushalt? Geschlechterspeziefische Bereiche im postsozialistischen Polen', in C. Hann (ed.) *Postsozialismus. Transformationsprozesse in Europa und Asien aus ethnologischer Perspektive*, Fankfurt and New York: Campus Verlag, pp. 147–174.

Portelli, A. (1992) 'History-telling and time: an example from Kentucky', *The Oral History Review*, 20(1/2): 51–66.

Portelli, A. (1997a) 'Oral history as genre', in A. Portelli (ed.) *The Battle of Valle Giulia: Oral History and the Art of Dialogue*, Madison: University of Wisconsin Press, pp. 3–23.

Portelli, A. (1997b) 'There's gonna always be a line', in A. Portelli (ed.) *The Battle of Valle Giulia: Oral History and the Art of Dialogue*, Madison, WI: University of Wisconsin Press, pp. 24–39.

Roth, K. (1999) 'Praktiken und Strategien der Bewältigung des Alltagslebens in einem Dorf im sozialistischen Bulgarien', *Zeitschrift für Balkanologie*, 35(1): 63–77.

Roth, K. (ed.) (2004) *Arbeit im Sozialismus – Arbeit im Postsozialismus: Erkundungen zum Arbeitsleben im östlichen Europa*, Münster: Lit-Verlag.

Roth, K. (ed.) (2006) *Arbeitswelt- Lebenswelt: Facetten einer spannungsreichen Beziehung im östlichen Europa*, Münster: Lit-Verlag.

Shlapentokh, V. (1989) *Public and Private Life of the Soviet People: Changing Values in Post-Stalin Russia*, New York and Oxford: Oxford University Press.

Siemer, K. (2002) 'What is red on the outside and white inside? The topic of the Soviet rule in Estonian life stories', in T. Jaago (ed.) *Lives, Histories and Identities*. Studies on Oral Histories, Life- and Family Stories, vol. II. Individual. Society. Life Story. Contemporary Folklore 3, Tartu: University of Tartu and Estonian Literary Museum, pp. 188–203.

Verdery, K. (1996) 'What was socialism, and why did it fall?', in K. Verdery (ed.) *What Was Socialism, and What Comes Next?*, Princeton, NJ: Princeton University Press, pp. 19–38.

Verdery, K. (2004) 'Anthropological adventures with Romania's wizard of Oz, 1973–1989', *Focaal: European Journal of Anthropology*, 43: 134–145.

Wedel, J. (ed.) (1992) *The Unplanned Society: Poland During and After Communism*, New York: Columbia University Press.

Yurchak, A. (2005) *Everything Was Forever, Until It Was No More: The Last Soviet Generation*, Princeton, NJ: Princeton University Press.

Zdravomyslova, E. and Voronkov, V. (2002) 'The informal public in Soviet society: double morality at work', *Social Research*, 69(1): 50–69.

6 Let me tell you a sad story

Soviet Russian immigrants in independent Estonia

Aili Aarelaid-Tart

Anti-Soviet revolution and Russian immigrants

The social changes that accompanied the collapse of socialism in Estonia in the 1990s replaced its former socialist legacy with new and yet abstract-seeming democratic ideas, transformed the command economy (of shortages) into an immature ultraliberal free market economy (of plenty) and raised the ethnicity-based self-confidence of the Estonian people. This tumultuous transition period was followed by a rapid increase in the complexity and number of rather ambiguous developmental tendencies in Estonian society. The times were economically hard for everybody.

The restoration of independent statehood left the Russophone 'settlers' who had arrived between 1944 and 1991 in an unenviable position as immigrants without a clear picture of either what had happened or what was to come. They were not granted automatic Estonian citizenship, and there has been plenty of debate on the requirement of being able to speak Estonian before becoming a citizen. Soviet-period settlers were often labelled with unflattering names, such as occupants, colonizers, 'homo sovieticus', 'vankad', and 'inorodnõje'. For many Soviet migrants the new social order was unfamiliar, difficult to understand, and untrustworthy. Even 15 years after the restoration of independence, people without Estonian citizenship demonstrate 2.4 times higher levels of distrust towards the institutions of the republic of Estonia than Estonian nationals (EHDR 2008: 53).

Thus, after the collapse of the Soviet Union, hundreds of thousands of Russophones were resident in the territories of the Baltic republics. The proportions of these Soviet-period eastern-Slavonic immigrants (Russians, Byelorussians, and Ukrainians) according to national census data are very high: in Estonia 28.9 per cent (2008 census); in Latvia 33.9 per cent (2009 census) but in Lithuania 6 per cent (2009 census), which is closer to the western European EU-15 national averages of 6–10 per cent but higher than the average central and eastern European immigrant populations of 1–2 per cent. The Estonian population of 1.35 million consists of approximately 1 million ethnic Estonians and 350,000 ethnic minorities. The ethnic minorities consist of three citizenship groups (defined by their passports) of roughly equal size: Estonian passport holders,

Russian passport holders, and 'grey passport'-holders who do not have a clearly defined citizenship (non-citizens). Integration of immigrant ethnic minorities, especially the non-citizens, into the social and cultural structures of the small Baltic states is extremely complicated, because large groups residing so close to their ethnic country of origin have difficulty seeing themselves as minority communities. The eastern Slavonic immigrant populations of the Baltic states prefer to interpret themselves as the 'lost sons' of Great Russia and as members of a repudiated and humiliated 'near abroad' Diaspora.

Systems theoretician Niklas Luhmann (1979) argues that a concept central to immigrant populations successfully integrating into their host societies is 'trust'. When a social actor does not understand the nature of the social environment and its development, then they may become aggressive towards the system and give into negative feelings of alienation and mistrust. Luhmann claims that a lack of trust reduces the range of possibilities for rational action in an unfamiliar situation (1979: 21), whereas Sztompka (1999: 25) contends that trust is crucial in dealing with an uncertain and hard-to-control future. Luhmann also argues that trust is only possible in a familiar world and needs common history for a reliable background (Luhmann 1979: 20). But the historical retrospective is fundamentally different for the native peoples and the Soviet immigrants. The Soviet immigrant populations are not monolithic and they vary quite a bit between the large urban metropolises and the rural areas and also small Russian dominated towns, as well as between older and younger generations. But at the mainstream level we have the classical rivalry of the triumph of the natives in restoring their statehood and the tragedy of the newcomers in losing their previously dominant position.

Many members of the Russophone population feel that they are not treated on an equal level with the Estonians. The main cause for this forlorn identification has been their social inertia in adapting to the fundamentally changing circumstances. The main factors restraining the Russophone community in coming to grips with the post-socialist social landscape are: (i) Russian immigrants during the Soviet period (1944–1991) were granted various privileges such as guaranteed employment in heavy industry or construction work, priority in accommodation and the use of Estonia's infrastructure which was significantly more developed than Russia's; (ii) the collapse of socialism led to the disappearance of many jobs, especially in heavy industry and the military ordinance industry, which were sectors of the local economy that Moscow had directly managed and controlled; (iii) rapid technological innovation meant that many Soviet period vocations became meaningless and immigrant workers were less able to adjust to the changing conditions in the labour market and therefore occupied the lower-paid positions that required lower qualifications; (iv) the Soviet period had provided a monolingual secure environment, which had been replaced by great social insecurity and ontological anxiety. The global requirement for human resource and technical managers to know at least one other language (not just Estonian) is a very disturbing aspect of the new social economic environment. Immigrant generations born before the 1970s have had the most difficulties adapting to these conditions.

The farewell to the Socialist past was a cultural trauma for many Russian immigrants, since they had perceived socialism and their privileges as 'elder brothers' to be eternal (Yurchak 2003). The Baltic revolutions stripped them of their values, and worse, the Russian federation left them at the crossroads on their own. Their choices came down to three primary variations: (i) return to Russia, where people are Russian or at least speak Russian willingly, but where the economic situation is a lot more uncertain; (ii) migrate to another country outside the former Soviet Union, and become Russian immigrants of dubious status and prestige; and (iii) stay in Estonia and find a new way of relating to the ethnic natives and their views of independent Estonia. About three out of four of the later waves of migrants chose the third option, which however proved to be as complicated a choice as any of the three. Several decades earlier many immigrants had arrived in Estonia as 'rank-and-file soldiers' of a huge Kremlin project aimed at the development of communism. That project failed throughout central and eastern Europe (CEE) and millions of Poles, Czechs, Hungarians, Balts, and others started to construct a new order of living. The Russians (mostly those in or related to the Soviet military) left the CEE area, much as the one million French soldiers and administrators who evacuated Algeria in 1962 after France's failure in the Algerian War (for independence) 1954–1962. Immediately after the Second World War, Lithuania, Latvia, and Estonia saw a massive influx of people who belonged to or were connected to militarized institutions: Soviet army bases and garrisons, militsiya (police), border guards, and the workforce of the military-industrial complex. The imported labour of later decades consisted primarily of workers for heavy industry and construction projects. Unlike the CEE countries, 'Pribaltika' (consisting of Estonia, Latvia and Lithuania) had entire new cities developed for the immigrant colonists such as Narva and Sillamäe (Estonia), Daugavpils (Latvia) and Visaginas (Lithuania). In the 1980s, the immigrants accounted for about half of the population in the capitals of Riga (Latvia) and Tallinn (Estonia). When the Soviet regime ceased to exist in the Baltic countries more than a million Russophones decided not to return to their Motherland and thus chose to try to meet their uncertain post-socialist future alongside the ethnic peoples.

Biographical ways to study the Russophone mentality

For a deeper understanding of the inner psychological crises as well as the difficulties in adapting to a rapidly changing social system, the biographical approach is quite feasible. The biographical method is a modern qualitative move towards keener insights into the intimate worlds of the social actor (Atkinson 1998). One of the central topics among researchers in the biographical field is the method of forming generalizations based on the subjectivity of their empirical material (Bertaux 1981; Ochberg 1996; Rustin and Chamberlayne 2002). While comparing and generalizing scores of orally recorded and transcribed life stories, I have developed two ways for analysing such texts: the leitmotif method and the frame analysis method (see the specific subsections).

The empirical database comprising of the 43 life stories of Russian-speakers resulting from extensive fieldwork by myself and my Russian-speaking assistants was assembled in 2001–2007. I chose to gather biographical records of Russian-speaking individuals living in Estonia. Although I speak Russian and have previous experience in biographical interviewing, the Russian-speaking respondents still perceived in me 'a danger of espionage' right from the start. Being an Estonian social scientist was sufficient to be mistrusted, even up to outright refusals to be interviewed. So I had to get the life stories by using interviewers who could speak Russian, although they were not necessarily ethnically Russian, but were Jewish, Azeri, and Armenian. I employed nine interviewers, each of whom interviewed between one and ten respondents with whom they had a trusting relationship. But even some good acquaintances refused to give interviews. My diligent guides to the Russian-speaking respondents were Aida Hachaturyan, Irina Belobrovtseva, Grigori Utkof, Boriss Baljasnõi, and Maria Tolbast. Aida Hachaturyan was inspired to transform her fieldwork into an article containing a very interesting inside look at the life in restricted-area Russian garrison complexes (Hachaturyan-Kisilenko 2003).

Some of the interviews were gathered in 2001–2003 in the course of writing biography-oriented pro-seminar theses with students of history and sociology at Tallinn University. The students were tasked with recording a three-hour biography with a person they knew well, and subsequently transcribing the material. We familiarized ourselves with the basics of the biographical method, and afterwards everyone had to write an interpretation of their interview based on the historical context. An example of this work, the transcript of Vera's biography, appears in this chapter.

The collection includes life stories from communal Russians, which with another sub-sample consisting of ex-military personnel who stayed in Estonia and their children ensure the data set differs from other collections.[1] The main feature of this sample was the military background of the first and second generations and a secondary feature of special interest consists of interviews with bilingual Russian intellectuals who hold important positions relating to local Estonian–Russian cultural contacts.

Crises in society 'always affect the substance of our biography because they put at risk any reconstructable or anticipated continuity of our self-plan' (Alheit 1994: 310). In life stories, the rapid changes and value collapses in the social environment are interpreted as personal turning points, after which the previous identity could no longer be retained. The value collapse confuses one's everyday routine, the self-evident repetition of customary events. Every respondent lived through such a situation according to their own sense of danger and tried to pass through the distorted times by means they can personally comprehend and manage. The disruption of everyday life of a social group does not become visible by opening just a few 'windows' of life stories but only becomes evident in comparing the views of the past as seen through many 'windows', thus creating a broader panorama.[2] The respondents have their personal ways of talking about these disturbing practices (individual), and generalizations and comparisons can only be made after listening to a sufficient number of interviews (universal).

Table 6.1 Number of respondents by generation and gender

	Pre-First World War generation	*Victory in the Second World War generation*	*Soviet colonists' generation*
Birth period	1900–1917	1918–1939	1940–1970
Location of birth ($n = 43$)			
Estonia	1	2	12
Russia		5	19
Latvia			2
East Germany			2
Gender mix ($n = 43$)			
Men	1	6	16
Women	0	1	19

When are there sufficient narrations for generalization? Daniel Bertaux has established the generalization-enabling numerical sufficiency of interviews in terms of 'saturation', which Miller (2000: 77) defines as 'the point at which new interviews failed to provide additional information but merely reiterated previously noted patterns'. In the case of interviews conducted with the Russianspeakers in Estonia, saturation occurred after listening to about 30 interviews, at which point subsequent presentations of traumatic feelings and unpleasant social practices started to be repetitive.

Leitmotif method in the analysis of the essence of cultural trauma

There have been several different approaches to the problem of identifying common themes in life stories. Daniel Bertaux studied biographies of bakers by fixing typical life trajectories (Bertaux and Bertaux-Wiame 1981), Jeja Pekka Roos has placed emphasis on identifying the tragic points and moral hardships when analysing the Finnish middle class (Roos 1987), and there has also been research based on gathering people's explanations for being unemployed (Leana and Feldman 1992). The idea of a leitmotif has been used by Anna Rotkirch in *The Man Question* (Rotkirch 2000). In this chapter, leitmotifs are taken to be certain themes, which occur repeatedly in many of the texts of a particular sample, not necessarily in the form and choice of words, but at least in basic content.

My sample of 43 life stories contains biographic interviews ranging from two to three hours in length, which equates to approximately 20–40 pages of written text for each interview. Finding leitmotifs in such an extensive amount of data means the researcher must have a specific target, which in this case was the narration of the restoration of the independence of Estonia as an unpleasant experience in the respondent's life. Russian speakers' life stories possess a number of other leitmotifs, clearly distinguishing them from both homeland and exiled Estonians. For instance, there is the leitmotif of characterizing the atmosphere of one's childhood home as normal ('semeinõje otnoshenija bõli vsegda normal'nõje'). Another reappearing theme is the emphasis of how cultured and silent ('kul'turno, tiho') Estonia appeared when they came here for the first time, i.e. how work was so well organized, etc. A third leitmotif concerned the understanding that all Estonians spoke Russian with them in a quite friendly manner. While interpreting leitmotifs, the researcher must not rush to the conclusion that the frequency of occurrences is in direct correlation with the objective social reality of a theme. Leitmotifs primarily echo values and a subject's positive or negative opinions on certain stances. Tom Wengraf warns about making the distinction between the 'told' life and the 'lived' life (Wengraf 2000). So one must not automatically assume that the childhood homes of most respondents had uniformly '*normal'no*' (normal) atmospheres. The high frequency of such an evaluation rather hints at the traditional stance of using a common phrase when speaking in a neutral manner of one's parental home. The researcher should also not take the Estonians' universal Russian language skills at face value. The poor Russian language skills of the average Estonian was actually a common headache for the officials in Moscow. A more fitting explanation might be that the newcomers came into contact with only specific social groups (Communist Party and Executive Committee functionaries, directors of some enterprises, and other high-ranking individuals), who at least immediately after the war were Russian-speaking Estonians, and later had to have at least minimally acceptable Russian language skills.

When talking about the leitmotifs pertaining to crises, the researcher must respect every single experience, yet also try to find a common denominator for the phenomena mentioned in many or most of the stories. Such research has been called the leitmotif method, and is used to find the common communications about unpleasant and threatening events and emotions in a particular community of memory. Obviously, life story narrators do not specifically refer to 'value collapse' or 'cultural trauma' (CT); rather, they tell their story from the point of view of suffering and living through the conditions of invisible political and social changes. The lived life of the narrator follows a sequence of real everyday events, authentic episodes taken from critical situations, but the narration imposes a new order on them, one that is significant for the narrator at the moment of the story-telling. Crises in society always affect the substance of an autobiography and the individual remembers them in a very tragic manner, which could be called the trauma discourse. In life stories, radical value shifts in the social environment are interpreted as quick and unpleasant personal turning points, after which the previous identity could no longer be retained. The value collapse confuses one's everyday routine, the self-evident repetition of customary events. Collective trauma is directly connected with mistrust; it creates social instability and evokes imagery of living in a dangerous world that is unresponsive to personal needs and interest. By selecting and grouping leitmotifs, we can create a description of the discourse, giving us a picture of the impact of the value collapse on a particular community of memory.

The manifestation of leitmotifs in the traumatic discourse of Russophones could be called the 'The Fall of the Dreamland'. In the life stories of both Russophones and ethnic Estonians there exist several post-socialist traumatic discourses like 'Lives Interrupted by Occupiers' (Kõresaar 2004), 'Brave Freedom Fighters' consisting of a constant fear of being betrayed and falling into the grasp of the Soviet reprisal system, and confrontations concerning one's entry into the Komsomol and the CPSU (Aarelaid-Tart 2006: 62). Among other biographical discourses, the 'The Fall of the Dreamland' is the most current and most painful, and more importantly is still in the making. The last aspect strongly relies on the fact that the Russian Federation has never acknowledged the occupation of the Baltic states in 1944, and on the international level wishes to depict the Russian population staying in Estonia and Latvia after 1991 as victims of ethnic discrimination. Baltic Russophones are very responsive to the Russian propaganda machinery, which presents them as people losing national and citizens' rights. The Estonian Russophones' stormy and controversial search for identity began at the same time as the ethnic Estonians' mass mobilization for restoring their national independence in 1988. There is still a nationality-based rift in interpreting the Soviet order, although the specific emphases of several confrontations have shifted over the years.

Based on numerous biographies, the Estonian Russophones' course of the 'The Fall of the Dreamland' echoes the respondent-disturbing leitmotifs (for details see Aarelaid-Tart and Belobrovtseva 2004) as:

1 an intense dissonance between the 'bad' Estonian present and the 'good' Soviet past;
2 the forceful and humiliating visa regime Estonia has with Russia, which is of importance because many Russophones have close relatives living in Russia;
3 a painful acknowledgement of the presence of ethnic Estonians and the requirement to learn their complex language;
4 Estonian authorities' interference with their habitual life;
5 Estonians insultingly labelling them as occupiers.

We provide three examples:

> I had never thought that Estonia could ever withdraw from the Soviet Union, and that the Soviet Union itself could break up. For me, Estonia was one of the republics, the technical equipment of which was better than of the others. The fact, that there is so called native nation, I realized in 1988–1989, when Estonian intellectuals started writing about the independence. After all, of course, the questions arose – what will come out of all of that, what will happen to us? I have two daughters, also by that time I have already had four grandchildren. And till now I haven't yet got a clear answer for these questions.
>
> (Man, born 1934)

> The whole system of values was turned upside down. The holidays were abolished. But did they think about what a person lives for? Probably most of the holidays should have been retained. Everything should have been thought out and planned ahead. Now, everything is just destroyed in a revolutionary manner.
>
> (Man, born 1941)

> Nobody could remain indifferent to the events of the 1989. All that is new, scares. Predictions of those days, unfortunately, came true. First of all, that after the restoration of independence the priority of the Estonian language would be established. Our children are absolutely not prepared to such a life however they have to set to learn Estonian seriously. Second, I predicted that it would become difficult to get education in Russian. In the days of our youth anyone could enter any high school, or technical secondary school – and be

> sure that he would definitely get a job after finishing. But our children go to different kinds of paid schools, but nobody guarantees them employment. Third, I predicted the rapid decline of life standards – and it became the dreadful reality. Unfortunately, you have to pay for everything – be it medical care, education, or anything else.
>
> (Man, born 1943)

Combining the leitmotif method with analysing public media can yield rather surprising results. Aida Hachaturyan[3] has presented a content analysis of Russian newspapers in a previous article of hers (2003), and we thought of trying to compare biographical and journalistic narratives. This comparison showed that the biographic interviews conducted in the 2000s directly relate to opinion pieces in local newspapers on the pitiful and humiliating status of the Russian community in the case of Estonian independence (Aarelaid-Tart and Khathaturyan 2006).

One must mention that not all of the 43 respondents portrayed their present identities according to journalistic pessimism. On the contrary, the Soviet nostalgic self-presentation was present in perhaps only half of the life stories. We can therefore only conclude that among other identity-creating methods, the Estonian Russophone community also possesses the mentality of a marginal Diaspora, which in turn was initially generated through mass media and has become the cornerstone of the Estonian Russophone memory community. Consequently they do not see their identities tied to the country they live in, but rather to some mythical homeland, a proto-Motherland, which is closely patterned on the Soviet Union that no longer exists but is still fondly remembered. Their decisions to remain in Estonia and their separation from the Motherland have had tragic consequences for these people. They have lost any hopes for a brighter future and in their new country they feel pressured into the peripheral areas, as aliens constantly opposed to the 'Others' (Estonians). As a typical conservative and poorly integrated diaspora, they want to preserve their original way of living, and do not want to learn any languages besides their own. The national regulations of their present location are taken as social harassment and human rights' violations.

Principles of frame analysis in biographical research

The leitmotif method is quite coarse and for a closer scrutiny of biographical comparatives a more flexible method is needed. The ambivalence of the respondents' self-assessments gives rise to the more general methodological problem of whether it is actually possible for the researcher to regard CT life stories in a neutral manner. In order to do that, a researcher must initially deconstruct the unreflective assumption that their narrators simply describe what has happened (Ochberg 1996: 112). Furthermore, it is evident that one person does not recall historical events more correctly than any other and no one can be offhandedly accused of fabricating false memories (of course, some persons are actually more reliable witnesses because they have a better memory for details or less ideological involvement). Rather, it is possible to group respondents according to their communities of memory (Burke 1989; Irwin-Zarecka 1994), which reflect the narrator's social position and their sense of belonging together with other people who have had similar life experiences.

In the following, I shall present a theoretical scheme that includes the main components a researcher should keep in mind when analysing an interview made with someone who has had CT-related experiences. It is a rather broad scheme and is primarily based on the frame-theories of Erving Goffman, Olaf Struck, Gerhard Riemann, and others. Goffman's classical frame theory tells 'about the organisation of experience – something that an individual actor can take into his mind – and not the organisation of society' (Goffman 1974: 13). He described social frames as 'guided doings', which 'provide background understanding for events that incorporate the will, aim, and controlling efforts of an intelligence, a live agency' (Goffman 1974: 13). Frames bring together both the actors who respond and the world they are responding to.

I also use the idea of 'keying' (Goffman 1974: 43) and claim that there exists an actor's subjective 'keying frame', which is created through the interpretation of personal past as well as any present actions in the subject's biographical narration. That frame also contains explanations of the coping strategies. This 'keying frame' is a behavioural and self-reflective personal set of conventions for finding relevant answers for how to transform the actor's behaviour to be acceptable and to conform to the new 'frame in society'. Keying is 'the process of transcription' (Goffman 1974: 44) to answer questions about what 'own' and 'right' refer to in a particular social situation, and how an actor should be involved in this changing and frequently unclear reality. My scheme, similar to Struck's (Struck 2003: 213–215), is based on an opposition of 'inner' and 'outer' frames and thus has direct connections to the treatment of human time as internal and external. Thus, my aim is to find some evidence and justification for biographical continuity in situations in which it becomes hard to manage the sharply transformed temporal order of external realities. There are six methodologically important notions in the research of post-traumatic reshaping of self-identity:

1 The outer frames of the value constellations for a social actor, which are interpreted as 'a potential world that answers all questions about what it is that shall be taken by participant as real, and how is that they should be involved in this reality' (Struck 2003: 214). Such a frame in society has developed for an individual, but independently of their actions and is perceived as a taken-for-granted social reality. The most characteristic feature of CT is the sharp and usually violent replacement of this frame with another, and the subject normally is incapable of quickly and immediately accepting this as real. There are two frames in society coexisting at the same time for a longer or shorter period, and one of them is the approved and accepted reality of the new power-holders, while the other reality is forbidden and condemned. It is often vital for the subject whether and how they can and are able to distinguish between the approved and forbidden outer frames.

2 When analysing the told story of a respondent who has encountered a CT situation, one must find out the previous habitual disposition of the actor. *Habitus* 'is the system of categorisation and thinking that are employed to order one's perception of the social environment' (Humphrey *et al.* 2003: 6). Certainly education and professional skills are important for an individual's success, but a previously cultivated worldview is also important, the more so because it has to undergo some serious corrections due to the CT circumstances. While managing a CT, the habitual disposition can change a lot, which means adaptation to a new frame in society (Segert and Zierke 2000).

3 A part of the analysis that requires a substantial knowledge of the cultural context is determining the 'community of memory' of the person who is telling the life story. Iwonna Irwin-Zarecka assumes there are 'communities of memory formed by individuals with not only common experience but a shared sense of its meaning and relevance' (Irwin-Zarecka 1994: 54). The situation is complicated by the fact that after the frame in society has changed, all communities of memory are no longer equally legitimate and the respondent may begin to hide or forget the common memories that are unsuitable in the renewed circumstances.

4 It is very important to describe an actor's mental and behavioural capability for reframing self-identity according to changed outer frames. Often this means an internal strength to intentionally act even in a hopeless situation and find the 'ways of making out' (Goffman 1974: 9). This inner capability reflects the actor's flexibility to change their socially adapted habits and 'to act in unpredictable and unfamiliar decision-making situations' (Struck 2003: 214). This 'coping capability' (Vago 1980: 353) or 'capacity to get back on their own feet' (Rustin and Chamberlayne 2002: 11) is released during a value crisis, directed towards achieving a stable understanding of the actor's life trajectory, and its reshaping of the self-identity could be perfect, or contrariwise, disadvantageous.

5 The next component of the analysis is the teller's skill of using all available recourses to keep their personal self-continuity during the discrete social processes. The personal sufferings in a CT situation are mostly 'inner events, which are not accessible to direct empirical observation' (Riemann and Schütze 1991: 339). The most extreme events of suffering can manifest in the life stories even as suppressed or hidden memories and these may not be talked about at every turning point in their lives. But the researcher can find out, which of the realistically available possibilities for managing the situation have been presented by the respondent. The usual resources for surviving sharp turning points are education, professional skills, frequently used language skills, but also the ability to use any existing social networks to fit into the changed frames in society.

6 The researcher must pay special attention to the inner censor, through which the narrator wishes to present themself in a manner suitable for the context at hand. The respondent's inner censor tries to exclude the uncomfortable

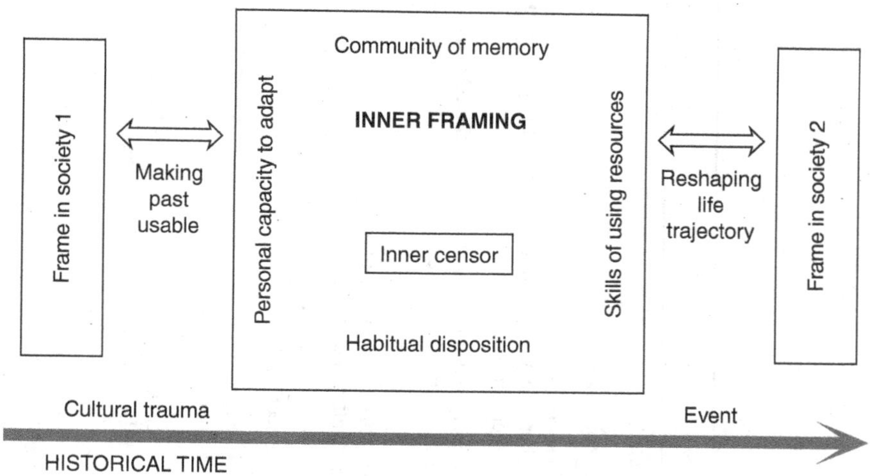

Figure 6.1 Relations between components in the frame analysis of a cultural trauma life story.

moments in life during the narration of the story (Roos 1992: 4; Passerini 1992: 15) and merely picture personal value decisions as having been made due to compulsion or the malice of fellow citizens. In most cases the past is also retouched to better fit into recent political currents.

Vera and Victor – two ways of dealing with a changed Estonian society

Below, I provide a brief comment on two rather different life stories of Estonian Russophones and then examine them through the prism of frame analysis. The complete text of Vera's life story (translated into English) is available in my book (Aarelaid-Tart 2006: 331–338). A student of mine recorded Victor's life story, which is available as a Russian language appendix to her BA work (Borovskaja 2007). I provide a quick overview of their lives in the format of *Curriculum vitae* (see Table 6.2).

On the basis of the data in Table 6.2 and the details of their life stories, I have constructed a table of Vera and Victors' inner framings (see Table 6.3).

This construct enables me to conduct frame analysis on their opportunities and abilities to cope with social change in the context of reshaping their life trajectories and facing the post-Soviet period of their life. Vera and Victor represent two different communities of Estonian Russophones: Estonian citizens and non-citizens. This does not just mean that they have different relations with state authorities, but there are also primarily fundamental differences in their previous ways of living. Vera and Victor have had varying degrees of success in integrating with the new frame of society because they have had quite different habitual

Table 6.2 Curricula vitae of Vera and Victor

	Vera	*Victor*
Year of birth	1947	1961
Place of birth	Tallinn (Estonia)	Liepaja (Latvia)
Parental status	Unmarried Father: unknown Mother: unmarried	Married Father: official of a military ship-building company Mother: dressmaker
Upbringing	Childhood and youth with grandmother in Russia in a small and poor village. Aged 16 years returned to Tallinn and her mother's second family, which did not fully accept her	Friendly and strongly patriarchal family. Aged 6 years, his parents moved to Estonia
Education	(i) village school in Russia; (ii) Russian night school in Tallinn; (iii) Railway Institute in Leningrad; correspondent course student	(i) Russian high school in Tallinn (ii) Tallinn Polytechnic Institute
Qualification	Engineering diploma	Engineering degree
Working career, pre-1991	(i) postal worker (ii) worker in an engineering plant manned by the Soviet army (iii) specialist for the state-run railway (iv) supplier in a textile	(i) engineer (ii) senior engineer (iii) head of a working group, all in a special construction factory, which was liquidated after the collapse of the Soviet Union

Working career, post-1991	(i) Russian-oriented family business in rubber technology, which collapsed during the economic blockade of 1992–1993 (ii) unemployed for a year (iii) Accountant for several small private hairdressing salons (iv) Retired in 2007	(i) unemployed for 6 months (ii) locksmith, fitter and technical director in a ship-building company, which went bankrupt in 1996 (iii) self-employed in real estate (iv) unemployed from 2009 during the world-wide economic recession
Partner status	Husband:	Wife: Russian – native born
Nationality	Russian	Does not have Estonian citizenship
Qualification	Engineering degree	Engineering degree
Current work status	Entrepreneur in apartment repairs. Information not available	Assistant kindergarten teacher
Marital status	Divorced, but living with her husband; 3 children (1 deceased)	Married with 2 daughters
Language skills	Russian (fluent), Estonian (elementary)	Russian (fluent), Estonian (fluent), English (elementary)
Citizenship	Estonian alien's passport ('grey' passport)	Estonian

Table 6.3 Comparison of Vera and Victor's inner framings

Components of inner framing	*Vera*	*Victor*
Habitual disposition:		
Family	Poor relations with her mother, excellent rapport with her grandmother, a simple village woman	Fully supported by his family, successful as a father, but authoritative
Education	Lacking basic formal schooling, but completed in applied education institutions in Russia	An academic diploma in independent Estonia
Work experience	In predominantly Soviet-style institutions before 1991; Russian-speaking collectives only	Before 1991, worked in a well-known manufacturing plant, which was innovative, R&D-based and produced a unique building material; mixed Estonian–Russian collective
Community of memory	Memories from the Russian-oriented working collectives; Neighbourhood and close friends only; Ignorant of Estonian language and customs Identifies initially (a) with the 'true' Soviet citizen Identifies after Estonia regained independence, (b) as a second-rate human, and finally (c) adopts the role of a modest actor who has come to terms with the changed circumstances.	Belongs to the group of Russians living in the Baltics who had adapted to a bilingual learning and working environment; Tolerant of Estonian and Latvian language and customs; Identifies with those Russians who can understand the indigenous ethnics' desire for freedom and who can succeed in the new nation-state.
Personal capacity to adapt	Satisfactory, more successful in known circumstances and less succesful under uncertain conditions	Good, achievement-oriented in any circumstances
Skills of using resources	Is unable to use all of the resources available and does not cultivate new ones very well	Capable of using all resources at hand
Inner censor	Did not elaborate on her relations with her mother	Only a few comments about his interactions with his wife's parents, who left Estonia after the restoration of independence

dispositions and communities of memory. Victor was educated in Tallinn where he also got his first working experience in an Estonian–Russian multi-ethnic collective. His language competence allowed him to receive Estonian citizenship and he is quite tolerant of the Estonian state and nation. Vera studied and worked in a mono-lingual environment for many years and became truly integrated into the official Soviet value system. She knew nothing about Estonian ideals, she did not need to speak Estonian at all, and she had no Estonian acquaintances. With these limited social and cultural recourses she became a person without citizenship in the restored Republic of Estonia.

Victor grew up in a family with cordial relations and common experience in adapting to changing living conditions. Victor and Vera have both lost their 'for-life' Soviet-time jobs and have experienced temporary unemployment. Victor's father offered him a new job as a locksmith, which paid well but was professionally crippling. Victor soon redesigned his career and was able to become a technical director. Following the bankruptcy of the company, he had sufficient energy and know-how to start over as an entrepreneur. He continued working as a real estate agent, a job demanding language skills and competence in ethnicity-based preferences in home design. Victor grew up in a Baltic environment (attended a Latvian kindergarten in Liepaja and an Estonian students' sport-club in Tallinn) and flexibility in inter-ethnic communications was second nature to him.

Vera had difficult times with her parents, and her relationship with her husband was not very stable either. The collapse of the Soviet Union was a catastrophe for her, because this changed the general purpose and quality of her life. Vera's family survived quite well during the start of the market economy in Estonia as they managed to set up a Russian-oriented business in rubber technology. The business went into decline after Estonia developed its national currency, the kroon, to replace the rouble, which to Vera seemed to be profoundly offensive to Russian national pride. The Russian economic blockade of Estonia in the beginning of 1990s placed Vera and her husband in an extremely difficult position. They did not have much experience in networking with Estonians, with the native cultural background and currently rapidly changing social environment. This seriously diminished their capacity to utilize habitual resources. Lacking any help from their relatives, Vera and her husband's family were simultaneously hit with unemployment, the danger of losing their home, and consequent health problems. A year later Vera had acquired a new (but lower-level) vocation in accounting, and had also learned a minimum of Estonian necessary for everyday communication with her Estonian colleagues. Vera does not plan to leave Estonia.

In conclusion, I will quote Vera and Victor themselves, as they give their final and largely positive judgments of their lives:

VERA:
It seems that the period from 1996 to 2004 has been more or less peaceful for us. I think that if there was not the issue of age, we would have no

troubles any more. Now I am already 56 years old and I cannot earn a normal salary any more.... Looking back, I think that at that time when we lost our jobs we could still have contributed a lot for our Homeland – Estonia, but, alas, we turned out to be, I do not know who (grey people). But anyway, I still take to heart all the bright changes in Estonia. What concerns studying the Estonian language, personally for me bad hearing created the biggest obstacle, but I can say that I understand something on the elementary level.

VICTOR:
Yeah, I am satisfied with my fate. Achievement, happiness – everything is included. How to formulate it? If you would like to be happy, then do so. To complain will be a sin. Working place I have, hobby I have, good family I have, even parents are alive. I am satisfied because I am socially engaged. It is most important. When one has a clear social engagement then one is happy.

Conclusion

In conclusion I can say that politicians who invoke sharp socio-economic turns always think they lay the foundations of institutions and values as new social frames, which they see as eternal and indisputably correct in guiding the general public path through their life stories. Yet in social reality, every individual lives a single life, and these great cataclysms and breakthroughs greatly disrupt their routine behaviours and mental standards. Biographical narratives demonstrate the ways people employ new thought patterns with old ones in most unexpected ways; first, in opposition to any changes and second, in finding out how to adapt better and fit in with the new environment. In doing so, they become the actors who create the new social reality, who transform the abstract schemes of the power-holders into concrete chains of social events, full of human suffering, double-dealing and white lies, but also full of joy and accomplishment.

The Russian population that settled in Estonia (or the Baltics in general) after the Second World War had to follow two completely opposite political doctrines. During the Soviet period, the political merry-go-round has given rides to three and in some cases even four generations. Of those who arrived in the 1940s, most have already passed away and even their children are now grey-haired grandparents. The participants of the second significant immigration that happened in the 1970s have also finished raising their children. Now, Russian youths born in independent Estonia are on the brink of adulthood.

After the third change of regime in 1944, the Kremlin depicted the newcomers as the liberators of the Baltics from Hitler and the bourgeois enemies of the state. The 1944 communist ideological change created a favourable environment for the Russian speakers, one in which they did not have to adapt to the local language and customs and could live for decades without coming into contact with the worldview of the indigenous people. The official ideology portrayed

Russophones as the prototypes of progressive Soviet man, allowing most of the immigrants to enjoy their national superiority and a number of intentional everyday benefits. Some of those who arrived just after the war did learn to live with the locals, taught their children to respect Estonians and fortunately such an attitude has only deepened with the passing of generations. But during the post-Second World War decades, the authorities brought into Estonia (and Latvia and Lithuania) ever-greater numbers of new Russian-speakers, primarily to aid the development of the heavy and military ordinance industries. The construction sector was also booming and entire areas were evolving with a drastically reduced Estonian presence (e.g. districts in the capital of Tallinn and entire towns in north-east Estonia). In these locations, the newcomers could easily come to the conclusion that they did, indeed, live in a great country called the Soviet Union. Unfortunately for them, that entity ceased to exist at extremely short notice and the Russophones who had moved to the Baltics in the Soviet period became foreigners overnight.

The abrupt 1991 decision by the Kremlin to remove all support for Russophones in Estonia impacted on the elder generations who keenly felt they had been abandoned to the designs of the youthful Estonian politicians of Mart Laar's government of the 30-year olds. In 1989, Estonian had been declared the conditional official language, making Estonian, in 1991, the language of the majority of bureaucratic or public procedures. The 'open' regional border between Estonia and Russia became a 'controlled' international border once economic and social interactions with Russia were no longer of primary interest to Estonia. The Russophones who chose to remain in Estonia were expected to learn the language and respect the small independent country, but feeling respect was hard, as many Russophones felt harassed and humiliated. When Vladimir Putin came to power in Russia, diplomatic relations cooled significantly, with Russia branding Estonia as a fascist midget state that violates the human rights of Russians. This particular Russian propaganda topic has both adherents and opponents, and the views of the middle-aged and elder Russophones are not summarily decisive.

The members of Russophone generation, who were born and brought up during the collapse of socialism or afterwards in independent Estonia, are the ones now making up their minds about their relationship with Estonia. They have studied Estonia's history and constitution and learned the language sufficiently to enable them to acquire Estonian citizenship with minimal effort. They are consequently able, not only to easily work in a multi-ethnic environment, but also to serve with the Estonian defence forces. But does this mean that they want to become 'true' Russian-speaking Estonians loyal to the land of their birth? There is not a single all-embracing answer. This generation is every bit as divided as any that came before.

The riots of the 'Bronze Soldier nights' that happened in April 2007 consisted mainly of groups of Russian-speaking youths incited by Putin's propaganda. A consequence of the riots was an increase in the number of young Estonian-born Russians who opted for Russian citizenship. Although a sociological survey conducted in 2008 indicated that almost half (49 per cent) of the Estonian-born Russians do not think of a future in Estonia, the other half feels that they are unquestionably a part of Estonian society. A vivid example of such an attitude was the incident in March 2009, when the leader of the Students' Representative Assembly for Russian schools in Estonia, Sergei Metlev, courageously opposed the Russian ambassador to Estonia, Nikolai Uspenski, when the latter spoke of the repression of Russian language schools and Russian teachers in Estonia. In an article in the Estonian newspaper *Postimees*, Metlev (2009) said that Russian-speaking 'children of liberty' had no desire to become the playthings of the great eastern neighbour's mass media and wished to be prosperous members of a multicultural Estonia.

Notes

1 See Aarelaid-Tart (2006: 16) for details of the three collections of life stories compiled by the author.
2 Paul Thompson (1978) devised the 'window' method.
3 Hachaturyan also spelt as Khachaturian; Khathaturyan.

References

Aarelaid-Tart, A. (2006) *Cultural Trauma and Life Stories*, Helsinki:Kikimora Publishers.

Aarelaid-Tart, A. and Belobrovtseva, I. (2004) 'The (im)possibilities of Estonian-Russian dialogue in the conditions of cultural trauma', in A.P. Klemeševa (ed.) *Na perekrestke kultur: russkie v Baltiiskom regione*, vol. II, Kaliningrad: Baltiiskii Mezhregionalnyi Institut Obchcestvennyh Nauk.

Aarelaid-Tart, A. and Khathaturyan, A. (2006) 'Diskurs kulturnoi travmy v russkojazychnoi srede Estonii' ('Discource of cultural trauma among Russian-speaking community in Estonia'), *Sotsiologicheskije issledovanija (SocIs)*, 10, pp. 57–65.

Alheit, P. (1994) 'Everyday time and life time', *Theory and Society*, 3(3): 305–319.

Atkinson, R. (1998) *The Life Story Interview*, *Qualitative Research Methods*, 44, Thousand Oaks, CA: Sage.

Bertaux, D. (1981) 'From the life-history approach to the transformation of sociological practice', in D. Bertaux (ed.) *Biography and Society: The Life History Approach*, London, Thousand Oaks and New Delhi: Sage.

Bertaux, D. and Bertaux-Wiame, I. (1981) 'Life stories in the bakers 'trade', in D. Bertaux (ed.) *Biography and Society: The Life History Approach*, pp. 29–45. London, Thousand Oaks and New Delhi: Sage.

Borovskaja, A. (2007) Vera ja Viktor – kahe eesti-venelase elulugu (Vera and Victor – life stories of two Estonian Russians), unpublished BA theses in sociology, Tallinn University.

Burke, P. (1989) 'History as social memory', in T. Butler (ed.) *Memory, History, Culture and Mind*, Oxford and New York: Blackwell, pp. 97–113.

EHDR (Estonian Human Development Report) 2007 (2008) Tallinn: Eesti Koostöö Kogu.

Goffman, E. (1974) *Frame Analyse: An Essay on the Organisation of Everyday Experience*, Cambridge, MA: Harvard University Press.

Hachaturyan-Kisilenko, A. (2003) 'An attempt to describe life in a Soviet military garrison through biographical material', in *Pro Ethnologia, 16: Studies on Socialist and Post-socialist Everyday Life*, Tartu: Publications of the Estonian National Museum.

Humphrey, R., Miller, R. and Zdravomyslova, E. (eds) (2003) *Biographical Research in Eastern Europe: Altered Lives and Broken Biographies*, Aldershot and Burlington: Ashgate.

Irvin-Zarecka, I. (1994) *Frames of Remembrance: The Dynamics of Collective Memory*, New Brunswick and London: Transaction Publishers.

Kõresaar, E. (2004) 'Insights into memory, history and life story in post-Soviet Estonia', in E. Kõresaar (ed.) *Memory and History in Estonian Post-Soviet Life Stories: Private and Public, Individual and Collective from the Perspective of Biographical Syncretism* (Dissertationes Etnologiae Universitatis Tartuensis 1), Tartu: Tartu University Press.

Leana, C.R. and Feldman, D.C. (1992) *Coping with Job Loss: How Individuals, Organizations, and Communities Respond to Layoffs*, New York, Oxford, Singapore and Sydney: Lexington Books.

Luhmann, N. (1979) *Trust and Power*, Chichester: John Wiley.

Metlev, Sergei (2009) 'Täisealise valik' ('The choice of an adult'), *Postimees*, March, 27.

Miller, R. (2000) *Researching Life Stories and Family Histories*, London: Sage.

Ochberg, R.L. (1996) 'Interpreting life stories', in R. Josselson (ed.) *Ethics and Process: The Narrative Study of Lives, 4*, London, Thousand Oaks and New Delhi: Sage.

Passerini, L. (1992) 'Introduction', in L. Passerini, (ed.) *Memory and Totalitarianism: Vol. 1, International Yearbook of Oral History and Life Stories*, Oxford: Oxford University Press.

Riemann, G. and Schütze, F. (1991) 'Trajectory as a basic theoretical concept for suffering and disorderly social processes', in D.R. Maines (ed.) *Social Organization and Social Processes: Essays in honor of Anselm Strauss*, Howthorne and New York: Aldur de Gruyter.

Roos, J.P. (1987) *Suomalainen elämä: Tutkimus tavallisten suomalaisten elämäkerroista (Finn lives: Reseach on ordinary Finnish life stories)*, Finland: SKS.

Roos, J.P. (1992) 'European Lives: The question of cultural comparisons through life stories: Childhood as a cultural constant', paper presented at the workshop 'Constructions of childhood', Voss, May 1992.

Rotkirch, A. (2000) *The Man Question. Love and Life in Late 20th Century Russia*. Department of Social Policy, Research Reports 1, Helsinki: University of Helsinki.

Rustin, M. and Chamberlayne, P. (2002) 'Introduction: from biography to social policy', in P. Chamberlayne, M. Rustin and T. Wengraf (eds) *Biography and Social Exclusion in Europe*, Cambridge: The Polity Press.

Segert, A. and Zierke, I. (2000) 'The metamorphosis of habitus among East Germans', in P. Chamberlayne, J. Bornat, and T. Wengraf (eds) *The Turn to Biographical Methods in Social Science: Comparative issues and examples*, London and New York: Routledge.

Sztompka, P. (1999) *Trust: A Sociological Theory*, Cambridge: Cambridge University Press.

Struck, O. (2003) 'Trajectories of coping strategies in Eastern Germany', in R. Humphrey, B. Miller and E. Zdravomyslova (eds) *Biographical Research in Eastern Europe: Altered Lives and Broken Biographies*, London: Ashgate.

Thompson, P. (1978) *The Voice of the Past*, Oxford: Oxford University Press.

Vago, Ṡ. (1980) *Social Change*. New York and Chicago: *Hold Rinehart and Winston*.

Wengraf, T. (2000) 'Uncovering the general from within the particulars: from contingencies to typologies in the understandings of cases', in P. Chamberlayne, J. Bornat and T. Wengraf (eds) *The Turn to Biographical Methods in Social Science: Comparative Issues and Examples*, London and New York: Routledge, pp. 140–164.

Yurchak, A. (2003) 'Soviet hegemony in form: everything was forever, until it was no more', *Comparative Studies in Society and History: An International Quarterly*, 45(3): 480–509.

7 Rural belongings

Baltic Russian identities in Estonian and Latvian borderlands

Laura Assmuth

Introduction

There are hundreds of thousands of ethnic Russians and Russian speakers living permanently in the Baltic states of Estonia, Latvia, and Lithuania. Some are citizens of the Baltic states, or Russia, or other former republics of the Soviet Union (e.g. Ukraine, Belarus, Kazakhstan). In addition, quite a large percentage of ethnic Russians or Russian speakers living in the Baltic states are stateless people. Since very large numbers of Russians and Russian speakers moved to the Soviet Baltic republics in the Soviet period, their whole presence has often been seen as a legacy of only the Soviet period. The way the Baltic Russians are seen and discussed is further complicated and distorted by the attempts of the Russian federation to use their status and condition as political leverage against Estonia and Latvia (in Lithuania the number and percentage of Russians has consistently been smaller and has thus created less controversy). Moreover, in the public and political discussions, Russians in the Baltics are almost always represented as a more or less homogenous group. In this chapter, I wish to draw attention to some neglected aspects of the Russian presence in the Baltic states of Estonia and Latvia. First, I discuss ethnic Russian people and groups of people who have 'always' lived in the territories of today's Estonia and Latvia; and second, I point out the great variation of identities among the different members of the Russian population. The ways in which ethnic identities intertwine and interact with linguistic, religious, citizenship and local identities of individuals are analysed, based on the research results of an anthropological research project. The chapter concludes with a discussion of possible new identities of people with Russian and Soviet backgrounds living permanently in the Baltics.

My approach to the Baltic Russians is informed by my disciplinary background in social anthropology where individuals' experiences and identities are primarily explored through the methodology of ethnographic fieldwork. When an anthropologist meets, observes, participates, chats, and discusses with individual people in face-to-face encounters during prolonged periods of fieldwork, in particular communities, they necessarily pay attention not only to similarities but also to variation among groups of people. This type of a personalized and localized micro-level research approach is balanced and enriched by the outsider's viewpoint that being a foreign researcher means that, especially in a politicized atmosphere of ethnic or other tensions, people often find it much easier to talk openly to a stranger. A relaxed yet focused interview session with an interested outsider, the anthropologist, provides the respondent with a welcome possibility to ponder about and spell out their thoughts about issues that matter personally – also identity issues which are often taken for granted and therefore not discussed with family, kin, friends, and neighbours. In this chapter I wish to contribute to the discussion on Baltic identities by focusing on rural Russians whose social realities are surprisingly little known even in Estonia and Latvia, not to mention Russia and elsewhere.

Our small team of Estonian, Finnish, Latvian, and Russian anthropologists has for several years studied the complexities of daily life and identity formation in the border area between Estonia, Latvia and Russia.[1] We have conducted interviews on ethnic, linguistic, and religious identity, everyday life at the border and local and family history in various borderland communities in the three countries; we have carried out participant observations in selected locations, and collected written materials from high-school students. Among the key research questions are: What does ethnicity mean to the people who live at or close to the border? What relevance does ethnic identity have in their everyday lives? How are the residents' identities constructed? Do they think of themselves primarily as Estonian, Latvian or Russian citizens, or Estonian, Seto, Latvian, or Russian by ethnicity, or speakers of Russian, Estonian, Latvian, Seto, or other languages, or as inhabitants of their respective villages, regions, and towns? Or perhaps some or all of these identities in different situations and in different contexts? In this chapter I focus on the Russian-speaking borderland residents of Estonia and Latvia and their own understandings of being Russian. The discussion is based on in-depth thematic interviews with local Russian speakers who were willing to discuss their identities with a foreign anthropologist and her local colleagues.

The discussion is based on intermittent ethnographic fieldwork in villages and towns in the borderland between Estonia, Latvia, and Russia; see Assmuth (2003, 2005, 2007) for detailed descriptions of the research area. The main research data are transcripts of long theme interviews conducted during 2000, 2004, 2005, and 2006 with men and women of different ages, nationalities, citizenships and social positions. Besides the transcribed interviews, the other large corpus of research data consists of essays (n = 110), written by school pupils (aged 17–18 years) from the study areas in 2000, on the themes of ethnic and local identity and the border. These were collected by way of a writing competition organized in local schools by interested teachers.

Although we have not done explicitly biographical but ethnographical research, a biographical element is very much present in the interviewees' way of speaking and thinking about their identities. The narrated descriptions of significant life events, in which identities become heightened, altered or just visible in a novel way are the material on which I base my analysis. Also our fieldwork methodology brings us quite close to biographical (narrative) research: to start with an open and informal discussion about themes such as border and identities we usually asked the interviewee simply to 'tell us about their life'. Some of the interviews can thus be considered more biographical than thematic, and in all of them, biographical, personal events formed the background to our more thematic concerns.

Ethnicity at a post-Soviet borderland

Anthropologist Bruce Kapferer has written, in the context of the ethnically motivated war and violence between the Tamils and Sinhalese in Sri Lanka, that 'ethnicity is not merely a social construction and therefore a cultural construction but it assumes the dimensions it does through the cultural logics embedded in the institutions of the modern state' (2002: 5). Therefore, social and cultural forces such as ethnicity must be understood and studied in the context of political entities and forces, i.e. states. In a borderland situation states from two (or more) sides affect the lives of local people in many concrete ways. What is more, both the policies of the states in question and the actual borders frequently change. People living in the borderlands '[n]ot only have to deal with the institutions of their own state, but with those institutions of the state or states across the border, entities of equal and sovereign power which overshadow all border relations' (Wilson and Donnan 1998: 8). Ethnicity intermingles with these complex forces, and easily becomes politicized. More generally, ethnicity and ethnically motivated political claims need to be taken into account and taken seriously in the process of trying to create democratic state structures and civil society.

Also political scientist George Schöpflin reminds us that '[D]emocracy is composed of three key, interdependent elements: civil society, the state and ethnicity. These three are in a continuous, interactive relationship' (1997: 1). Using Schöpflin's argument in our case we can say that in the Soviet era the uniform communist state was all-powerful and omnipresent, civil society almost non-existent, and ethnicity a controlled and suppressed force in the hands of those in power. In the post-Soviet situation there are now three different states as actors in this area; ethnicity has become a matter of personal identities and choice, and civil society is developing, albeit hesitantly and slowly, especially on the Russian side (see Alapuro *et al.*, 2004). The time and place of our exploration of (Russian) identities is of crucial importance here: it is the specific context of the post-Soviet societies of Estonia, Latvia, and Russia, each of which is involved in redefining and rebuilding its nationhood in the 1990s and the first half of the 2000s. First, in this study context identities are very much in a state of flux and second, discourses involving ethnic and other identities necessarily become political. We have with our research methodology participated in ongoing discourses on a personal and local level, and provided a space for the interviewees to ponder about the changes from their point of view.

A discourse about ethnic identities is of course present in a multi-ethnic borderland context of the former Soviet Union, but ethnicity is usually presented and understood as one significant identification among many. In the research area Seto ethnicity certainly has become more pronounced and appreciated lately; one can even speak of a Seto cultural revival. Kaiser and Nikiforova (2006) have even linked the development of Seto ethnic identity and the Seto cultural movement specifically to the establishment of the present state border. On the basis of our interview material, I would rather conclude that in the circumstances of the nationality policies of the Soviet Union there was a clear ethnic dichotomy between Russians and Estonians, and no room for a Seto ethnic identity to develop. Our Estonian-speaking interviewees, both in Estonia and in the Pechory district in Russia, frequently said they had always felt themselves to be Estonians, even in Soviet times. The language and customs, and the obligatory designation of *natsional'nosti* (ethnicity, nationality) on personal documents, had marked that basic distinction quite clearly in a multicultural environment. Thus, ethnicity had always mattered and ethnic boundaries had always been there, but only lately had a specific Seto sub-ethnicity come to the fore. People were now making finer distinctions than before; 'gradually I began to realise that I was and I had always been Seto, not just Estonian', as one male interviewee explained.

But ethnic (or national) identity[2] is not the only kind of identity that was important to our interviewees. As noted above, ethnicity seems to be very important to most Setos (see also Võro Instituut 1998). Many Estonians and Latvians in the region, on the other hand, take their Estonianness or Latvianness very much for granted; for them other distinctions, such as language (dialect) and locality are at least as important markers of identity as ethnicity (cf. Võro Instituut 2000). A local village identity is very important in the Russian village of Lavry with its distinctive history of ethnic Latvians and Russians having lived under Estonian rule during 1918–1940 (first Estonian republic).

The ideas of the ethnic Russian interviewees living in the Russian Pechory district, bordering with both Estonia and Latvia, about what it means for them to be Russian also vary a great deal. In just one village, Lavry, which is very close to the Latvian border, opinions and ideas range from extreme, chauvinistic Russophilia to the idealization of the Latvian history and heritage of the village. In the first case, Russianness is constructed in firm opposition to other identities and peoples, and is seen to be far superior to either Estonianness or Latvianness. In the second case, Russianness is constructed on the basis of a multicultural local identity, which means that it is flexible and changeable. As in many other instances we have witnessed, women are the active agents in 'tradition work' of ethnic groups: in the families that have a Latvian origin women pass on the stories, pictures, and documents that relate to Latvianness, and are the ones most likely to be able to speak Latvian. Among the local Russian population the female librarian/local museum curator collects and preserves the Latvian heritage of the village.

By contrast, in the predominantly Russian-speaking villages on the Latvian side of the borderland interviewees commonly referred to themselves as 'Russian Latvians', even when they were not Latvian citizens. Many people made it absolutely clear to us that they feel different from Russians in Russia proper and that they get treated differently as being viewed as Westernized, Latvianized, or

Estonianized, by Russians on the other side of the border or while visiting Moscow or St. Petersburg.

The story told by Anastasija (45 years old), a Russian Latvian woman from the Latvian village of Pededze, three kilometres from the Russian border, is a typical example of 'Othering'. She told us how she is considered different, Latvianized, by her friends and relatives who live in Russia and whom she visits.[3]

INTERVIEWER: How do your relatives in Russia see you when you visit – do they treat you like a foreigner by now? [Anastasija has lived in Latvia since the 1980s.]

ANASTASIJA: Let me tell you a story. It seems paradoxical, but this is how it is. I have this girlfriend whom I hadn't met in 20 years. She lives on the outskirts of St. Petersburg. Last time I was there, I happened to pop into her – I was travelling by tram, got off, and there she was, standing, just by chance! Imagine, in a big city like St. Petersburg!

'Well, we hugged each other of course and started chatting, and then she told me, sort of jokingly: "Well well, there is clearly something Latvian in you!' But when I came back [from Russia to Latvia], another girlfriend of mine immediately told me: 'But now you really look like a real Russian, a Russian Russian!" That was really funny for me, how differently people see you. That old girlfriend in Russia was so certain that something Latvian had stuck in me. I wonder what that might be?'

Anastasija tells the story in an ironic tone since she wonders herself what that mysterious 'Latvianness' stuck in her might be. She has clearly thought about the matter a great deal, as have most of our Russian interviewees living in Estonia and Latvia. In some situations and contexts they wished to stress their Russian or (Russian village) identity, in other contexts they emphasized more the differences between their own Russian Latvian or Russian Estonian culture and that of the 'true Russians'. Hilary Pilkington (1998), in her study of ethnic Russians who migrated from the former Soviet republics to Russia, also notes that Russians who have lived among other nationalities often develop a heightened sense of their Russianness. They feel different or superior to Russians in Russia, and definitely get treated differently by them. This is clear in this typical quote from one of Pilkington's interviewees: 'Although we are Russians (*russkie*), we are not the same kind of Russians that live here' (Pilkington 1998: 191). Also Irina Novikova (2008), in her research on Russian-speaking elderly women in Riga, discusses how eagerly Russian-speaking residents of the capital city of Latvia nowadays distance themselves from 'those Russians in Russia'.

As Norwegian anthropologist Fredrik Barth noted in his classic study '*Ethnic groups and boundaries*' (1969), ethnic identities are formed at the boundaries around and between ethnic groups, through the contrast with other groups. Borderland people or others living in a multi-ethnic environment observe and discuss these variations daily and thus participate in the reformulation of significant differences between the groups. However, Barth's analysis did not deal sufficiently with the status differences between ethnic groups, which is where Pierre Bourdieu's (1984) concept of distinction comes in useful. Individuals from different ethnic groups struggle for prestige and higher status for themselves and their group, and try to distance themselves from groups and individuals with a lower status. Status hierarchies are of course changing through the course of history, and very much so in the rapidly changing post-Soviet societies. For example, the disparaged 'old values' culture of the Setos has become prestigious in its exoticism, and being a European or Baltic Russian is definitely preferable to being an ordinary Russian of Russia (cf. Pilkington 1998; Novikova 2008).

Ethnicity in relation to language

On the western shore of Lake Peipus (Peipsi), which separates Estonia from Russia, are the villages of the orginal Old Believer migrants from the sevententh century: Nina, Kolkja, Kasepää and Varnja. Nina is one of the oldest settlements of Russians in Estonia. The majority of the villagers are Russian speakers, most of them are also Russian Orthodox by religion. In Nina we encountered many very different kinds and understandings of Russian identity. For example, there is the strong and firm Russian Estonian identity of Vladimir, a local man in his seventies, a former Soviet soldier, prisoner-of-war and 'enemy of the Soviet state' who spent years in concentration and labour camps both in Germany and the Soviet Union. He insisted on speaking only Estonian (which he had mastered perfectly) with us, and willingly and without prompting defined himself as '*a proud citizen of Estonia who learned Russian as his first language*'. But we also spoke with Svetlana, 50 years old, born and raised in central Russia, who had come to work in Soviet Estonia 'just by chance', married and stayed, and suddenly found herself living in a foreign country. Adjusting to that new situation had been very hard for her, especially language-wise. Technically, both Svetlana and Vladimir are Estonian citizens whose mother tongue is Russian, but their ideas about being Russian Estonians were almost the opposite. From the start, Svetlana had problems with the question 'what is your ethnic, national identity?' Only when we asked her repeatedly and in many different ways (in Russian,) she replied: 'You might simply call me a Russian person who lives in Estonia, because that's what I am'.

Vladimir's certainty (and pride)with the same question and Svetlana's hesitation taught us researchers an important lesson: for our interviewees, either or both ethnic and national identities were issues that were relevant and spoken about in relation to something else, not as separate, well-defined identity categories. In Vladimir's case, his Russian Estonian identity was related to locality, citizenship and language; for Svetlana, the crucial thing was her Russianness related to birthplace, family and language and unaltered by (Estonian) citizenship and long-term residency. In yet more cases, people would talk about their ethnic identities mainly or only in relation to religion.

The research methodology of doing ethnographic interviews made it quite natural to start discussing the relevance of language and language use for our interviewees. The researchers worked in pairs so that each interviewee was able to choose the preferred language of the interview; very often it happened that both Estonian and Russian or Latvian and Russian were used.

Ivan was born in 1945 in Soviet Russia, in the Pechory region, which had belonged to the Estonian republic in 1920–1940. He now lives in the town of Võru in south-east Estonia. Ivan is married, and his wife is also Russian. He told us that he had come to live and work in Soviet Estonia in the 1960s, like tens of thousands of Soviet citizens from all over the USSR. The interview with Ivan took place in the Russian language.

INTERVIEWER: When you came to live here in Estonia, you did not speak any Estonian?

IVAN: No I didn't. My mother could speak some Estonian but she has a strong Russian accent to it. I did learn something from her when I was a child, I could at least count up to ten … And when I came here to work I could understand at least something. But not much. Later at work I learned more and more, everything related to work [as a bus-driver] I know pretty well. I can manage. I only regret I could not go to school here … I know most words but nothing of the grammar. My workmates of course can understand me even when I don't speak properly.

INTERVIEWER: At home you speak Russian, but outside of the home, according to which language is required?

IVAN: That is correct. My children speak Estonian very well, they went to the kindergarten here. At school they studied in Russian, but still, their Estonian is fine. Both my children's spouses are ethnic Estonians.

INTERVIEWER: So that your grandchildren are half Estonian, half Russian?

IVAN: Yes. My three-year-old granddaughter spends a lot of time at our home and she can speak Russian also.

Besides the crucial differentiation of who speaks what as their native language, ethnic differences are often expressed with regard to living standards and quality of life. All our interviewees in Estonia and Latvia with connections to Russia, regardless of their ethnicity, eagerly participated in a discourse of comparison between 'here and there, West and East'. This was also the case with Ivan:

INTERVIEWER: Is there a difference between Russians in Russia and Russians in Estonia?

IVAN: Well, for sure there is … Here I live a better life. Although my wages aren't much, I can get by. Life is better here and it is easier to live your life … Of course, this applies if you have got a job and get a decent salary for it.

INTERVIEWER: There's no difference with regard to language [between Russians in Estonia and Russians in Russia]?

IVAN: Well, I don't know … When I visit in Russia my sister tells me I speak Russian with a clear Estonian accent. Naturally I argue against that and say there can't be any difference.

INTERVIEWER: In Russia, do people consider you as an ordinary Russian just like anyone, or do they consider you as a Russian Estonian? Do they see you to some extent as a foreigner or just as one of them?

IVAN: Well, among my closest relatives I am of course one of them. But others ... well, they don't always treat you so well ... I think it has to do with the relations between Estonia and Russia which aren't so good.

INTERVIEWER: Maybe they are envious of you?

IVAN: Maybe envious or else a little bit hostile towards you because you come from Estonia. Not everybody of course, there are all kinds of people in Russia, just like everywhere. You just get that feeling over there, I can't explain it. You don't belong. Fully.

Ivan's experiences with some Russians in Russia being suspicious of and even hostile to a Russian person from Estonia is a sad but typical example of state-level politics entering into and having an effect on personal relations. Powerful stereotypes about the qualities of Russians, Estonians, Latvians, and others are there already, and nationalistic and xenophobic politics play on and exaggerate them, in all directions. Concurrent with the decline of personal, face-to-face encounters across the borders, people increasingly rely only on media representations about the neighbouring countries and peoples, as they do in this rural area (see Manakov 1999: 131). This makes them more prone to prejudiced views and attitudes about the inhabitants of the neighbouring country. According to results from various opinion polls and surveys conducted in the three countries, negative stereotypes about Russia and Russians are indeed very common both among ethnic Estonian and ethnic Latvian youth. Young Russians in Russia tend to take a more positive view of Estonia and Estonians than of Latvia and Latvians, which again reflects the very negative media representations in Russia concerning Latvia (Kuldin 1999). Increasingly, young people's opinions about 'what the Russians/Estonians/Latvians are like' are formed in the national capitals in events like the Bronze Soldier riots in Tallinn, not in relationships of proximity among the borderland peoples themselves.

Ethnicity and religion

Valentina was born in 1961 in Beresje, a village in south-east Estonia. She now lives in the university city of Tartu where she works as a nurse. Valentina's mother tongue is Russian, but since she is married to an ethnic Estonian she is practically bilingual. Valentina chose to be interviewed in Estonian and the children are also completely bilingual. Language for Valentina is not, therefore, the defining criterium for self-identification. Instead, as an Old Believer (pre-seventeenth century schism of Russian Orthodoxy), her religion is a very important marker of identity for her and also sets her (and her home village) apart from 'Russian Russians':

INTERVIEWER: So you are saying that there was always a cultural border [between Russian Russians and Russian Estonians]?

VALENTINA: Yes, a cultural dividing line. Like, we have never thought that they were just like us, although they are Russians like us, in Russia.

INTERVIEWER: Yes, that I find very interesting and unexpected, somehow.

VALENTINA: We [Russian Old Believers living in Estonia] have always considered Russian Russians as different from us. We live separately from them ... And of course, it has to do with religion. We have our own religion. That explains a lot.

INTERVIEWER: And your religion is the Old Believer's faith?

VALENTINA: Yes, that is the relevant thing.

INTERVIEWER: And is it still adhered to? Is it important for you personally?

VALENTINA: Yes, I guess. Although I don't follow all the strict rules anymore ... You know, these days it has become like a tourist attraction, they have discovered that here [in the village] we still practice religion in the old way, it has become appealing ... [laughter]. They even repaired the road to our village so that the tourist buses can come in. And the people [tourists] watch us [laughter]. Followers of the Old Faith.

VALENTINA'S DAUGHTER (born in 1985): I don't really know how important the old faith is for me, but I have had my child christened according to our traditions. Also my sister's child is. We can't really do otherwise, it just feels right. That is what makes us Russian Old Believers, the ancient traditions. Not the strict rules which they had in the old days, but I guess there are some remnants of that even now.

As Valentina notes, the ancient and quaint traditions of the Old Believers and their picturesque villages have in independent Estonia become a tourist attraction of sorts, which might paradoxically help to keep the traditions alive. All the Old Believers we have spoken to consider religious identity to be of paramount importance: to be Russian by ethnicity has little meaning, but by contrast being a Russian Old Believer matters a great deal. Interestingly, although there are also Old Believers in Russia, mostly in peripheral regions, the Baltic Old Believers draw a clear dividing line between themselves ('we in Estonia') and Russians in Russia, whom they consider to be 'just ordinary Orthodox Russians'.

Both Zenovja (born 1916) and her daughter Ljudmila (born 1947) were born and still live in the Old Believers' village of Nina. Zenovja and Ljudmila are ethnic Russians and practising Russian Orthodox believers. Their whole family was deported to the Ural region in central Soviet Union during the Second World War and Ljudmila was born there. The interview went on in Russian.
Interviewer: Did you always have an Estonian passport?

ZENOVJA, THE MOTHER: Yes, the passport of the state of Estonia all along.

LJUDMILA, THE DAUGHTER: My father had his passport from the [First] Estonian Republic kept hidden. And my forefathers are buried here from the early 19th century and even before that. Our family has always lived here, in Estonia.

INTERVIEWER: Do you feel Estonian or Russian?

ZENOVJA: Well I am Estonian because I live in Estonia.

LJUDMILA: I am Russian ... [both laugh]

ZENOVJA: But to be a real Estonian one would have to speak Estonian...

INTERVIEWER: Maybe you are both Estonian and Russian?

ZENOVJA: Yes, I have nothing against that. But I am Russian [Orthodox] and when I die, they will bury me in a Russian [Orthodox] cemetery...

LJUDMILA: But mother, anyone can be an Orthodox follower of Christendom – a Russian, a German, anyone.

Mother and daughter have somewhat diverging opinions about what makes a person to be of a particular nationality; the elderly mother stresses the importance of linguistic ability to truly belong. Still, she can think of herself as both Russian and Estonian, having been born in Estonia and having carried an Estonian passport through the many years of changing political regimes. On the other hand, the daughter born in the Soviet period considers herself firmly to be Russian, as this was the natural and preferred choice for a Russian-speaking person in the Soviet Union. The distinguishing criterium between ethnic groups that Zenovja uses, who is buried in which cemetery, is an interesting one we encountered frequently during fieldwork. We often heard from elderly people that 'during our lifetime we are all the same and equal, but it in the end, what really matters is where and with whom we are buried'. The strong link that is made between Russianness and Russian Orthodoxy reminds us of the continuous power of religion to shape and define identities (Kormina 2003).

Again, Zenovja, and Ljudmila came to notice their 'different kind of Russianness' through a contrast with a different kind of reality:

INTERVIEWER: Is there a difference between an Russian Estonian and a Russian Russian? When you visit Russia, do you feel yourselves at home or abroad?

ZENOVJA: Of course it is not like home there in Russia! Home is here...

LJUDMILA: No, I have no intention whatsoever to move from here. When we lived in Russia [during and after the war], even then we were always called and considered Estonians, not Russians.

INTERVIEWER: Your mother tongue is Russian, and you were still treated as Estonians?

LJUDMILA: Yes, definitely.

Zenovja's and Ljudmila's war-time experiences about being called, considered and treated as Estonians while living in Soviet Russia are related to how Baltic residents were viewed in the Soviet Union in general. Despite the forceful propaganda that the Baltic states of Estonia, Latvia, and Lithuania had been liberated exclusively by the Red Army from the occupation by Nazi Germany and had joined the Soviet Union voluntarily, there was always a popular understanding among Soviet citizens that the Baltic republics were 'different from the rest'. In the context of the Soviet Union, they were the Soviet west: the most developed and the most envied part of the country, 'the model socialist republics' (see Assmuth 2001). During the Second World War, some nationalities like Germans or Finns were designated as 'enemy nationalities' and persecuted collectively, and during the Stalinist regime belonging to any minority nationality could always become a serious liability. However, depending on circumstances and individual luck, even in localities experiencing forced deportations there were Soviet citizens who viewed Estonians, Latvians. and Lithuanians with high regard, as being (more) cultured, civilized, and generally advanced.

Multiple identities, or remnants of Soviet identity

Fjodor, a Russian Estonian Old Believer (born 1913), has lived all his life on the small island of Piirissaar [translates as 'border island'] in the middle of Lake Peipus. The majority of islanders are Russian speakers and also Old Believers. At the time of the interview Fjodor was the eldest resident on the island and a very well liked and respected figure. The interview went on both in Estonian and in Russian – Fjodor shifted very easily between languages, almost without noticing it. His flexible language use reflects an unproblematic mixed identity as a Russian speaker (linguistic identity), Estonian citizen (state identity) and Russian Old Believer (religious identity).

INTERVIEWER: Did your parents also come from here [the island]?
FJODOR: Yes. All of them, all my family is from here.
INTERVIEWER: And you have been a fisherman all your life?
FJODOR: All my long life [90 at the time of the interview].
INTERVIEWER: Did you go to school on the island?
FJODOR: Yes, here on Piirissaar.
INTERVIEWER: A Russian language school?
FJODOR: Russian language.
INTERVIEWER: But you also learned Estonian at school?
FJODOR: Also at school, but mostly because I worked as a young boy for four years on the mainland – working as a farming hand on a big farm. There I also spoke and learned a lot of Estonian.
INTERVIEWER: Do you still need the Estonian language in your everyday life here on the island?
FJODOR: Yes, I do. When somebody from the mainland comes here who doesn't know Russian, I use Estonian. But you know, here on Piirissaar all the local Estonians speak Russian: maybe at home they speak only Estonian amongst themselves, but with others, with us Russians, they all speak Russian. Some speak Russian with a slight Estonian accent, but others have no accent whatsoever. Then you can't tell whether they are ethnic Estonians or Russians, there is no difference. My Estonian used to be like that when I needed it more, now it has become rustier.

As Fjodor explains, for him and his generation of Russian speakers, biligualism in Estonian and Russian and an identity as a Russian Estonian were quite natural. My own fieldwork experience in the Russian villages of south-east Estonia confirms this. I could easily 'test' the residents' ability and willingness to chat with me in Estonian since my Estonian is fluent but my Russian is elementary. As a consequence, I was usually sent to either children or youngsters who learn Estonian at school, or else to the elderly 'who all speak Estonian as well'. The middle generations of Russian Estonians, those who grew up and got their formative education and work experience in the Soviet Union, had not had any use for Estonian in a language environment where Russian was the lingua franca.

People with mixed (multiple) identities like Fjodor are often bi- or multilingual from childhood. Bilingualism as an ability and willingness to interact in more than one language is rightly seen as the key to succesful intergration for minorities and migrants, but I hold that it would be equally important for people of ethnic and lingustic majorities. The Baltic Russian speakers are interesting in this respect since their language is a minority language in the countries in which they live, but a powerful majority language in the adjacent neighbouring country, Russia. Due to Soviet language policies, Russians mostly had neither need nor incentive to learn languages other than Russian whereas people of all the other 200 officially recognized linguistic groups were obliged to know Russian (see Nettle and Romaine 2000).

Vasilly (born 1922) is an ethnic Ukrainian and a Russian speaker. He lives in Pededze (north-east Latvia) and was interviewed there in the Russian language. Vasilly's case is instructive in showing how crucial the knowledge of Latvian, the language of the ethnic majority would be in order to be an active citizen and avoid feeling alienated.

INTERVIEWER: What TV programs do you watch?

VASILLY: Only Russian language programs. I don't understand Latvian.

INTERVIEWER: You don't speak [any] Latvian?

VASILLY: I can't, I don't understand anything. I have become so stupid [laughs].

INTERVIEWER: And how do you communicate, in what language?

VASILLY: In Russian. At least I can speak Russian. And Russian by now is easier for me than Ukrainian. I have already grown out of Ukrainian.

INTERVIEWER: Do you still remember Ukrainian?

VASILLY: Yes, but not proper Ukrainian. Because in Western Ukraine where I come from there is no such thing as proper Ukrainian. Just a mixed language. Mixture of Russian and Ukrainian.

INTERVIEWER: But you told me that you will have to learn Latvian? Why?

VASILLY: Because I don't understand anything. I always have to ask someone [for help]. For example, this document that I need for my passport has to be filled in Latvian. I will have to try to learn Latvian. In the shops I do understand the language but to write it … I hate that I have to pay someone to write things for me. I just hate it.

Vasilly's inability to speak Latvian marks a clear difference between him and ethnic Latvians. On the other hand, there is an equally sharp difference between him and the Russians of the village; knowing the language well is not enough to make him feel Russian. Therefore, what is left for Vasilly is the category of a relative outsider, 'a Ukrainian living in Latvia'.

INTERVIEWER: Do you feel yourself to be a Russian, a Latvian, a Ukrainian, or a Russian-speaker in a Latvian environment?

VASILLY: I have never been either a Latvian or a Russian, I have always regarded myself as a Ukrainian. A Ukrainian living in Latvia. I just talk Russian, because the Russian language is more common in Latvia than the Ukrainian language. I would never say that Russians are better or something, but I can't say that I'm a Latvian either, because I don't understand the language. How could I say that I'm a Russian – I understand Russian very well, I can speak it but I can't be a Russian if I'm not.

Vasilly describes himself as someone who does not fully belong. Being an ethnic Ukrainian Russian speaker living in Latvia actually makes him like the millions of citizens of the former Soviet Union who were encouraged to became 'true Soviet people', *homo Sovieticus* who were supposed to give up all feelings of belonging and attachment to a specific place and instead be ready to settle anywhere in the huge country. As with Vasilly, a loss of native language and roots in one's local culture frequently results in deep alienation (see for example Russian Karelia, Melnikova *et al.* 2005). To make matters worse for Vasilly and others like him, in the post-Soviet independent states one cannot anymore expect to get by with just the Russian language.

Ethnicity and citizenship

Zučika (born 1947) lives in Alūksne, the administrative town of the district of the same name in north-east Latvia. Zučika chose to be interviewed in Latvian since she is completely bilingual in Latvian and Russian. This is how she explained her citizenship, nationality, and identities:

ZUČCIKA: My nationality is Russian, but I have never lived in Russia, not even in the Soviet times. I have always lived in Latvia only.

INTERVIEWER: Where were you born?

ZUČIKA: According to my documents I was born in the Pskov region [now Russia], but that is true only in the documents. Because it was the year 1947 and all these different regions belonged to the Soviet Union. Since 1947 we have lived here in Alūksne. My parents come from the region of Abrene, you see, a region that used to belong to Latvia before the war, in the Latvian times. My parents left that region for Alūksne in the beginning of the Soviet times. Because of this I am a citizen of Latvia and therefore I don't have all these problems that real Russians face. I mean those Russians who are more connected with Russia. I don't have such problems. I cannot even tell you about those problems, because I am such an odd Russian, such a strange Russian.

When we asked about her identity, Zučika defines herself as 'a Latvian with a Russian touch'. This is completely logical since she has lived all her life in Latvian territory, speaks both Latvian and Russian, and is a Latvian citizen. 'Russianness' for Zučika is like an additional, spicy ingredient to her 'Latvianness'. However, Zučika is also aware of the many subtle differentiations that others make between Latvians and Russians:

INTERVIEWER: Do you feel as a Russian in Latvia or a Latvian Russian, or how would you characterize yourself?

ZUČIKA: My personal feelings I could characterize so that I feel that I'm like a Latvian with a Russian touch. There isn't even a proper word to characterize my true feelings.

INTERVIEWER: Do you feel there is a difference between Latvians and Russians? Do you feel different from an ethnic Latvian person?

ZUČIKA: Maybe I do feel somehow different, somehow.

INTERVIEWER: In what way, how does the difference manifest itself?

ZUČIKA: You see, those who know that I am not Latvian, they also perceive me like a Russian. But those who don't know that I am a Russian, they don't perceive me like a Russian.

Zučika is here referring to the many prevailing assumptions and prejudices about 'how Russians and Latvians are really like'. In the multi-ethnic and multilingual environment of north-east Latvia where each person's acquintances and personal encounters cross ethnic and language lines, stereotypes are both posivive and negative. For example, Russians are both criticized and praised for being 'sentimental', Latvians for being 'rational'. Zučika's point is to resist the definitions made by others, and to work out and choose what Russianness means for herself.

Jelena (born 1968) is ethnic Russian and a citizen of Russia. She says she speaks Latvian badly (the interview was conducted in Russian). She and her husband are farmers. Her husband is also ethnic Russian but speaks Latvian, since he was born in Pededze where bilingualism in Latvian and Russian is common. The couple's children know Latvian well. Jelena was born close to Leningrad. Jelena and her husband moved to Russia in 1992, immediately after Latvia's independence, for fear of persecution of Russians, but came back and settled permanently in Pededze in 1995. Jelena now feels very much at home in the village and Latvia.

INTERVIEWER: How do you feel, are you mostly an inhabitant of Pededze, of the Alūksne district, of Vidzeme region, of Latvia, or of Russia? What would you say, where do you belong to?

JELENA: Actually, I am a citizen of Russia, but it's not because of my conviction, so to say, but it's because that when I drew up my documents for a visa and a residence permit they told me short and sweet that in Latvia there are already enough aliens, meaning people with residence permits but no citizenship. They told me: you have to decide, you must have some citizenship.

> Well, which citizenship? I could only get the citizenship of Russia. So, for this reason I got the Russian citizenship. But during all these years, albeit with a small interruption, I feel myself to be an inhabitant of Latvia. Latvia, Alūksne district is my second motherland now. So, I don't want to go anywhere [from here].

Jelena is an ethnic Russian whose mother tongue is Russian. She is also a citizen of the Russian federation while being a permanent resident of the state of Latvia. She may not be the most 'typical' Russian citizen living in Latvia, but her 'case' is not unique either. There are many ethnic Russians who, like Jelena, clearly identify themselves with their Baltic homeland. Possessing a passport of a neighbouring state does not necessarily mean identification with that state: the choice of citizenship (or the choice of remaining a stateless resident) is often presented as a purely practical choice. In the conclusion, I discuss what a post-modern cultural atmosphere of conscious individual choice and identity politics might mean in the case of the rural Russians living in the Baltic states.

Conclusion – making choices: becoming a local Baltic Russian

People everywhere are recreating and re-enforcing local, ethnic, linguistic, and religious identities, and the same processes are definitely under way in the countries that used to belong to the Soviet bloc. The paradox of the twenty-first century is that the increasing homogenization of economies and societies is paralleled by cultures becoming more and more heterogeneous. People living in the European peripheries have indeed become thoroughly modern and still want, and make the decision, to retain their cultural distinctiveness. Many of our interviewees are now making new choices with regard to their identities as Seto, Russian, Latvian or Estonian, or some combination of these. But modern identities are not exclusive: the people who live at the border between these three different post-Soviet states will continue to want to choose their distinct ethnic, linguistic and religious identities. They might also feel that they are 'borderlanders', village people, members of congregations, citizens of their nation states or Europeans, depending on the context. In the modern world, people can and will hold multiple identities and increasingly, even in the national peripheries of Estonia, Latvia and Russia, they are doing so quite consciously.

When I started doing research on Estonia in the mid-1990s, my first hesitant attempts to suggest to ethnic Estonians and Russians that there might, in the near future, exist a category of people living in Estonia who would see themselves and who would be seen as 'Russian Estonians' was met with laughter, scepticism, and suspicion. These reactions came from urban people living in Tallinn where the social realities of the two groups, Estonians and Russians (or non-Estonians), were quite separate and remain so to this day. Later on, fieldwork in the peripheral regions of south-east Estonia and north-east Latvia taught me and my colleagues that identity categories as 'Russian Estonian' or 'Russian Latvian' did exist, and there were people who would actually identify themselves in this manner. This was perhaps not so surprising in the case of the 'old Russians', having generations' long family backgrounds locally, but as I have showed in this chapter, many Soviet-era migrants to the area are also choosing to think of themselves as 'Baltic Russians'.

In my view, the glue that ties the Russian Estonians and their Latvian counterparts to their Baltic countries of residence is a strong sense of local identity. What we have found during the research process in this border region are localized, grounded versions of being Russian, Estonian, Latvian, or Seto. In the case of the Russians, this simply means that being Russian and living in villages like Nina and Beresje (Estonia), and Pededze (Latvia) is not the same as being Russian and living in Tallinn or Narva (Estonia) and Riga (Latvia), and wholly different to being Russian in Russia. Crucially, with a local identity comes a feeling of *belonging*; if a person does not feel that they belong they will always remain, in the opinions of self and others, a relative outsider. This is the simple but important lesson that the borderland peripheries of Estonia and Latvia and the people living there have taught us, and it is a lesson that hopefully has implications in other contexts as well.

Notes

1 Research projects 'Ethnic identity and everyday life in the borderlands between Estonia, Latvia and Russia' (1999–2001) and 'Russia and the new EU-neighbours on a local level: a comparative ethnography of the border area between Estonia, Latvia and Russia' (2003–2006), funded by the Academy of Finland and the University of Helsinki (Network for European Studies, Helsinki Collegium for Advanced Studies). Besides the author, the researchers were: Dr. Jeanna Kormina and Dr. Marina Hakkarainen from the European University at St. Petersburg; Sanita Vanaga and Aija Lulle from the University of Latvia; and Dr. Aili Kelam from Tallinn University.

2 I am here using the terms ethnic and national identity interchangeably. Here I follow Katherine Verdery, who even uses the concept 'ethnonational identities' to stress that ethnic and national identities and ideologies cannot be separated from each other in this part of the world. Verdery writes: 'I say "ethnonational" so as to emphasize that in this region [former socialist countries in Europe] the idea of "nation" has long had primarily an *ethnic* sense rather than the political one more familiar to North Americans' (Verdery 1998: 293; emphasis in the original).

3 The direct quotations in the text are from the following research materials: interviews conducted in Estonia by the author (in Estonian); interviews conducted in Estonia by the author and Uno Saar (in Russian); interviews conducted in Latvia by Vanaga and Lulle (in Latvian), by Vanaga, Lulle, and Kormina (in Russian); and interviews conducted in Russia by Kormina, Hakkarainen, and Lulle (in Russian). Translations from Estonian into English are by the author; from Latvian into English by Vanaga and Lulle; and from Russian into English by Kormina, Hakkarainen, and Kirichenko.

References

Alapuro, R., Liikanen, I. and Lonkila, M. (eds) (2004), *Beyond Post-Soviet Transition: Micro Perspectives on Challenge and Survival in Russia and Estonia*, Helsinki: Kikimora Publications.

Assmuth, L. (2001) 'On the margin, at the centre: a view from a northern European periphery', in L. Assmuth and A. Kelam (eds) *The Baltic Sea islands of Estonia: A Periphery in transition*, Tallinn: Estonian Academy Publishers.

Assmuth, L. (2003) 'Nation building and everyday life in the borderlands between Estonia, Latvia and Russia', *Focaal – European Journal of Anthropology*, 41: 59–69.

Assmuth, L. (2005) 'To which state to belong? Ethnicity and Citizenship at Russia's new EU-borders', in T.M. Wilson and H. Donnan (eds) *Culture and Power at the Edges of the State: National Support and Subversion in European Border Regions*, Münster: Lit Verlag.

Assmuth, L. (2007) 'Politicizing language at a post-Soviet border: an Estonian school in Russia', *Suomen Antropologi* (Journal of the Finnish Anthropological Society), 1/2007: 36–46.

Barth, F. (1969) *Ethnic Groups and Boundaries: The Social Organisation of Cultural Difference*, Bergen: Universitetsförlaget.

Bourdieu, P. (1984) *Distinction: A Social Critique of the Judgement of Taste*, Cambridge, MA: Harvard University Press.

Kaiser, R. and Nikiforova, E. (2006) 'Borderland spaces of identification and dis/location: multiscalar narratives and enactments of Seto identity and place in the Estonian-Russian borderlands', *Ethnic and Racial Studies*, 24(5): 928–958.

Kapferer, B. (2002) 'Ethnicity, nationalism, and the culture of the state', *Suomen Antropologi* (Journal of the Finnish Anthropological Society), 27(2): 4–23.

Kormina, J. (2003) 'Oral stories about a village sacred place. The social dimension of narrative tradition'. Available: www.anthrobase.com/Txt/K/Kormina_J_01.htm (accessed 11 June 2009).

Kuldin, S. (1999) 'The border influence on the conscience and economic behaviour of the people along the Pskovsko-Chudskoe Lake', in O. Brednikova and V. Voronkov (eds) *Nomadic Borders*. Proceedings of the seminar held in Narva, November 13–15 1998, St. Petersburg: Centre for Independent Social Research.

Manakov, A. (1999) 'Border factor in the life of the population of the Petchory area (Pskov region, Russia)', in O. Brednikova and V. Voronkov (eds) *Nomadic Borders*, Proceedings of the seminar held in Narva, November 13–15 1998, St. Petersburg: Centre for Independent Social Research.

Melnikova, E. (ed.) (2005) *Granitza i lyudi (The border and the people)*, St. Petersburg: The European University.

Nettle, D. and Romaine, S. (eds) (2000) *Vanishing choices: the extinction of the world's languages*, Oxford and New York: Oxford University Press.

Novikova, I. (2008) 'Babushka in Riga – age and power in Russian-speaking translocal contexts', in I. Novikova (ed.) *Gender Matters in the Baltics*, Riga: University of Latvia Press.

Pilkington, H. (1998) *Migration, Displacement, and Identity in Post-Soviet Russia*, London: Routledge.

Schöplin, G. (1997) '*Civil society, ethnicity and the state: a threefold relationship*', paper delivered at the conference 'Civil Society in Austria', Vienna, 20–21 June 1997. Cene for the Study of Nationalism, School of Slavonic and East European Studies, University of London. Available: www.ssees.ucl.ac.uk/gs1.htm.

Verdery, K. (1998) 'Transnationalism, nationalism, citizenship, and property: Eastern Europe since 1989', *American Ethnologist*, 25(2): 291–306.

Wilson, T.M. and Donnan, H. (1998) 'Nation, state and identity at international borders', in T.M. Wilson and H. Donnan (eds) *Border Identities: Nation and State at International Frontiers*, Cambridge: Cambridge University Press.

Võro Instituut (1998) *Ku kavvas Setomaalõ seto rahvast jakku. Ajaloolise Setomaa põlisasustuse säilimise võimalused* (*How Long will there be Setu People in Historic Setumaa*), Võru: Võro Instituut.

Võro Instituut (2000) *A kiilt rahvas kynõlõs … Võrokeste keelest, kommetest, identiteedist.* (*And the people spoke their language … On the language, customs and identity of Võru people*), Võru: Võro Instituut.

8 Exit from communism

Career decisions of the Lithuanian young communist functionaries

Vaida Obelenė

Introduction

The scope of this chapter is restricted to the generation born after the Second World War (see Chapter 1, p. 2); yet to a segment of individuals who were preselected eventually to replenish the ranks of the communist elite. This chapter explores how these individuals explain events in their careers at the onset of post-communism, during the months when independent Lithuania reemerged and individuals associated with the former communist regime increasingly became a stigmatized group. Observing how the interviewed individuals describe their moves as 'entering', 'exiting', and 'returning' offers insights into the subjective orders of their social mobility. It is with reference to the larger group of interviewees who adopted the perspective of 'exit' to describe their first post-communist jobs that the title of this chapter emphasizes exits from communism rather than entries into post-communism.

Komsomol and functionaries of Cekomol

Lithuania's Komsomol was a republican branch of the All-Union Leninist Young Communist League, the organization in the former Soviet Union for young people aged 14–28. When the decision to split from the All-union Komsomol was taken by the Congress of Lithuanian Komsomol in June 1989, the autonomous organization was renamed as the Communist Union of Lithuanian Youth. This chapter focuses exclusively on Lithuania's Komsomol (further Komsomol) and Lithuania as a milieu for social mobility.

The individuals involved in this study, and referred to as functionaries, could be characterized as the most significant segment of the Komsomol personnel structure. They were employees charged with the performance of functions relating to planning and co-ordination of various policies in the field of youth as well as control organizational processes and resources – the so-called principal staff. Moreover, they were all employed in the secretariat and apparatus of the highest standing administrative body of Komsomol, the Central Committee. It is with reference to this body that the secretariat and apparatus of the Central Committee colloquially was known as Cekomol. Anyone gaining a Cekomol post had to have initially progressed through the hierarchical structure of Komsomol. Besides, they had to have completed higher education; they may have been older than 28, but desirably not above 40, and preferably members of the Communist Party.

The target group of this project were male functionaries who worked at Cekomol between 1986 and 1989. The exhaustive list of 102 names was constructed by conducting research on Komsomol documents available in the Lithuanian Special Archives. The information collected enabled me to place each functionary into one of the three hierarchical groups: top, intermediate, and subordinate. The sample of individuals from each of these three groups were chosen at random and invited to participate in the study. The recorded live history interviews were conducted in the winter and spring of 2005 with 36 individuals. While the individuals were sampled with reference to their hierarchical position in Cekomol, the significance of their functional allocation as economic and ideological functionaries became apparent from data. Given the importance of the distinction between ideological and economic functionaries, this study adopted the distinction to emphasize that either practical or abstract tasks predominantly characterized the work of a functionary at Cekomol.

Change in career prospects

The significance of Komsomol is indicated by references to being 'a state within a state' (M. Pastukhova quoted in Riordan 1995: 88). The structure of this organization mirrored the organization of the Communist Party, and indeed Komsomol committees worked in close co-operation with the Communist Parties' committees. By and large, Komsomol was an avenue for young adults who wanted to play big or to add meaning to their lives by engaging in projects in which they believed. For example, my interviewees presented themselves as young adults who were escaping from the realities of their parents' lives, such as standing at conveyor belts in manufacturing plants day after day (Tadas),[1] to live full and creative lives. Komsomol was also a tool that enabled them to outpace time by accessing a diverse array of special privileges, usually available only to experienced top-ranking executives, such as travel abroad and housing. Last but not least, Komsomol was an important gateway to the communist elite. Komsomol functionaries had fast-track access to positions in other sectors of Soviet society by the age of 30, such as jobs in the Communist Party apparatus, government bodies at executive and legislative levels, managerial positions in educational, economic and cultural organizations, and positions in law enforcement structures and the trade union system. While Komsomol functionaries were privileged to preferential access to an attractive future, there was the widespread belief among them that career progression did not involve a return to the specialist field of their university degree or vocation. Consequently, the ideas of promotion and career progression shaped their life projects. Typically, Komsomol functionaries were snapped up as preferential candidates by employers. This applied particularly for the 1986–1989 cohort of functionaries who worked through the Perestroika period when rejuvenation was the aim of the Communist cadre recruitment and promotion policies.

For example, Vytas graduated as an engineer in 1980, but Komsomol intercepted his allocation process and Vytas, clearly not without his own willingness, became a Cekomol employee. Here remarkably quickly within three years, by making one step upwards Cekomol's hierarchy each year, he reached a top position. In his account, Komsomol emerges as a playground of future elites; it represents opportunity for the young ones, the prospective communist elite, to be close to the established communist elite and to learn from them. In the early spring of 1987 Vytas was invited to the Council of Ministers of Soviet Lithuania where he was offered a position. He recalls:

> I was not planning to go and work there [he was not planning to quit Cekomol as yet, V.O.], so I said 'no' to them for the first time. Then in April they invited me to come there again, and so I said 'no' to them for the second time. And finally in June the third conversation took place, and when I responded 'no', the deputy of the chairman of the Council of Ministers said: 'Child, where else in Lithuania will you get a job if you say "no" to us?' Well, so I thought then that perhaps I behave naively [he decided to accept the position, V.O.].
>
> (Vytas[2])

However, the fall of the communist regime, more specifically disintegration of the communist recruitment and promotion system (see e.g. Harasymiw 1984; Antanaitis 1998) for information about the system that existed as a web of lists of key positions, whose prospective occupants had to receive confirmation of a Comminist Party organization in order to assume a post), meant that these fast-track, upwardly oriented career paths became if not obsolete, then at least less institutionalized, more problematic, and in certain cases less desirable (e.g. jobs as CP apparatus functionaries). The interviewed functionaries began recognizing difficulties or, to put it more precisely, the lack of attractive opportunities already in the second half of 1989. The process was enhanced by ongoing structural and functional reorganizations of Komsomol (see Table 8.1), which involved first demotions and sackings of staff.

For example, not interested in working as an engineer after graduation in 1986, Algis decided on an academic career: he was put on a waiting list for a postgraduate position, aspirantura. In parallel he worked as a part-time functionary at his faculty's Komsomol. However, his Komsomol career progressed faster, and within a year Algis was offered a position at Cekomol, where he soon established himself as one of the active reformers of Komsomol. During the first half of 1990 he was still entirely immersed with the projects of Komsomol, when rather suddenly he began experiencing sluggishness and lack of activity.

> Indeed, well, when I used to sit there [at Cekomol] and contemplate … When there already was [unoccupied, V.O.] time, so I already was contemplating

> what should I do. So it came to me then that I really have to return to my vocation. Because the processes are changing very quickly … I have to begin thinking how I will be earning my bread. Anyway, the family is growing … And while I worked at Komsomol … Anyway how helpful Komsomol was [to me]? I was able to go abroad, which was a great value back then. To see the other world … And again, English language … Somehow we were trying to develop ourselves. In Komsomol we even had created a circle, where we were learning English … Once one had started traveling [abroad], one realized that one needs it. And so I thought that somehow it would be great – this type of activity … And so I had very much the desire that I could combine [as his next job, V.O.] my profession [pre-Komsomol vocation, V.O.], a sort of experience I had had [international experience he had while at Cekomol, V.O.] and try something. Well, and there was an excellent opportunity. By the way, earlier one former komsomoler had left there as well. … My colleague, my former coworker, invited me …, I agreed.
>
> (Algis)

When speaking about achieving his positions at Komsomol, Algis said: 'You could not apply for this job, you had to be invited.' Algis implied that within the communist recruitment and promotion system, he was not expected to take a proactive role in getting positions at Komsomol. The system was evaluating his performance and offering appropriate positions. Just like in December 1989 when the reorganization of Cekomol was undertaken and Algis was invited to continue working in the office amid sackings of Cekomol staff.

However, soon after the proclamation of independence of Lithuania in March 1990 and only several months after his last Cekomol appointment, Algis was beginning to realize that Komsomol lost its purpose and energy. There is a sense of disassociation from Cekomol and his colleagues when he recounts his experience of that period when Cekomol was speedily 'dissolving' to turn into an office where Algis was only expected to 'sit' without activity; he appears as a loner preoccupied with 'contemplating' his own relevance in the emergent society. Algis did not see himself as part of his Cekomol peers' endeavours in business or politics, and even though for a brief period but Algis was uncertain in which direction should he proceed. The solution to the problem came when from his former Komsomol colleague Algis learned about an opportunity to work as an engineer at a state company of international significance. The colleague not merely introduced Algis to the management of the company, but supported him in navigating the corridors of power when Algis was declined by his immediate superior-to-be, the head of a department, due to his Komsomol past. Algis admitted the growing divide in society when he recounted ultimately receiving the job offer directly from the director of the company who associated his Komsomol background with desirable skills.

The stories of Vytas and Algis serve to highlight the change in the situation of Komsomol and developments in career prospects of former functionaries. It is important to consider that while Komsomol lost capacity to channel its employees to positions in other sectors of society, communists increasingly were stigmatized and stereotyped as untrustworthy, disloyal and possessing inappropriate skills and judgement. Former Komsomol functionaries had to respond to the challenges posed by the rapidly shifting and uncertain environment. Most of the 36 interviewees had, by the middle of 1990, moved onwards from their positions in Cekomol to other employment; only one interviewee had an experience of working at the Lithuanian Komsomol (Forum) (see Table 8.1). Particularly the first half of the year 1990 may be characterized by an extensive exodus of employees. Besides, in March 1990 the independence of Lithuania was proclaimed, which involved gradual but pervasive reorganization of institutional structures and mechanisms in the country. This meant that the employment conditions of the 19 functionaries who quit Cekomol at an earlier point (before December 1989) also had been affected by initial post-communist reforms.

The positions taken by former Komsomol functionaries between January and July 1990 were classified into four categories: entrepreneurs, government, non-specialists, and specialists (see Table 8.1, row 5). In case of multiple positions, the functionary was classified in relation to the first job taken. However, the slots of the interviews that were analysed covered all positions taken by every functionary during this period.

Functionaries describe their first post-communist jobs as either Komsomol or Komsomol-unrelated. Staying in government option is associated with the perceptions of remaining within the milieu of their Komsomol roles. However, while during communism it was common that former functionaries would seek management jobs in industry, they typically did not return to their specialists' positions. Therefore, the decisions to become economic sector specialists at the outset of the post-communist period meant that these functionaries were trying to reverse the effects of Komsomol on their careers. The decisions to either seek employment within the emerging private business sector or as a self-employed entrepreneur typically involved a buy-and-sell type of business and marked total breaks from their career paths within Komsomol. However, two interviewees were involved with consulting services that implied continuation of their Komsomol activities. Interestingly, the options of following the established structures were equally viable with just a fraction more than half my sample of functionaries turning towards the emergent, uncertain, and highly unstructured domain of the private business sector. This chapter aims to discover why Komsomol functionaries assumed these employment positions at the onset of the post-communist transformation in Lithuania.

Social mobility and desire

Inquiry into the fate of the communist elite in the process of the post-communist transformation became a buoyant field of research (e.g. Steen 1997; Matonytė 2001; Steen and Ruus 2002). Scholars studied Komsomol-related issues from various angles (e.g. Pilkington 1994; Solnick 1998; Wallace and Kovatcheva

Table 8.1 Timeline of Komsomol related events and dynamics of principal staff of Cekomol

Timeline	*Event*	*Formal title (abbreviation)*	*Effects on principal staff of Cekomol*
January 1986	Lithuanian Komsomol, established in 1941, is part of All-Union Komsomol	Leninist Young Communist League of Lithuania (Komsomol)	27 of the 36 interviewees already had taken up positions in Cekomol
January 1989	Reorganization of Cekomol	Central Committee secretariat and apparatus (Cekomol)	Functionaries assigned new functions, occasional demotions 24 of the 36 interviewees worked at Cekomol
3 June 1989	Komsomol splits from All-Union Komsomol	Young Communist League of Lithuania (Komsomol)	No evidence of impact on principal staff neither from documents nor from interviews, i.e. not a single Cekomol functionary quits in disagreement
November 1989	Reorganization of Cekomol as Komsomol seeks for both social and political relevance in emerging socio-politico-economic environment		Principal staff shrinks significantly, but several departments were reorganized as semi-autonomous organizations;new organizations were established 17 interviewees worked at Cekomol or at organizations associated with Komsomol
January–July 1990	Independence of Lithuania proclaimed (March 1990) Exodus of Cekomol employees		Posts taken by former functionaries: Entrepreneurs ($n = 13$): posts as businesspeople or self-employed in the private sector Government ($n = 6$): posts in public administration and political parties Non-specialists ($n = 11$): posts in private sector businesses or well-established state enterprises Specialists ($n = 6$): posts in well-established state enterprises
October 1990	Komsomol reorganizes as socially and economically oriented youth organization	Youth Forum of Lithuania (Forum)	1 interviewee worked at Forum, while moonlighting in business Importantly, while interviewees are classified as entrepreneurs and employed in private businesses, these organizations often have associations with Forum (from merely using the resources of Forum to having Forum as a stakeholder)

1998). However, research in post-communist social mobility that analyse Komsomol is quite rare, other than Kryshtanovskaya and White (2002, 2005), who argue that individuals with a 'Komsomol background' form an influential segment of the new business elite in Russia. While social stratification researchers were eager to explore whether there was, to put it in words of Sorokin (1959: 133), 'social climbing' or 'social sinking' of former elites, the role of subjective factors such as personal beliefs and desires in the social mobility of former elites has interested scholars to a lesser extent.

In describing the process of downward social mobility (sinking), Sorokin (1959: 133–134) wrote 'the first case of "sinking" reminds one of an individual falling from a ship; the second of the sinking of the ship itself with all on board, or of the ship as a wreck breaking itself to pieces.' The words of one of the interviewees, Saulius, complement this perspective with a focus on subjective experience: 'We were a squad of people who fell out of the ship, each of whom were assessing situation in our own way and sought to ride out the condition. We had no understanding [of what was out there, V.O.].' Saulius draws our attention to the fact that people fall from ships not only alone but in 'squads'. This refers to what researchers of social mobility describe as 'the degradation of a whole social group' (Sorokin 1959: 134). However, Saulius, contrary to Sorokin, proposes that the ship does not have to sink with all on board. Saulius manages to successfully capture the fact that former Komsomol functionaries felt they were part of the ship, at first part of the Revival movement and then part of the independent state. The progressive role of the Lithuanian Komsomol functionaries, for example, was apparent not only in the split from the all-Union Komsomol in July 1989 but also that the Lithuanian Communist Party half a year later followed Komsomol's lead in breaking away from the all-Union Communist Party. Their youthful readiness to embark on new career ventures combined with the best training the communist system could provide; their forward-looking approach to life and their amenability to transform along with society meant that the environment of change was full of opportunities for them. This chapter by delineating on an array of desires describes how endeavours, which initially propelled these young adults into communist structures, were converted towards post-Communist undertakings.

Primarily, in this chapter, desire is taken as a broad category: wishes, wants, goals, inclinations, preferences, and aspirations to name just a few common synonyms. Desires are multiple, and just as the word 'desire' means that an individual wants to achieve something, it might mean that the individual also wants to avert something. However, experiencing a desire is different to remembering a desire. Most importantly, how do humans explain their past choices? It seems that their explanation is likely to be focused on their reasons for action, which primarily will concern their desires and beliefs (Malle 2004). In other words, the array of desires that result from this analysis are not only what former functionaries directly admitted that they had desired but also inferred desires; these are inferred by exploring what interviewees believed had been the circumstances of their mobility.

Desires that explain the career events

This section endeavours to delineate the occupational goals and wanted situations that appealed to the functionaries and influenced their movements, and describes them as an array of desires. The question is: What did former Komsomol functionaries desire at the onset of post-communism?

No desire to start from the beginning again

Vilius, a top ideological functionary, and Algis, a subordinate ideological functionary, admitted that during the Communist period they had only a vague understanding of the variety of employment spheres available to them when leaving Cekomol and claimed to have been fairly open to various career possibilities. The interviewees did, however, have an elaborate understanding of the levels of command to which their Cekomol positions would convert. In other words, they were not interested so much in the domain they would enter but rather on the level of command that they would attain. If we observe how the functionaries' perceived choices are linked to the rank of their Cekomol positions, we see that rank in the hierarchy plays a major role. While Algis, a subordinate rank functionary, was ready to accept low-level subordinate positions, Vilius, a senior ranking functionary, believed he was entitled to more, which inevitably generated a pattern of contrast in achieving their desired outcomes: success for the subordinate rank functionary and failure for the top- rank functionary. Still, Algis had to make a significant effort to gain new post. For example, he had to learn a foreign language in just three months and pass several interviews to become an engineer in one of the prosperous manufacturing companies despite the support of influential friends when applying for the post.

By contrast, Vilius was also seeking to leave Cekomol during the first half of 1990. Vilius received some work offers but declined them, once as he remembers on the advice of a senior party official: 'As it [the position] was, so it [the position] will remain irrelevant'. Finally, Vilius was advised by a communist Party functionary that there was a job opportunity for him in an office of a newly established institution with good prospects for the future. However, when Vilius arrived at the office where he was supposed to present himself to the leadership as willing to take a vacant position, he encountered stiff opposition from subordinate staff members. Disturbed by the experience, he left the office without even trying to meet the person in charge.

> Well, I went there and told them what I am, told something in general, presented my résumé and so on. And they, as if they had it pre-planned, launched an attack on me: what kind of human being I am, what type of insignificant Communist I am, and so on in this way.... Well, they moralized that I am wicked, appalling and so on, and surely I should not hope to get a serious job. And if, so to say, I still want to achieve something with my life, I have to start from the lowest, so to say, rank.... Well, then I told

> them: 'You know, dear ladies, it is not for you to decide – I say – however it is, it is not for you to decide what I am. I myself know perfectly what I am. I know what kind of experience I have and so on. It might be, if we already talk like this, that you are anything but close to me – a functionary of the Central Committee who has passed ten years of the Komsomol School. You are not even nearly close.'... And afterwards I left. Then I didn't even go upstairs [to see the person he was supposed to talk to about the job, V.O.], because I was so irritated for they had this appalling way of looking at this Komsomol member and party member, so to say, looking at a person who had the Komsomol and the [Communist] party ties. I say, if then at that time, so to say, if I had managed to get a job there, if nobody had tried to offend me, to disdain me or something else, perhaps even then I would not have moved to business.
>
> (Vilius)

Vilius was not prepared to start from the lowest rank, because he believed that what he had deserved until then, his achievement as Cekomol functionary, was relevant when applying for the next position, his first post-communist job. He did not even contemplate returning to his specialist vocation as Algis did. In summary, the likelihood of achieving the desired employment favoured the subordinate rank functionaries compared to the top-rank functionaries.

No desire to talk politics, desire to pursue practical projects

Rokas, an economic functionary, did not hesitate to abandon politics and turn to 'purely' economic matters; there was he explained simply not another option available to him: 'But indeed there were only two options: either political activity, or, so to say, private business.' Rokas maintained that his transfer to business was a smooth transition, which followed on from the type of work he had always preferred and were precisely the functions he was assigned to at Cekomol. Similarly, Jonas, an economic functionary, claimed that from the very beginning he was more interested in practical work, even when he worked at Cekomol.

> I liked that it was not some kind of ideological company or department but a purely practical, such an economic ... as I said I was fond of technical drawing, calculating, such practical work, not some kind of slogans, ideas.
>
> (Jonas)

This lack of interest in political matters, which is explained by them being preselected to the ranks of Cekomol functionaries as being inclined towards practical problem-solving, explains why these functionaries opted for jobs in industry or business. When Communist Party membership and pursuing political participation were no longer a prerequisite for success in any endeavour, they solved the question in a 'simple way' as Rokas: they took their opportunity to withdraw from the political domain.

What about the functionaries who were not economically minded? Petras provides an interesting perspective that highlights the contrast between the two types of functionary: the economic functionary and the ideological functionary. Petras began the interview by saying that his life was 'clear' and without 'ambivalence'; he proposed himself as a down-to-earth person and an economic functionary. He did, however, witness the top-ranking ideological functionaries make their first uneasy and uncertain steps into the post-communist environment:

> You see, one reason why they were throwing themselves to all sides, I can tell you, you see, they were all ideological. How could I say it? They used to be soldiers at the ideological front, let's refer to them this way. They had to face the problem of discovering themselves. Because from the [idea] of life being linked to ideology they had to come back down to earth. I did not have to do that because I always stood on earth. (Laughter) Do you understand? So for me it was much easier. I simply did that work before, I knew that work, I was engaged with different tasks.... Everything I did was (going) to be linked to commercial activity. So it was simply much easier for me.... We had nothing to do with ideology – nothing, nothing.
>
> (Petras)

The ideological functionaries had a dilemma in deciding whether they desired working ties to the abstract ideas (e.g. of party politics) or dealing with more practical matters, which meant they had to reorient themselves. For example, Giedrius, an ideological functionary, indicates that his reason not to engage in politics was the disappointing encounters he had with the first politicians to promote Sąjūdis ideas of independence. He recalled a project that was aimed at helping to promote the Sąjūdis movement. Cekomol organized an expedition to Siberia to excavate the bones of the Lithuanian victims of communist purges. Giedrius recalls the unexpected appearance of a Sąjūdis politician in the expedition's camp in Siberia on the eve of the journey back. This encounter with one of the highly respected members of the Sąjūdis, who later became a controversial public figure, proved to be decisive for Giedrius in excluding politics from his career options:

> But at the same time instantly I saw that I certainly hadn't got the slightest desire to enter politics, because somehow I sincerely hated [the idea] of making a speech on a podium, of beating on my breast, once I had leaped out of that airplane ... And then it came out very clearly. It came out very clearly: who goes for what reason, who has what kind of motives ... Because those people were older, they understood what kind of politics was coming, how to enter it, how to become suddenly, well, a social star or a revolutionary star, and [they understood] that this was their chance. And we were naïve – I certainly was stupid. I remember our plane landed, [with]

> 120 [human] remains, [name of the Sąjūdis politician who became a prominent post-communist public figure] threw himself on a podium, all of them were saying speeches, were walking around with crosses, were burying those coffins that were hammered together and soldered by us – by the hands of Komsomolers, you know, but … And we very quietly [(walked] through the other exit of that huge airplane – as a matter of fact we also found and rented it ourselves … and we, all those who worked and did that work from beginning to end, we all quietly got into some kind of insignificant bus, I remember it as it were today, and left for Vilnius. And none of us were in that gathering. And those who wanted to, who already – one could see the signs that they were going into politics – those went, shouted, screamed, sung. In this sense, then it was very clear for me, that I did not want to get involved with that shit, and my place was somewhere else. Perhaps I did not name it [back] then but I think that this kind of clear distinction emerged. Because now every year I get offers to go into politics, to nominate myself in elections and everything else, but such a thought does not even occur to me. I understand that it is not for me – it is too dirty for me. I do not want that.
>
> (Giedrius)

There was one further group of functionaries to consider, the ardent believers in Communism, whom Naglis referred to as 'beets' while all the others, like Naglis, were 'radishes'. The study included five functionaries who either admitted to having been ardent believers in communism or whom their peers claimed to have been. This group, like the economic functionaries, were adamant that their choice was limited to a single business option.

Overall, when functionaries explained their departures from Cekomol, it was their affinity for either the ideological or the economic domain, which made them choose one direction over another. However, while there seemed to be a cluster of functionaries who were genuinely inclined towards practical work, such as commerce, others had to pick this choice simply because it offered open access at a time when access to other sectors was limited. However, in reference to the preceding section, another factor worth noting is that their position in the hierarchy as subordinate, intermediate, and top functionaries thus conditioned their preference of new jobs. The emergent private business sector was unfamiliar and unstructured, which enabled them to enter the sector without any feeling of demotion. Whenever functionaries failed to secure hierarchically appropriate posts in their preferred domain, they opted for a less desired sector of the private economy, with the exception of Tomas who prioritized a domain to hierarchical position and thus accepted the demotion. In fact, the experience of Tomas was sufficiently notable to act as a reference point for the other functionaries interviewed and his decision to forego the privileges concomitant with working at Cekomol was among the reasons for the interviewees to use Tomas's exit strategy as a frame of reference to evaluate their own desires, beliefs and achievements.

Desire to continue in the previous line of work

Cekomol functionaries clearly had different reactions to the change in the socio-political environment at the end of the 1980s. Several of them immediately left Cekomol to begin their careers in other societal domains whereas others stayed on but appeared to have undecided courses of action due to the uncertainty of the future: if they started a new career but communism survived, they might never be able to return; whereas, if they waited to see whether or not communism survived, they might leave it too late to find a worthwhile position. There were also functionaries who simply did not have any idea about their desired future careers when the number of attractive opportunities available to them was rapidly declining, and also those who were starting to moonlight in business development while keeping their Cekomol jobs. At the same time, a prominent number of functionaries were engaged in active efforts to facilitate innovation and change in the entrenched communist structures, such as the reorganizations of Komsomol. Consequently, a great many functionaries had good reasons to linger in their Cekomol posts.

Rytis, who accepted employment as a non-specialist in a private business, described his peers who got involved as entrepreneurs in the business sector as the 'lucky' ones. Moreover, he proposed that those functionaries drifted into business merely due to the forces of transformation: one day they just 'woke up' to realize that they were in a profitable economic sector. Rytis maintained that the experience of entering the business sector was not so extreme for those who had instead opted to become engaged in business projects using the skills developed at Cekomol.

> Take [he names other functionaries, V.O.]: so they based [their business] on Komsomol work, because they were engaged with [a certain work], so all that [activity] they did, it grew into their current work. They had it easier; it did not happen to me. If I had worked a couple of years longer at the Central Committee, perhaps it would have worked for me the same way.
>
> (Rytis)

According to Rytis, who exited Cekomol in 1988 before the pro-market economic reforms became widespread in society, entering the business sector as an entrepreneur was not possible for him because work that was necessary in the context of a socialist planned economy became obsolete in the market economy – he thus became redundant. Rytis in leaving Cekomol 'too early' was not knowledgeable enough to be able to work within the principles of market economy. His case helps to clarify the important phenomena that was caused by lingering in their Cekomol posts.

Functionaries who lingered in their posts performed their duties without having the time or energy for other activities such as managing their own careers. Kostas and Henrikas, for example, mention that their exits from Cekomol were not deliberate.

INTERVIEWER TO KOSTAS: Didn't you think of going into business at that point?

KOSTAS: Well, yes. So in a way ... Somehow it happened to us that we were the last in [the department of the Central Committee], and, so to say, all those centers were set up, all those enterprises. But there simply were not enough hands to do something, to think about ourselves.

INTERVIEWER TO HENRIKAS: Didn't you think about starting a business yourself?

HENRIKAS: No, there were no such thoughts. Because you understand ... Well, I was so busy with my duties. Those duties, they would simply drown everything else. It was simply like that. It simply did not even come to that. I do not know...

The act of lingering did, however, mean they were rapidly accumulating innovative knowledge about how to manage commercial and democratic processes. The functionaries succeeded, while performing their daily Cekomol duties, in moving from planned economy to market economy relationships without the gap that Rytis experienced (see above paragraph). Indeed, as Cekomol was central to the events and processes of 1989–1991, the functionaries would have been the first to know of any innovative courses of action or methods of work. Algis recalls how his Cekomol work accelerated the process of personal development and significant changes in his worldview:

> Naturally, participating in all these processes exerts an influence on you. And if, lets say, one day, for example, in the beginning of the year you are closer to some leftist views, you realize that towards the end of the year you already stand somewhere in the centre or you are already a rightist. So I felt this within myself. And very strongly. It was happening every day ... Perhaps it (the change in worldviews) was even faster in Komsomol, than if I had, let's say, had I been working conventionally in some plant as a proper engineer.
>
> (Algis)

It is important to clarify the general climate of support for the Sąjūdis among functionaries. Algis, for example, spoke about the uncertain situation of acting as a go-between between young people, eager to make a difference in a short time, and the established Communist elites, many of them being reluctant to change the existing structures and processes. It thus became apparent that the functionaries were not merely confused about where they should go, but they also considered themselves to be active participants in an effervescent society. While they lingered over their work, they tried to enhance the relevance of their lines of work in the transforming society.

No desire to market themselves

As Cekomol functionaries worked on communist-oriented assignments, many of which were concerned with the everyday life of young people, they were gradually conditioned to think in terms of what they were best at doing. Consequently, the interviewees, in relating their Komsomol experiences, tended to regard the work as a privileged and stimulating administrative job. If they performed their work duties well enough and demonstrated a potential for high performance, in time they would have been provided with attractive positions in other domains of communist society. In this context, the communist recruitment and promotion system may be thought of as a mediator between the functionaries' career aspirations and the work for which the system judged the functionary to be talented.

Importantly, functionaries considered themselves to be entitled to promotions and were able to predict their occurrence, although not with perfect accuracy. Even though factors such as personal chemistry between actors interacting within the recruitment and promotion system made a significant difference in their mobility outcomes, the system arbitrated the interaction between the actors in such a way that promoting a functionary was seen as a professional transaction and not a personal favour – it was an earned entitlement and a predictable outcome.

The collapse of the system meant the functionaries had to market and promote themselves to potential employers. Furthermore, the collapse removed both the system's guidance and the functionaries' chances of embarking on a gradual process of discerning what their talents were, as well as learning the norms, behaviour, and social skills appropriate to functionary's social position. Under the new circumstances they had to determine the criteria for recruitment and prioritize their options, which led to the chance of failure and the possibility of the unpleasant experience of being rejected. The threat of failure had always been present under communism, but the system had alleviated the threat through mediating mechanisms such as guidance, or even generously providing another chance. Finally, the professional transactions between the Cekomol functionaries were transformed into personal favours: in these new circumstances, a functionary had to ask for work as a personal favour. The decline of employment opportunities in the old system took place simultaneously as new practices and institutions of employment such as opportunities in the emerging state and private sectors were merely taking shape. The lack of best practices, rules, and procedures for handling the relatively recent phenomena, such as recruitment of new employees in the emergent post-communist labour market, resulted also in functionaries experiencing their job-seeking prospects as relying on personal favours from employers, which exacerbated the issues related to seeking such employment for functionaries rather than offset them.. In the following passage, Henrikas describes how he dealt with the uneasy experience of making an attempt to get a job and being rejected, after which he decided to be 'self-reliant' to build his own business rather than be employed by others.

> I don't know. I tried several times. I do not even know if I can call that an attempt or not, maybe it's better to say I nominated myself. During those turbulent times, this [business] of mine, it moved forward but it wasn't very

> active. And then I tried my old connections. I thought about getting a job at [name of organization] because several of our people [former functionaries] got jobs there. I had an interview, I do not know what prevented them from taking me, I do not know why, but they did not take me ... But maybe at that time they did not need new staff.... But they said that they will keep me in mind. But in practice ... Well how? They rejected me, they did not take me. Then I decided to go my own way. Somehow, I never thought about public service and I did not even want to do that because I realized that the best way is to do it yourself, to be self-reliant. You are responsible for yourself and you need no one.
>
> (Henrikas)

The entrepreneurial (self-employed) sector for some of the interviewees represented an activity which violated their standards of self-respect and required the special, inborn skill of entrepreneurship. Darius, for example, tried to enter the entrepreneurial sector, while simultaneously working at a well-established state enterprise, at the extreme micro-level of taking his wares (crammed into bags) to sell at open-air markets. His and several other functionaries' experiences of humiliation in the business world help to explain the alternative choices, being employed as specialists or non-specialists by other businesses.

In the context of the entry into the entrepreneurial sector Liudas was luckier than his peers. Once he was jobless and did not have a clear understanding of 'what to buy and where to sell', he got into the open-air market trade at the 'bag' micro-level. He did admit to finding it difficult to go and sell unless he was tipsy. The 'luck' occurred on learning at an open-air market a profitable opportunity at the macro-'container'-level. The chance to disengage from being an open-air market seller was the only reason he decided to stay in the entrepreneurial sector.

In summary, the Cekomol functionaries found it difficult to market themselves, ask for favours or prove they were worthy of a job; nevertheless, some functionaries chose to become self-employed businesspeople (entrepreneurs) because of these difficulties. The real and perceived humiliation of entering the entrepreneurial sector at the open-air market bag level did, however, make being an employee of a business a more attractive option.

Desire to avoid blame

Although the interviewees admitted to having different experiences of stigmatization (e.g. see Vilius above), many of them became businesspeople even without trying to get a different job elsewhere, because they expected attempts to discriminate against them because of their communist affiliation. Kostas describes the social atmosphere of the time and his perception of the processes that were taking place:

> Well, until there was still ... [when Komsomol was reorganized] we, [and another functionary], quit. We set up our enterprise. It was one of the first

> enterprises.... But it was also difficult afterwards, you know, when it all started afterwards: 'Look, there are those former Komsomolers.' The different laws came under consideration: 'The one who worked at the Party Central Committee, and Komsomol Central Committee, should not have the right to work in the state structures'. Well, you know, I really was consumed by black thoughts back then. You have no idea how this business will go: will it be successful, will it not? And here they just block your way. And you know what the most important thing was? What was really strange when I read that list of those who are supposed not to be allowed to do public service? The head of the Central Committee department gets onto the list, but the Party's Central Committee instructor is not on the list. Although the head of the department at the [Komsomol] Central Committee would only get a job as an instructor at the [Communist] Party Central Committee. And this was already considered a promotion.... And then you think: why is it so? And it is so because somebody there is pushing it this way, so that he himself won't get put on the list. And you were lower, or something of the sort, and you were on that list which would ban you from public service.... It was bad, a really bad feeling. Then you start thinking: have you really committed some crime or something?... So they did not adopt that law, they only were considering it. But anyway, it entails a moral pressure. It makes some kind of impact. It is painful for a human being.
>
> (Kostas)

No desire to work alone

Rytis, who exited Cekomol in early 1988, proposed that his life would have turned out differently if he had continued to work at Cekomol for even a few more years. The 'too early' exit also explains why Alvydas did not become a businessperson. They argued that if they had still been working at Cekomol at a later point, they could have conducted a smooth transition to business during the mass exodus of functionaries from Komsomol. Rytis reflects on this:

> It is difficult to begin if you are alone, but if there are several of you ... Somehow it did not happen in my life that there were a few of us who thought we could begin such a thing [private business].
>
> (Rytis)

The interviewees refer to Cekomol having a family atmosphere, in which the functionaries worked and socialized together, and until they gained a personal apartment (a key incentive for working at Cekomol) many of them also lived together in the same dormitory blocks, where the aspect of communal living was enhanced by having communal kitchens and playgrounds for the children. Clearly, the functionaries who did not have an accommodation entitlement and those who had been allocated their own apartments, particularly the top ranks, did not fit into this communal lifestyle. Still, there was the chance that one could socialize with them at the

Komsomol holiday homes during vacations. Cekomol functionaries, in essence, formed a tightly knit working and socializing community, whose members rarely took on any other interests beyond the all-consuming life of the Cekomol. The sense of being a member of a communal group was sufficiently strong for them to make communal decisions, particularly concerning business ventures, as Valdas explains:

> I am a loyal man perhaps. Making the decisions to leave for me … It took me much time to figure what to do. It is a pity to leave people with whom you grew into a team.
>
> (Valdas)

The distinction between ideological and economic functionaries is important in explaining how individuals approached the choice of going into business. For example, a subordinate functionary Giedrius suggested that being an ideological functionary like himself was a distinct disadvantage compared to being among the economic personnel. By that he means that the subordinate economic functionaries were the key personnel of communal businesses organizations, where the top-ranking ideological functionaries were the founders, because the latter needed to recruit the more practical down-to-earth economic subordinates to provide the skill base of the business. Giedrius simply says 'that was a problem' and proceeds to analyse the options he – as a subordinate ideological functionary – had at that point, or, to put it more precisely, his lack of options, which resulted in his choice of accepting a non-specialist job in a newly set-up business organization.

> I think the fact that I left … I nevertheless was from the Central Committee … I did not belong to economic personnel and that was a problem. I certainly had no friends in ancillary enterprises [he implies the public sector, V.O.], where I could do something, where I could work as some kind of white-collar worker there. Well, I was not interested in being a white-collar worker. But to go to some kind of higher position … Anyway, every ministry has its own personnel system for its senior officials. There is a circle of its [own] people and it is natural that those positions would be taken – the positions of managers of enterprises and all higher ministerial positions – by members within its [own] circle. So, I had nothing in common [with them].
>
> (Giedrius)

Absence of the desire to make a profit

The former functionaries never actually stated that they decided to become businesspeople in order to make a profit. Judging by their stories, profits only became an issue once they had gone into business and then their early experiences were simply and purely profit-making ventures. The fact that they did not prioritize the opportunity to make profits when deciding on entering the private business sector is an interesting perspective from which can be drawn three general insights into what their exits entailed for functionaries.

First, the absence of this desire occurred because they did not have a specific goal in mind. They simply sought to find their places in the transforming society and naturally, among other things, had to ensure they received sufficient remuneration. However, they were, as Kozielecki (1982: 138) defines, in a situation of 'total uncertainty', in which individuals deal with 'completely novel tasks' but 'show no preference for any' of the outcomes. Consequently, the situation was sufficiently unfamiliar to anticipate any definite outcomes such as profits.

The second insight is that they chose this exit strategy for non-material reasons but because they were unable to assume positions in the well-established administrative and economic sectors which they thought were an appropriate reward for their efforts and achievements in the communist environment. Their situation, at the time, was not characterized by a lack of finances and they considered the business exit strategy to be reversible because they could always return to their original vocations and opt for a less desirable administrative job. It is important to understand that the emergent private sector was poorly institutionalized and unstructured. Therefore it was able to serve as a social space where former functionaries did not feel degraded and discarded by society: the sense of losing their privileges was significantly watered down or removed altogether by the experience of the unfamiliar and emergent social space.

The third insight is that these functionaries did not even realize how they came to be businesspeople. Their fields of responsibility in Komsomol were becoming obsolete within the governmental sphere, and as these fields, with functionaries embedded in them, were being pushed out as irrelevant from the emergent institutional order, former functionaries merely had to rapidly and relevantly transform themselves and their lines of work for new relevance.

Consequently, their business reorientation was marked only by the new statutes that they had had to design to establish their new businesses; their day-to-day experience was no different from when they worked within the framework of Komsomol – they continued to do what they had been doing previously. Clearly, they had already, and for a while, been focusing on money-making activities. The interviews contain multiple examples of how the functionaries were profiteering from projects within Komsomol. There were, for example, misunderstandings that occurred when subordinates believed they had earned some profit for themselves but their superiors argued the money belonged to Komsomol. In other words, in these cases the first post-communist job as entrepreneur is merely a formality which conceals that the actual transformation from functionary to entrepreneur had already happened some time earlier; it was hidden by the façade of Cekomol.

Conclusions

This study was concerned with a particular segment of the first true post-war generation, born between 1952 and 1963, who worked within Cekomol, the secretariat and apparatus of the highest standing administrative organ of Lithuanian

Komsomol, between 1986 and 1989. In the communist system, Komsomol functionaries were supposed to be the successors of the established communist elites after the latter had been 'carried away in coffins' (Vytas); their position in Cekomol therefore signified that they were preselected candidates who would in time occupy high-ranking communist positions. However, during their time in this privileged office, in the late 1980s and the early 1990s, the communist organs with their satellite organizations were increasingly marginalized by the emerging social order in the Baltic countries. The collapse of the communist regime meant the system that ensured promotion, which their service at Cekomol entailed, became ineffective. Moreover, the stigmatization and discrimination of the former functionaries by employers and society became increasingly commonplace, which suggests their experiences of transition as being particularly interesting. However, while many functionaries left Cekomol in rather complex circumstances, it is important to recognize both the declining desired career prospects and the opening-up of new career opportunities. The post-communist pathways of former functionaries give rise to an irony that demonstrates the paradoxical essence of turbulent Baltic history: similar to those members of the republican generation who got the chance to realize their youthful abilities and aspirations by becoming the builders of communism, the Komsomol functionaries, even when unfavourably labelled as former communists, assumed active roles in constructing a post-communist society. The chapter has endeavoured to elaborate on the opportunities and constraints, the range of career options and alternatives that Komsomol functionaries had to choose from as their first post-communist jobs, and conceived an array of desires that were proposed as conditioning functionaries' decisions to move onwards, in one way or another, at that particular moment.

The chapter has highlighted the following desires, which came in varied configurations in accounts of former functionaries when they explained events in their careers at the onset of post-communist transformation:

- No desire to start a new career in posts that they perceived as lower rank posts, which included going back to being a specialist and moving to lower positions in the hierarchy. There was also a belief that their achievements within the communist environment, regarded as deserved entitlements by them, should count within the post-communist environment.
- Desire to be engaged purely with economic matters while disliking to participate in the political process.
- Desire to avoid stigmatization and attempts to discriminate against them due to association with the Communist Party, which went hand in hand with having an aversion to marketing themselves when seeking work within the post-communist environment.
- Desire for working in collective and group settings, partnerships, and no desire to work alone.
- Desire to preserve their previous lines of work that they believed to be valuable.

I would like to emphasize that the collapse of the communist recruitment and promotion system did not catch the Komsomol functionaries either unsuspecting or unprepared. The work of Komsomol functionaries was in a parallel, even ahead of, developments in society. In order to illustrate the circumstances of their exits from Cekomol, one of the interviewees, Irmantas, offered the metaphor of locking the doors by themselves. He meant that the functionaries who personally lock the doors are embarking on new lives without being abruptly forced to do so. It seems therefore important to acknowledge that the processes of the functionaries' exits from Cekomol that lasted throughout a two-year period resulted in the concept of a natural withdrawal or disengagement (Ebaugh 1988: 9).

> I imagine, I do not know how others would think, but I had not experienced any kind of great shock or high tension. And I never felt as if I was cast ashore, so to say, like I couldn't breathe or somebody mistreated me. Secondly, I never was too attached to that Komsomol so that I would claw at it with my horns, nails and teeth and everything else. I always looked at it in a natural way, from the side, and I never worried that something might happen with me. And I did not worry that the Komsomol was changing, that the situation was changing, that the structure was shrinking and so on.... Well, we left and I certainly did not feel harmed. I left with my head high and I did not feel like anyone had done something wrong to me. I was in a good mood.... It all went naturally for me ... and all those processes were not painful for me. It might be that some other people took it painfully, that somebody was offended when the Perestroika came, and everything began to crumble and deteriorate slowly, perhaps somebody hoped that things would last. [They thought]: that it was good the way it was three or five years ago and that it should stay that way; that they would have something, that they would work at the Central Committee of the Party; that they would have a bigger, three-room apartment in Antakalnis [prestigious neighborhood in the capital, VO]; that they would get a bigger salary; that they would have holidays ... All those things were not of primary importance for me. And certainly I had not the smallest, not any heartache. Pain did not visit me.... Everyone sensed the processes occurring in society and we had to more or less adapt to those processes, perhaps try to influence them more or less. We had to, but I couldn't describe the influence in some kind of bad sense. I would even think that the effort was made not to influence, but to adapt to the processes. Eventually, we tried to integrate [ourselves] somehow, eventually, to coincide or to identify with [the change in society].
>
> (Vilius)

Even though those initial jobs of the functionaries indubitably played an important role in their later lives, for example, as a source of understanding about what they desire to do or what they are best at, most of their choices should be regarded as provisional.

Notes

1 Interviewees are coded to protect their identities.
2 Translation of all the transcribed interviews is the responsibility of the author.

References

Antanaitis, K. (1998) 'Lietuviškoji sovietinė nomenklatūra' ('The nomenklatura of Soviet Lithuania'), *Darbai ir Dienos*, 7: 1–100.

Ebaugh, H.R.F. (1988) *Becoming an Ex: The Process of Role Exit*, Chicago and London: The University of Chicago Press.

Harasymiw, B. (1984) *Political Elite Recruitment in the Soviet Union*, Oxford: Macmillan in association with St. Antony's College.

Kozielecki, J. (1982) *Psychological Decision Theory*, Dordrecht: D. Reidel.

Kryshtanovskaya, O. and White, S. (2002) 'Generations and the conversion of power in postcommunist Russia', *Perspectives on European Politics and Society*, 3: 229–244.

Kryshtanovskaya, O. and White, S. (2002) (2005) 'The rise of the Russian business elite', *Communist and Post-Communist Studies*, 38: 293–307.

Malle, B.F. (2004) *How the Mind Explains Behavior: Folk Explanations, Meaning, and Social Interaction*, Cambridge, MA: MIT Press.

Matonytė, I. (2001) *Posovietinio Elito Labirintai (The Labyrinths of Post-Soviet Elite)*, Vilnius: Knygiai.

Pilkington, H. (1994) *Russia's Youth and Its Culture: A Nation's Constructors and Constructed*, London: Routledge.

Riordan, J. (1995) 'The rise and fall of a youth elite in Russia', in J. Riordan, C. Williams and I. Ilynski (eds) *Young People in Post-Communist Russia and Eastern Europe*, Dartmouth: Aldershot.

Solnick, S.L. (1998) *Stealing the State: Control and Collapse in Soviet Institutions*, Cambridge, MA: Harvard Univeristy Press.

Sorokin, P. (1959) *Social and Cultural Mobility*, New York: The Free Press.

Steen, A. (1997) 'The new elites in the Baltic states: recirculation and change', *Scandinavian Political Studies*, 20: 91–112.

Steen, A. and Ruus, J. (2002) 'Change of regime – continuity of elites? The case of Estonia', *East European Politics and Societies*, 16: 223–248.

Wallace, C. and Kovatcheva, S. (1998) *Youth in Society: The Construction and Deconstruction of Youth in East and West Europe*, London: Macmillan press Ltd.

9 Catching up with the West?

An insider's perspective from Lithuania

Herwig Reiter

Introduction[1]

When the former socialist countries associated with the Soviet Union entered a process of transformation in the early 1990s the outcome of the change for these countries could not be predicted. After several years and a period of 'shock therapy' (Gligorov 1995; Standing 2002) of becoming accustomed to the new economic and welfare systems, it became clear that some, like the Baltic countries, would at high speed transform into capitalist market democracies and be economically and politically associated with the European Union. Some scholars conceptualize the process of transformation normatively as 'delayed or catch up modernization' (e.g. Zapf 1992: 12) that essentially involves the successful development of welfare and, more precisely, the following elements: competitive democracy, market economy, welfare state, and mass consumption. The replacement of the former life course model of the authoritarian welfare state with one that institutionally, politically, and biographically frames people's movement from birth to death according to the requirements of the new system (Kohli 1986, Leisering and Leibfried 1999, Leisering 2003,) accompanies the transformation process.

The application of an ethnocentric notion of modernization in a functionalistic tradition (Parsons 1964) to describe the transformation of post-communist countries in central and eastern Europe is debatable, although the idea of 'returning to Europe' was not alien to the region (Outhwaite and Ray 2005). Parson's notion was adopted not only by research assessing the process (e.g. Delhey 2001) but also in key policy documents instructing the European Union's enlargement process (European Commission 1997). The accession of all three Baltic countries to the European Union in 2004 quasi-ratified the success of their transformation (and the prescribed therapy) at least in institutional terms.

Economic, social and political change does not occur without the involvement of individuals. Agency is the substance of structure, and social history does not evolve independently from life histories (Sieder 2004). This chapter examines what happens beyond, or below, the institutional level of 'catch-up' modernization in the context of Lithuania, a country that with its Baltic neighbours went through a particularly radical institutional transformation (Barr 2005). The story of a single individual serves as a window into the lived experience of the transformation and indicates answers to the following questions concerning key institutional aspects of the transformation: How are they perceived? How are they accommodated in biographical narratives? How do they impact on the orientation of biographies? In other words: How does lived experience crystallize into transformation knowledge?

Mustafa[2] was one of 30 respondents, all of them young Lithuanians (aged between 15 and 24) in transition to the world of work, who were interviewed in 2004. The study researched the meanings of work and unemployment in a society, which after decades of constitutionally guaranteed access to labour suddenly confronted mass unemployment in the course of socio-economic transformation (Reiter 2008). The reason for choosing young adult respondents was because they hold a significant position in the process of knowledge renewal as they have to negotiate 'old' meanings and bear them onwards into the new society. Due to the research focus on work and unemployment, the four developmental dimensions of the normative model of 'catching up', democracy, market economy, welfare state, and consumption, were not explicitly addressed during the interview; yet they came to be indirectly but repeatedly represented in the material. The interview with Mustafa, who was a loser of the country's transformation, is unique in that aspects of these four developmental dimensions appear in one single account. Mustafa's story is a striking example of how a society's institutional transformation penetrates into and is assimilated in biographical accounts and articulated as 'knowledge' (Schutz and Luckmann 1973) about the new system.

The interviews of the study were conducted following the methodological programme of the problem-centered interview designed by Witzel (2000). This type of interview constitutes a systematic integration of inductive and deductive elements in the research process by combining strong narrative elements with a targeted interest in specific research issues. In this way the method provides the openness that is required for biographical research, as well as the possibility to apply a certain comparative grid to all interviews. The interviews were carried out and transcribed by trained Lithuanian and Russian speaking interviewers and were subsequently translated into and analysed in English.[3] In-depth analysis was limited by the unavoidable 'foreignization' associated with the processing and manipulation of the interviewee's language (Temple and Young 2004).

Extensive biographical case reconstructions, however, were crucial within the process of analysis that followed the suggestions of Kluge (2000) to systematically organize findings from qualitative research into empirically grounded typologies. The construction of empirically grounded types was done in four steps. First, the relevant dimensions were identified and developed out of the material on the basis of extensive single case analyses. Second, the interviews were grouped according to the established categories and subjected to comparative analysis, gradually unfolding the empirical space covered. Third, the attribute space was consolidated and the types were created by contrasting cases, and by assessing individual cases against the background of the emerging types. Finally, the constructed types were characterized along the main dimensions identified and described through prototypical cases. The study in the background of this chapter produced three classifications: (i) patterns of youth transitions and related time perspectives of biographical uncertainty (Reiter 2010b); (ii) young women in gender-work relations (Reiter 2010c); (iii) a heuristic typology of relations between individuals, the state, and the unemployed in society. Mustafa is a prototypical example of one of the types constructed in the third classification.

The analysis of Mustafa's life story, which addresses the critical aspects of the institutional change in his perspective, is structured in three sections. Preceding the analysis is a brief background, which introduces the main features of Mustafa's biographical situation, the micro-historical container, in which his perception of the changing world is embedded. The first analytical section reflects some of the consequences of the interplay of the comprehensive monetarization of everyday life and the normalization of employment in the new economy for consumption and the establishment of a life course perspective. The second analytical section reveals problematic issues of work and unemployment in the market economy as well as Mustafa's dissatisfaction with the responses of the state and its agents to obvious societal problems. The third analytical section is dedicated to the way Mustafa's evaluation of the current situation and his discontent is articulated on the level of (projected) action and self-perception; political, social, and identity aspects can be distinguished.

The final part reviews the findings from this one case, especially the indicated responses to the transformation, in the light of two approaches to theorizing and analysing social change, both of which imply a distinct notion of time. The first approach discusses social change under the label of 'social acceleration' (Rosa 2003, 2005; Eder 2004) and draws our attention to the consequences of the necessary speeding-up of individual lives in the process of a society's 'catching up'. The second approach, in addressing social change under the label of 'cultural trauma' (Sztompka 2000, Aarelaid-Tart 2006), invites the reflection of possible consequences of the economic 'shock therapy' for the transition into the new society in the sense of a disruption of a routine over time.

Background

At the time of the interview – in February 2004, only a few months before Lithuania became a member of the European Union – Mustafa was 22 years old and worked as a craftsman for the minimum wage in Vilnius. He grew up in the lands bordering Belarus and was trained as a forester and woodcutter. But in the new market economy this profession, like so many others, was useless: 'When I graduated we were already, the third generation of foresters and there were a hundred of us.' When he was a teenager Mustafa worked in the construction industry, repaired cars, and became involved in illegal trading before another member of his family offered to join him on the job as a craftsman, which he had done a couple of months before the interview. Mustafa's father has had a variety of different jobs in the course of the transformation ranging from veterinarian to tinker, which is indicative of the flexibility necessary in the years after the breakdown of communism. His mother has been unemployed ever since she decided to give up her job in order to take care of his older sister's child; her attempts to get back to work after a few years remained unsuccessful. Mustafa's second, younger, sister works as a saleswoman.

Mustafa's self-perception of not having a nationality is rather untypical for people from this area, who tend to emphasize either their original Baltic or their Russian identities. Yet the difficulty of tying him to a certain national identity is representative of the changeful history of the area and the contemporary struggle for an integration of Baltic, post-Soviet, and neo-European Union shares. Mustafa claims to be 'international', and says:

> For example, I did not write any nationality in my passport (...), because, for example, one of my grandfathers is Polish, the other Byelorussian. One grandmother is Russian, the other – Ukrainian. So who am I? (...) I finished a Russian school. I know Lithuanian. (...) My parents speak Russian. I talk in Lithuanian with my father. With one sister I speak in Russian, with the other in Lithuanian.

In many ways, Mustafa is a good example of a young adult in the Baltic region experiencing multiple transitions and between various cultures and traditions. Mustafa's transition to adulthood and regular employment is framed by the country's transformation from a Soviet republic to an independent nation and then member of another supranational entity, this time European, which yet again raises questions of collective belonging (Karlsson 2002). This tension becomes evident throughout his interview recorded only a few months before Lithuania became a member of the European Union. In the following passage the tension is rather explicitly articulated as a form of scepticism and uncertainty, or even fear:

> You will see what will happen here. That's for one hundred per cent; there will be a big change. Only chaos, prices will grow, salaries will wait [not be paid – H.R.] for a couple of months. (...) Then we have a year or so with all this bureaucracy and new laws and regulations and only then we'll start living normally. (...) There are a lot of friends; they all intend to run away from here, I can almost guarantee this. All of them. 'Because', they say, 'the first year after joining [the EU – H.R.] we have to leave, because there'll be a great mess and people of thirty, thirty five years old, you have experienced this and seen how Lithuania became independent.

The following sections substantiate Mustafa's uneasiness about the forthcoming change, which is rooted in his observation of the society's change under the new circumstances.

The monetarization of society – education, consumption, and later life

At the beginning of the interview when he starts responding to the opening question that addresses the last five years of his life, Mustafa introduces one of the main topics of the interview: the meaning of money in the new society. This issue, which he repeatedly takes up, provides a good starting point for exploring his perception of the transformation.

Leaving school with 'very bad marks' and no chances to enter state-funded further education, he has to realize that the alternative of private education is not accessible without the necessary means.

> After finishing studies, after the graduation from school I went to a tech (technical school; H.R.). After finishing the tech I started to look for a job, because there were no possibilities to enter some higher school, for there was neither money nor conditions for that as I finished the school with very bad marks (…) I tried to apply, but what I didn't have was good marks (…) The alternative was, everywhere one needed money, money in order to enroll at some fee-paying school.

The new quality of money represents real value which motivated his involvement in illegal activities as a teenager – 'I started this when I was seventeen'. Instead of focusing on his school performance and attending further education Mustafa started to earn his living from small scale-smuggling across the border to Belarus. Only after a while he understands that this activity would not get him anywhere, as a dramatic narrative consisting of ingredients like 'guns', 'violence', 'fights', 'blood', 'slit throats', as well as the criminals' 'fear for their families' emphasizes. Although he continues to characterize this period as 'the best time of my life, because (…) I saw all life, all the good and bad things', he is about to withdraw from all the associated activities by 'trying to set all those mistakes straight now'. However, his 'skills' from those days did somehow remain useful. When he started working in a regular job he was at first irritated by the necessity of being content with a very small salary, which still needed to be supplemented by additional income; for example, by 'making a few calls'.

> For example, when I work here, when I started earning this money, it makes me laugh. I see how much money I get and it already changes my attitude to the money that I earn normally. For example, with this money, well, I don't know, the last time I bought something with my salary money, I bought a CD on my salary money. And everything else, you could say, the salary is for the flat, to pay debts and that's it. For example, all my clothes, all the accessories, everything that I need, for example, to look well, to go out somewhere, to a bar or someone's birthday party, all these things are bought not on my salary. Well, anyway, I earn money, but I don't want to tell you how. I go home, I make a few calls, I find out, someone needs this, the other

> one needs that. So I bring these people together more or less, and then there's some per cent for me. So you could say I dress on this per cent.

Regular employment gradually made him differentiate between two types of money. While his salary from employment is for more conventional consumption and basic personal maintenance, his income from illegal trade primarily enhances his social standing and represents a form of luxury consumption whose significance and rules he had already absorbed. The more he settles into his 'normal job', the more he understands that in the common world of consumption money needs to be used in an economic way. Furthermore, as the following paragraph indicates, he associates a normal job with becoming a 'responsible person' as well as with having a family, which requires an individual to have a 'good basis under (their) feet' and a 'concrete job':

> When I started doing a normal job, I began to treat money more seriously. Because earlier somehow if I had money … OK, there was money, I would go and spend this or that much, I did not count money that I used to spend. Now, for example, I earn this salary and every time I go to a shop I count: 'OK, if I spend this much today, how much will I have for tomorrow? How much will there remain for me for the rest of the week?' (…) … Of course, the job, here, is very necessary. Here you have some kind of responsibility for some work. For example, you come, even going to work every day, you already are responsible for something. 'I have to come to work, I have to work.' But most often this work responsibility is for money. Because, for example, if you want to become a responsible person, OK, find a chick, give birth to a child and look after it, and you will have your responsibility. But here is something completely different. Every job is about money.

Mustafa's experience and knowledge of the norms of the new society as well as its standards of achievement enables him to provide a working model of socializing a child into understanding the link between working more and harder and the improvement of one's access to desired commodities. After briefly reflecting the childhood of his nephew whom he describes as being spoilt, Mustafa defines the educational programme that he proposes for his own future child:

> But in general, I know that my child, for example, when he is twelve or thirteen, if he says to me: 'Give me money', I will find some work at home for him so that there's something that I can pay him for. Because, for example, as my father taught me, he would also give me money but if I needed more to buy something, some better jacket, father would give it to me: 'Here's the money for you, go and buy the jacket.' It is ridiculous what a jacket you can buy for such money. Somehow, you want to buy a better one, but you don't have the money. You go to your father: 'Give me more money.' 'Do you want money? Then go and tidy up the garage. Do something else and I'll give you more.' So you work. You work and you know that you will earn

> money and you know why you need it, that you want to buy a better jacket. For example, I want to buy some computer, a cassette, or a CD or something else, anything. In general, the child has to see this.

Another feature of work associated with the value of money in the new system is the establishment of a balance between achievements, earnings, and consumption over the life course. The necessary initial incentive, at least from Mustafa's point of view, consists of not earning enough from which paid employment triggers an upward spiral of aspiring and achieving: 'When you work and earn less you want to find a better job in order to earn more money, for example, to achieve more in life, to support your family better'. In line with the specific life course model of capitalist societies that creates tight interdependencies between the major life phases (Kohli 1986; Leisering 2003), the quality of life in old age is essentially determined by finding this balance at an earlier life phase. Furthermore, it becomes obvious that Mustafa approves of the inherent concept of morality and the 'good life' that now needs to be passed on to the next generation. This rather complex feature of the new system is ratified in the following passage in which he uses an imagined dialogue between an unemployed father and his child to illustrate how it can all go wrong in the instance of being unemployed.

> Well, it is an obligation for a person to strive for something in life and not to stay at home, for example, without job thinking: 'Oh, I do not have a job, I do not have money.' And when you work, you somehow want to achieve much more. As for example, in his old age any person wants to live in a good flat and to have some little house in a suburb and to finish his life normally so that he could relax normally and say: 'I have achieved everything that I could in my life. I supported my family as good as possible. I brought up my children the best way I could.' And everyone wants to bring up his children the best possible way. In order to bring them up, for example, you have to show your children that you work and that you are doing your best, because, for example, non-working parents, children themselves when they, their parents are not working, (they) perceive all this somehow differently … 'Here, my father doesn't work. Father, why don't you work?' 'Because I don't want to work, there is no work.' They grow up and also sit at home thinking, 'Here, father doesn't work, maybe I also don't have to?' The same shit.

The changing world of work – unemployment and the irresponsible state

Apart from unemployment, which is discussed below, Mustafa describes the phenomenon of working poor as a real threat in the new system. A statistics of the EUROSTAT (Bardone/Guio 2005) assessing the poverty risk of employed and unemployed people shows that in Lithuania more than 40 per cent of the population beyond the age of 15 at risk of poverty are actually employed. In short, the opportunity costs of regular employment are very high. Talking about his current job, Mustafa illustrates how he struggles to make ends meet from the income of his regular employment alone. The job was difficult to get, although he earns only the minimum salary of 400 litas[4] a month; and he manages to get by only because he can share at least some of the costs with other people in the same situation.

> For example I have been without a job all winter, there isn't any job. So you sit here with four hundred Litas and now, when problems occurred, even less. And you have to survive in Vilnius, to rent a flat, food, to get home somehow. Well, it is a bit easier with going home now, because some friends came to work in Vilnius. So we agree and come here together, and we live together. But otherwise, by living here, and this work, I could say I am working into debts here, because for me ... During the winter I accumulated – with all this living, paying for the flat, buying something to eat and the most interesting: you get the salary, you pay back all debts and you keep on borrowing – so by and by I get into more and more debts. Because for example, as I counted, 'Jeez, I incurred so many debts here, to live in Vilnius, to do this job.'

Unemployment was one of the biggest problems characterizing the transition of the Lithuanian economy and society along Western standards. With the end of both the constitutionally guaranteed right and duty to work and the 'communist taboo against unemployment' (Baxandall 2000) unemployment rates skyrocketed from zero to double digits within a few years (European Commission 2006). Although the general level of welfare remained low in Lithuania (Aidukaite 2004) the image of the idle unemployed as a new figure in society became quickly available as a general stereotype (Reiter 2007a). Facilitated by novel official standards of appropriate behaviour worthy or unworthy of state support – as, for instance, established by official institutions of unemployment management (Juska and Pozzuto 2004), a general suspicion of welfare abuse became widespread and tenacious. It can even be found among young people whose families are affected by unemployment (Reiter 2008).

Also Mustafa shares some of these prejudices towards unemployed people, 'They receive benefits, they drank it away, and here they sit again'. Yet he remains critical of the capacity and willingness of the state to actually support people in this situation. The labour exchange offices are not able to provide jobs; they are little more than contact points that officially establish an individual's insurance status as an unemployed person like, for instance, with regard to graduates from education:

> Everybody after finishing the tech registered that they didn't have jobs. Those who didn't enter any school go to the job centre and stand there. Well, as if they were looking for a job already. But in fact you go to the labor exchange only to register.

Furthermore, *valstybė* (the state) and its agents are directly criticized. 'The state has to take more care of its citizens' is Mustafa's general opinion concerning public welfare provision. This principle is particularly relevant when it comes to the problem of unemployment, where the state does not seem to be ready to initiate the above-described mechanism of striving for more by offering to put people on the right track.

> I don't know, the state would have much more … I don't know, well, for example, our state, well, what can it do? It promises millions, it promises there will be no unemployed, there won't be anything. Look yourself how many people are mooching around without jobs, how many beggars there are. Well people, 'Beggars, I understand, their life is difficult.' There, X (the mayor of Vilnius; H.R.) opened a couple of lodging houses for them. Well, what's the use of those lodging houses for them? They spend a night (there) and start mooching for the whole day again. Offer them a job, any job. Let them earn kopecks. But you'll see that when a person starts working he will earn that money.

Mustafa accuses the state and its democratically elected representatives of showing little interest in the problems of the people. He laments the 'bad government', and provides examples of 'corrupt police officers' co-operating with smugglers and other criminals. Responding to the interviewer's question about what had changed after the collapse of the Soviet Union, Mustafa articulates his frustration about the ignorance of politicians thus expressing a deep crisis of confidence in politics prevalent in the area. In this personal perspective, politicians constitute an idle ruling class that is perceived as being selfishly involved in scandals of obvious corruption and self-enrichment. Mustafa also accuses them of manipulating the unemployment figures to their political advantage.

> Look at our Seimas (the Lithuanian Parliament; H.R.). That's ridiculous. They sit there with those party member tickets hidden somewhere in their closets and they are happy doing politics. And you could say that their politics is very much the same, they only take money (now). They take the money and they don't care. 'Ha, I got some money, I need to have one more villa built.' This is how they do it. Hm, in case there is an investigation (…): 'Look, where did you get so much land?' Where do you think an ordinary Speaker of the Seimas, whose salary is six thousand Litas a month at the most, bought all this, (even) if he worked two tenures? (…) For example, where do such people get their land? One piece of land is an estimated one hundred thousand [Litas, HR] and they have six, seven or eight of them. Where do they get so much money? And in fact these people say, 'Ah, I inherited this from my grandma.' I see, grandma somehow inadvertently bombarded the Swiss bank. Because in fact, this is ridiculous, where do such people get such money? Of course, bribes make a lot, contact number one did this, the other did that. (…) Really this is ridiculous, so what can you say about such a government? This government ate

everything up. You could say they care only for themselves. They look: 'Is it good for me?' 'Yes.' And you will live on somehow. They care little for a single person. (This is how) they care for Lithuania in general: 'Ah, here they work, here they don't. Well, if we mix, fine, it's not high unemployment.'

Citizen, emigrant, or legacy? The corrosion of identity

There are three main outcomes that can be distinguished with regard to how Mustafa (as well as other young people in the sample) may respond to the assessment of the current situation. The order in which the outcomes are presented reflects their increasing relevance for Mustafa's personal identity: (a) as a citizen he is frustrated with the political climate; (b) he is frustrated with the prevailing unfavourable living conditions and life chances; and (c) as an individual perceiving weak ties to the current system, he lacks the recognition as a valuable person in the context of the new society.

Mustafa's disappointment with political agents, the first outcome, has the clear consequence that he lost interest in participating in democratic procedures. However, by generalizing the problem and rationalizing it into a common phenomenon he manages to somewhat moderate his anger about the democratic culture in his country. 'I am disappointed with Lithuania', he says, before he specifies the reasons for his dissatisfaction.

> Well, I could say with the government of Lithuania, because there are lots of them in Lithuania ... Well, I could say, the government is the same everywhere. I don't know, for example, I have been living in Lithuania, I haven't lived somewhere in Poland or Russia I don't know what's going on there. Maybe also the same. For example, I don't know, for me the government of Lithuania, I don't even go to elections now. Because I know that whatever you elect it will be the same thing.

The evaluation of the living conditions and life chances in his home country, the second outcome, against the background of what he knows about other contexts causes his determination to leave. There is first of all the comparison of the new with the old system. While life does not seem to be much better now than during the Soviet Union, in Mustafa's opinion, it is not worse. In short, there is a certain trade-off between the two systems.

Although Mustafa has a rather clear opinion about the Soviet period, 'The Soviets reduced all the Baltic countries to poverty (...) the Soviets ruined all the states', he does subscribe to some of the Soviet nostalgia, to which the other interviews collected by the study also refer. For instance, he reproduces a popular metaphor of post-communism: 'In Soviet times, there was work but there weren't things to buy. Now there are lots of things to be bought, but there is no work'.

The comparison of Lithuania with other Western European countries and especially the European Union makes Mustafa feel desperate to go abroad for work. First of all he reiterates the argument that he would earn much more in his field of work, 'I will try to go abroad, because money is bigger there, because it doesn't exist here somehow. This work is not valued here.' On the other hand, he complains about the prevailing low level of development of his country, which narrows down his future perspective to the one chance of leaving. Considering his current job, he says: 'As far as I have noticed, there is only one chance here, one chance for my future: to leave this place and go abroad. There is nothing about it in Lithuania'. This perspective is, however, embedded in a rather long-term view on the trajectory he expects Lithuania to perform after joining the European Union, which this brief dialogue with the interviewer, who is probing for Mustafa's opinion, indicates.

MUSTAFA: I can't even imagine. In five years, five years, so it would make 27. Well, I don't know. If I continue to work as X (current occupation; H.R.), if I do, that's a very big question, then ... I think if I'm still an X, I'll be in Lithuania no longer. Surely, I will escape Lithuania. If there's a possibility, I escape Lithuania immediately. I know that Lithuania will join the European Union and will reach the level in 30 years only. So in 30 years I will be 50 and I will live there, you could say (...) in a way they will start living only later. So if I'm lucky, I will live those 30 years normally. Of course, there's no guarantee, because no one is sure what will happen in five years. I don't know, maybe I will fall ill the very next week...
INTERVIEWER: No, of course everything can happen but in general, if everything is fine. Do you think it would be easier abroad?
MUSTAFA: It seems to me that it is easier there.
INTERVIEWER: Anyway, if you go to work there, you go illegally.
MUSTAFA: No, why, it is possible. We will join the European Union and please go legally.
INTERVIEWER: So will you go there at once?
MUSTAFA: If there's a chance – at once, at once. There's nothing here, well, Lithuania has not reached that level yet, there's no living. (...)

The severest conclusion that Mustafa draws, even if perhaps not consciously, from his assessment of system change, is that he counts himself among those people that will need to disappear ('die off') in order for the country to recover. This is the third outcome of being a legacy, In other words, the prerequisite for erasing the Soviet legacy is the renewal of the people and their culture and competences by replacing those who lived under the old regime, including himself (at the age of 22!), by a new generation. In the following passage he first describes how a little town that he knew from his childhood turned into a ghost town during the last years, and then how people in professions associated with the Lithuanian nuclear power plant became redundant and have troubles adapting to the new situation. Once again he criticizes the state and finally implicates himself in the radical solution that could provide the next generation with the chance to live a normal life.

> Let's take a town X (name; H.R.), for example, so it died off as a town. The last time when I was in X, that was half a year ago, I drove around town and I

looked at it like this [the respondent makes his eyes big demonstrating how he looked at the town]. Some time ago, I don't know when, when I was about seven, I had an aunt living there. There was a town, a normal little town; there were block houses and everything, very tidy; there was a kindergarten working. Now when you go by, there are block houses, the doors are broken, the windows are broken. There's only one little light on the fifth floor in the whole block house. That's it. There isn't anybody. There isn't, they all died off. So you look at the house, a flat with three rooms costs one thousand Litas. 'Buy it!' 'I don't want to, what is such a room for? What will I do with this flat?' All people … are dying, are dying. And you'll see if they close the atomic [Nuclear Power Station in Ignalina; H.R.], you'll see, Visaginas [the town founded together with the power plant; H.R.] will die, the city. It will die because they do not have anything special. You could say that 70 per cent of residents work at this atomic. They closed the atomic – that's it. They can't do anything else; they have worked all their lives at the atomic. There, as far as I understood, one part is drivers, a driver will find work anywhere. But, for example, I don't know what a nuclear supervisor, who takes care of the nuclear, will do. Do you think he will go to, I don't know, at a computer to work as some computer man? He won't have an understanding, he would tell you everything about the nuclear from A to Z. He will tell you everything of what is going on there, but he won't be able to do anything else. Put him at a writing table now and ask, 'Write something for me.' He will sit and write and make mistakes. And he won't have an understanding of what should be done. And our state doesn't care for that. It seems to them that everything is nice, everybody is clapping their hands, they came and promised something, 'Please wait for three years.' So you wait. This is Lithuania. I don't know, someone said that in order for Lithuania to reach something and live well you must wait until all people who lived under soviets will die off. So when I die, maybe my grandchildren will see better times and will live a really normal life.

Conclusion

Mustafa's reflected account captures many dimensions that the young respondents in the sample relate to about the socio-economic change and addresses the temporal dimension of the socio-economic change of his country. In particular, the ideas of acceleration and breaking apart are implicit.

The term 'catching up' suggests primarily that within a Europe of different speeds (Eder 2004), an accelerated movement is performed by some societies in order to become equal to and perhaps even overtake a 'generalized' reference society in the sense of Mead ([1934] 1962). In the case of post-communist transformations towards European Union membership the 'generalized other' does not only represent an imagination and expectation that the decades of the Cold War had firmly established. The West has finally turned into the agent setting the rules of transformation and essentially extending the original economic notion of 'backwardness' (Gerschenkron 1962) to other areas of society. In this perspective

Mustafa's narrative can be read as the perception of change by an insider of a process of acceleration that also challenges established cultures of synchronizing everyday time with societal time (Rosa 2003, 2005). Mustafa essentially confirms and substantiates the relevance of the normative version of the modernization theory, involving the establishment of democracy, market economy, welfare state, consumption, and a new definition of the life course – and consequently the focus of this tradition on synchronization and, in welfare state terms, convergence. Mustafa comments on the new obstacles of finding work in what has become a 'market of labour'; he laments the poor performance of politicians as the agents of the recent democracy; he negotiates the new meaning and 'real' value of money in post-communism; he finds ways to respond to the pressures to consumption; and he critically observes the situation of those people in society that are not among the winners of the transformation. His readiness to abandon the idea of his national identity may indicate that he somehow sympathizes with the idea of becoming European. Yet, his political discouragement and the firm intention to leave the country suggests that in this overall evaluation he considers the country's development as not promising enough in terms of both speed and quality. The essential ambivalence of the transformation producing both chances and burdens for individual and society is expressed therein.

This normative perspective on the societal development is a source of discontent that can be resolved on the individual level by pursuing the option of 'exit' (Hirschman 1970, 1993), of leaving the country and its conditions of citizenship (Reiter 2007b). Yet, the second dimension of time inherent in Mustafa's account, which refers to a 'civilizational break' (Sztompka 1996) in the evolution of a society of which one is a member, is more difficult to cope with. It essentially implies a devaluation of the past and the individuals in which it is (still) represented. In academic terms, Sztompka's (1993) rash diagnosis of 'civilizational incompetence' of the peoples of a vast area of Europe is an example for such a perspective. It resurrects Zinoviev's (1986) 'homo sovieticus' as the bogeyman inhibiting the long awaited modernization and regeneration of formerly socialist societies.[5] One remedy is the fading of its significance or its existence. The very last quotation from Mustafa's interview substantiates the relevance of this academic perspective. His identity crisis is the individual biographical response to the 'shock therapy' applied to the socio-economic system. Essentially, he has difficulties locating himself meaningfully within the aftermath of the 'historical watershed' (Miller *et al.* 2003) that the collapse of the Soviet empire constitutes. The concept of 'cultural trauma' (Sztompka 2000, Aarelaid-Tart 2006) identifies some of the symptoms related to the challenge of suddenly being confronted with the necessity to reframe one's life and identity in order to establish cognitive continuity across experienced discontinuity. The transformation is here conceptualized as a rupture involving individual and collective disruptive experiences, going along with the transformation that establishes a clear distinction of past and present, and old and new societal frames of reference.

This second temporal perspective of rupture represented in Mustafa's account is severe as the established insufficiency lies within the actor and thus cannot be escaped, at least not with the speed of the transformation. The tension created by Mustafa's impatience at being unable to match the necessary speed for catching up, is resolved by suggesting a great generational break. Yet it makes him, in his own time and place, a stranger who is trapped in his biography even if his mind-set seems to have moved on. That he articulates this problem as a young man with little real socialist experience may entail that this sensation is common among all generations. Finally, in conceptual terms, I would suggest the notion of 'biographical alienation' to describe this phenomenon that the (individual and societal) past, the 'because' of life in the sense of Schutz (1967), loses some of its capacity to instruct the movement towards a meaningful biographical future.[6]

To conclude, the purpose of this contribution was first of all to provide, by means of introducing a particularly rich case, an interface for projecting some of the discomfort and disappointment concomitant with the scope of the societal change of post-communist transformations to market democracy in the Baltic countries. Most of the more critical aspects of the transformation introduced here were articulated by several young people in various ways (occasionally in a more exaggerated way). In this sense the aspects introduced here by means of presenting a single young person are 'valid' beyond the case and apply to the experiences of many young people in the Baltic area.

Notes

1 An earlier German version of this chapter was published as Reiter (2010a).

2 All the respondents who participated in the study were allowed to choose their own pseudonyms. The fact that Mustafa is not a typical Lithuanian name may be puzzling. Why he chose this name is not clear; yet there is no doubt from his comments concerning his nationality that he has mixed Lithuanian–Russian ethnic identity. The fact that he did not chose a Lithuanian or Russian name should not be exaggerated as there are also other young people in the sample that did not.

3 All translations are the responsibility of the author.

4 Litas, the exchange rate with the euro at the time of writing was 1 litas = 0.289 euro or 3.45 litas = 1 euro.

5 The culturalist assumption of inertia has many predecessors including the notion of cultural lag (Ogburn 1922), the principle of latency (Parsons *et al.* 1953) and the habitus concept (Bourdieu 1986). In essence, they all refer to the tenacity already inherent in the process of 'assimilating the new and accommodating the old' that Piaget (1954) describes in his genetic theory of cognitive development.

6 I use the term 'biographical alienation' following Riemann's (1987) sociological study of biographies of psychiatric patients with the title *Das Fremdwerden der eigenen Biographie*.

References

Aarelaid-Tart, A. (2006) *Cultural Trauma and Life Stories*, Helsinki: Kikimora Publications.

Aidukaite, J. (2004) *The Emergence of the Post-socialist Welfare State – The Case of the Baltic States: Estonia, Latvia and Lithuania, Södertörn Doctoral Dissertations No. 1*, Stockholm, Huddinge: Elanders Gotab, Södertörns Högskola.

Bardone, L. and Guio, A.-C. (2005) 'In-work poverty: new commonly agreed indicators at the EU level', *Statistics in Focus – Population and Social Conditions 5/2005*: European Communities. Online. Available: http://epp.eurostat.ec.europa.eu/cache/ITY_OFFPUB/KS-NK-05-005/EN/KS-NK-05-005-EN.PDF (accessed 9 March 2011).

Barr, N. (ed.) (2005) *Labour Markets and Social Policy in Central and Eastern Europe: The Accession and Beyond*, Washington, DC: The World Bank.

Baxandall, P. (2000) 'The communist taboo against unemployment: ideology, soft-budget constraints, or the politics of de-stalinisation?', *East European Politics and Societies*, 14: 597–635.

Bourdieu, P. (1984) *Distinction: A Social Critique of the Judgement of Taste*, London: Routledge & Kegan Paul.

Delhey, J. (2001) 'The prospects of catching up for new EU members: lessons for the accession countries to the European Union from previous enlargements', *Social Indicators Research*, 56: 205–231.

Eder, K. (2004) 'The two faces of Europeanization: synchronizing a Europe moving at varying speeds', *Time & Society*, 13: 89–107.

European Commission (1997) Agenda 2000 – Volume II – Communication: Reinforcing the pre-accession strategy, DOC/97/7, 15 July 1997, Brussels: Commission of the European Communities. Online. Available HTTP: http://europa.eu/rapid/pressReleasesAction.do?reference=DOC/97/7&format=PDF&aged=1&language=EN&guiLanguage=en (accessed 9 March 2011).

European Commission (2006) *Employment in Europe 2006*, Luxembourg: Office for Official Publications of the European Communities.

European Commission (2007) *Employment in Europe 2007*, Luxembourg: Office for Official Publications of the European Communities.

Gerschenkron, A. (1962) *Economic Backwardness in Historical Perspective: A Book of Essays*, Cambridge: Belknap Press of Harvard University Press.

Gligorov, V. (1995) 'Gradual shock therapy', *East European Politics and Society*, 9: 195–206.

Hirschman, A.O. (1970) *Exit, Voice, and Loyalty: Responses to Decline in Firms, Organizations, and States*, Cambridge, MA: Harvard University Press.

Hirschman, A.O. (1993) 'Exit, voice, and the fate of the German Democratic Republic: an essay in conceptual history', *World Politics*, 45: 173–202.

Juska, A. and Pozzuto, R. (2004) 'Work-based welfare as a ritual: understanding marginalisation in post-independence Lithuania', *Journal of Sociology and Social Welfare*, 31: 3–24.

Karlsson, K.-G. (2002) 'Europe's eastern outpost? The meanings of 'Europe' in Baltic discourses', in M. Malmborg and B. Stråth (eds) *The Meaning of Europe: Variety and Contention Within and Among Nations*, Oxford and New York: Berg.

Kluge, S. (2000) 'Empirically grounded construction of types and typologies in qualitative social research', *Forum Qualitative Sozialforschung/Forum: Qualitative Social Research*, 1(1), Art. 14. Online. Available: http://nbn-resolving.de/urn:nbn:de:0114-fqs0001145 (accessed 9 March 2011).

Kohli, M. (1986) 'The world we forgot: a historical review of the life course', in V.W. Marshall (ed.) *Later Life: The Social Psychology of Ageing*, Beverly Hills, CA: Sage.

Leisering, L. (2003) 'Government and the life course', in J.T. Mortimer and M.J. Shanahan (eds) *Handbook of the Life Course*, New York: Kluwer Academic/Plenum Publishers.

Leisering, L. and Leibfried, S. (1999) *Time and Poverty in Western Welfare States: United Germany in Perspective*, Cambridge and New York: Cambridge University Press.

Mead, G.H. ([1934] 1962) *Mind, Self and Society: From the Standpoint of a Social Behaviorist*, Chicago and London: The University of Chicago Press.

Miller, R., Humphrey, R. and Zdravomyslova, E. (2003) 'Introduction: biographical research and historical watersheds', in R. Humphrey, R. Miller and E. Zdravomyslova (eds) *Biographical Research in Eastern Europe: Altered Lives and Broken Biographies*, Aldershot, Burlington: Ashgate.

Ogburn, W.F. (1922) *Social Change: With Respect to Culture and Original Nature*, New York: B.W. Huebsch.

Outhwaite, W. and Ray, L. (2005) *Social Theory and Postcommunism*, Malden, MA: Blackwell.

Parsons, T. (1964) 'Evolutionary universals in society', *American Sociological Review*, 29: 339–357.

Parsons, T., Bales, R.F. and Shils, E.A. (1953) *Working Papers in the Theory of Action*, Glencoe, IL: The Free Press.

Piaget, J. (1954) *The Child's Construction of Reality*, London: Routledge & Kegan Paul.

Reiter, H. (2007a) 'Non-solidarity and unemployment in the "New West"', in N. Karagiannis (ed.) *European Solidarity*, Liverpool: Liverpool University Press.

Reiter, H. (2007b) 'The post-communist triangle of (non-)solidarity and beyond: youth and the perception of unemployment in the 'New West'', in L. Magnusson and B. Stråth (eds) *European Solidarities: Tensions and Contentions of a Concept*, Brussels and New York: P.I.E. Peter Lang.

Reiter, H. (2008) *Dangerous Transitions in the 'New West' – Youth, Work, and Unemployment in Post-Soviet Lithuania*, Ph.D. thesis, Florence: European University Institute.

Reiter, H. (2010a) 'Die nachholende Generation? Anmerkungen zur Beschleunigung der Generationslagerung Jugendlicher im Neuen Westen Europas', in M. Busch, J. Jeskow and R. Stutz (eds) *Zwischen Prekarisierung und Protest: Die Lebenslagen und Generationsbilder von Jugendlichen in Ost und West*, Bielefeld: Transcript Verlag.

Reiter, H. (2010b) 'Context, experience, expectation, and action — towards an empirically grounded, general model for analyzing biographical uncertainty', *Forum Qualitative Sozialforschung/Forum: Qualitative Social Research*, 11 (1), Art. 2. Online. Available: http://nbn-resolving.de/urn:nbn:de:0114-fqs100120 (accessed 9 March 2011).

Reiter, H. (2010c) 'In my opinion, work would be in first place and family in second': young women's imagined gender-work relations in post-Soviet Lithuania', *Journal of Baltic Studies*, 41: 531–551.

Riemann, G. (1987) *Das Fremdwerden der eigenen Biographie: Narrative Interviews mit psychiatrischen Patienten*, München: Fink.

Rosa, H. (2003) 'Social acceleration: ethical and political consequences of a desynchronized high-speed society', *Constellations*, 10: 3–33.

Rosa, H. (2005) *Beschleunigung: Die Veränderung der Zeitstrukturen in der Moderne*, Frankfurt am Main: Suhrkamp.

Schutz, A. (1967) *The Phenomenology of the Social World*, Evanston, IL: Northwestern University Press.

Schutz, A. and Luckmann, T. (1973) *The Structures of the Life-World*, Evanston, IL: Northwestern University Press.

Sieder, R. (2004) 'The individual and the societal', in J. Fikfak, F. Adam and D. Garz (eds) *Qualitative Research: Different Perspectives – Emerging Trends*, Ljubljana: Založba ZRC Publishing.

Standing, G. (2002) 'The babble of euphemism: re-embedding social protection in 'transformed' labour markets', in A. Rainnie, A. Smith and A. Swain (eds) *Work, Employment and Transition: Restructuring Livelihoods in Post-communism*, London and New York: Routledge.

Sztompka, P. (1993) 'Civilizational incompetence: the trap of post-communist societies', *Zeitschrift für Soziologi*, 22: 85–95.

Sztompka, P. (1996) 'Looking back: the year 1989 as a cultural and civilizational break', *Communist and Post-communist Studies*, 29: 115–129.

Sztompka, P. (2000) 'Cultural trauma: the other face of social change', *European Journal of Social Theory*, 3: 449–466.

Temple, B. and Young, A. (2004) 'Qualitative research and translation dilemmas', *Qualitative Research*, 4: 161–178.

Witzel, A. (2000) 'The problem-centered interview' [26 paragraphs]. *Forum Qualitative Sozialforschung/Forum: Qualitative Social Research*, 1(1), Art. 22. Online. Available: http://nbn-resolving.de/urn:nbn:de:0114-fqs0001228 (accessed 9 March 2011).

Zapf, W. (1992) 'Die Transformation in der ehemaligen DDR und die soziologische Theorie der Modernisierung', *MPIfG Discussion Paper Nr. 92/4*, Cologne: Max Planck Institute for the Study of Societies.

Zinoviev, A. (1986) *Homo Sovieticus*, London: Paladin Grafton Books.

10 Mobilizing capitals during transitions

The stories of Toomas and Nikolai

Raili Nugin and Aida Hachaturyan

Introduction

This chapter focuses on two case studies. We explore the life stories of two young men who experienced their paths from childhood to adulthood concomitantly with the societal transformation from socialism to post-socialism in Estonia in the early 1990s. The core issues of interest were the degrees of influence the social-economic transition (from a centralized and planned economy to the democratically based free market) had on those people who became adults during this period and, consequently, on their life paths. The cases are notably different: one is the life story of a successful businessperson who is a native Estonian (the ethnic majority) born in 1975, the other is a Russian-speaking (the largest ethnic minority) author and rock climber born in 1972. The biographical approach enables us to see how individuals reflect on their social choices and how social structures operate in their lives. We try to find out what kinds of resources they used when going through their individual transitions in those uncertain times. We also investigate their reflections on the role and impact of that social change on their personal transitions. In order to provide better answers to these questions, we used Pierre Bourdieu's (1986) concepts of capitals and habitus as analytical tools. Capitals (cultural, social, symbolic, and economic) are mediators between an individual and society, and thus we address the question of how habitus and the capability to mobilize capitals influence the course of transitions in a specific social context.

We show that in their specific cases both of our two respondents had acquired in their childhood the pattern of habitual behaviour they displayed throughout their lives, although the patterns varied according to different times and contexts. The agency of both respondents is extremely contextual and seems to be influenced by the general symbolic order of the society. Also, in both cases, ethnic identity played a certain role in the transitions. This is not to say that ethnic identity determines the outcome of a transition; we recognize that ethnic communities are far too heterogeneous for that. Rather, we point out that ethnic identity can influence one's habitual dispositions. Our analysis shows that the transitions in the lives of both those young men were influenced by the severe social transformations that took place at the time of their coming of age, yet both were influenced in their own particular way.

The chapter starts by presenting the social contexts of the time when the two respondents came of age. The aim of this section is to provide a brief introduction to the different social situations of the Russian and Estonian youth after the collapse of the Soviet Union. The symbolic order of the society did not support the upward social mobility of Russian youth, but was favourable to their Estonian counterparts. Next, we analyse the life stories by dividing them into three chronological parts: childhood (Soviet time), transition years (social transformation), and adulthood (stabilization period). This division is undoubtedly a bit arbitrary since life course is an ongoing process and it is hard to identify a specific moment when a new page is turned. There are always some activities begun in an earlier stage of life that continue into the next one. However, many life phases portrayed here coincide with developments in the society: both men were children in Soviet times, came of age during the years of vast social reorganization and finally matured during the period of social stabilization.

'Transition youth' in a transition society

The years of identity formation for an individual are often conceptualized as full of ruptures and uncertainty (Zittoun 2007: 196). For our respondents, Toomas and Nikolai,[1] those years coincided with the years of transformation in Estonian society, which can also be characterized by insecurity and ruptures. Their education and career development took place at a time when the entire society was in transition, politically and institutionally, as well as mentally.

After the dissolution of the Soviet Union, the economic state of Estonia was on the edge of collapse. After regaining independence, the subsidies of the previous system dropped overnight and GDP declined significantly (Keller and Vihalemm 2003: 196). Unemployment rates skyrocketed and shops were empty. Thus, even young people from families possessing better social, cultural and economic capital still went through hard economic times during their adolescence, especially if their parents worked for public institutions.

The first government cabinet of the restored republic introduced a number of liberal reforms, some of which had profound consequences for the disadvantaged strata of society. However, there are two sides to every coin. The liberalization of the economy and the subsequent free market regulation also meant new opportunities. Those who were more apt to do things differently and start new ventures gained the most from those reforms. Many of those people with open minds and the determination to become an entrepreneur were young (Helemäe *et al.* 2000: 38; Tallo and Terk 1998: 15; Titma 1999: 10), although a special group of the older generation also became winners; the elite former Communist Party personnel who had sufficient social and economic capital to profit from the privatization processes (Eyal *et al.* 1998; Steen and Ruus 2002).

The phenomenon of parallel transition (societal and personal) has come to the attention of social scientists in most post-socialist countries. While some studies have pointed out the disadvantaged state of youth after the fall of the Berlin Wall (see, for example, Gazsó 1992; Adelman 1994; Roberts 2003;

Williams *et al.* 2003), the opposite is the case in Estonian sociological research (Tallo and Terk 1998; Helemäe *et al.* 2000; Lauristin 2004), going so far as to create the term 'generation of winners' to refer to those who were at the threshold of their adult lives at this time period (Titma 1999). Yet, due to the focus of our chapter, we need to point out that the dissolution of the Soviet Union impacted differently on ethnic communities, which in the Estonian context refers to the (Estonian) majority and (Russian-speaking) minority youth. In the majority of cases, the ethnicity of the 'generation of winners' is the Estonian majority. Upward social mobility for 'transition youth' of the ethnic majority was rather high with 26 per cent of those who left school 1995–2002 gaining an initial post-graduate career in either a high-level managerial or a professional position (Toomse 2004: 26).

After the restoration of the republic of Estonia, the young generation of the Russian-speaking community in Estonia found themselves in a rather difficult position, as they (as well as their parents) were mostly only second or third-generation immigrants. Acquiring Estonian citizenship was highly dependent on their proficiency in the Estonian language. This was the period the Russian-speaking community began to feel suppressed by the mass media's use of neologisms of 'migrant', 'Russian speaker', 'occupier', 'alien', etc. (see also Chapter 6 by Aarelaid-Tart). Ethnic Russians, as a result of Estonia's independence, thus faced a crisis of societal positioning having to reorient from a position of belonging to Estonia within the mainstream of All-Union Soviet society to Russian-speakers in conflict with mainstream Estonian society. The problem of self-identity was a concern for the young in particular, since their formative identity-building did not get the customary support from their parents who were struggling with adjusting their own, already-formed identities.

Partly due to the language issues and partly their 'alien' identity and rejection by the Estonian ethnic majority, Russian-speaking youth had fewer choices compared to their Estonian coevals. In the media of the 1990s, the Russian-speaking minority were often held responsible for the Soviet occupation and the misery it had caused (Nugin 2003: 170). While Estonian youth were excited about political issues and had a positive outlook on the nation's future (Vogt 2005: 96–102; Nugin 2008: 197), Russian youth did not particularly identify with the overall political euphoria of independence.

Moreover, the high unemployment rates of Russian-speaking youth indicate they were not particularly among the 'winners'. This, however, does not infer the identity crisis and social exclusion applied to the entire youth of the local Russian community. A number of them were also among the highly socially mobile 'winners' and acquired economic capital far beyond that of their parents. Yet proportionally their number was smaller than that among ethnic Estonians. This may also stem from the fact that most Soviet-time immigrants were a manual labour force 'imported' to satisfy the needs of the Soviet industry. Such labourers were the social stratum that lost the most during the economic restructuring when Soviet factories were simply closed down and the manual workers lost their jobs.

Some Russian-speaking young people did take a serious interest in the political changes at the end of the 1980s because, unlike the older generation, they had not long experience of the previous social order and thus did not feel nostalgic about the Soviet regime. However, the social problems their parents encountered were still serious and influenced the life choices of the younger generation. Certain groups among the Russian-speaking community remained out of work, which induced young people to try out different ways of overcoming the employment challenge. In order to find regular work, some of them attempted to get a higher education, to learn Estonian and other foreign languages.

The cases of Toomas and Nikolai

The cases of Toomas and Nikolai were not chosen at random. Our aim was to find two young people who had transitioned to adulthood between 1988 and 1998, during which period the break with the old system, radical reforms, and economic stabilization occurred (Lauristin and Vihalemm 2009), and were 'successful' in one way or another. We looked for respondents of dissimilar ethnic, cultural, and social background, coming from different walks of life. Both respondents were male, single and without children. The biographical interviews primarily focused on their social activities. Thus we did not explore the reasons why their personal lives had not led to having their own families. But we did find it useful since single people usually dedicate more time to their social life, which was of interest to us.

How representative are those two cases of the other members of the same social or ethnic background? As a rule, such qualitative research can hardly claim anything about wider social or age groups. However, it can reveal some lines of reasoning or some reflections about choices or attitudes that were shared by other members of society. Many may have faced similar dilemmas, but solved them differently. Our task was to provide a picture of two possible ways of leading a life through these changes.

The data collection method was to conduct in-depth interviews about the respondents' biographies, which took place in spring 2008. We chose the biographical format because it allowed us to analyse the subjective meanings attributed to life transitions and the reflections of social impacts on personal life paths. The biographical approach allows us to treat identity as a process instead of a static state (Rosenthal 1997). By focusing on biographical case studies, we could follow the reflexive process of mobilizing and accumulating capitals through an individually acquired habitus. Our respondents talked about their lives in semi-structured, open-ended interviews with sufficiently broad questions that allowed them to narrate their lives in their own way. The interviews lasted for approximately two hours.

As we were mainly interested in the kinds of resources the respondents relied on, we had to define some heuristic categories to classify the different forms of resources (capitals). For this we used the concept of capitals of Pierre Bourdieu (1986, 1991). We found Bourdieu's concept of capitals useful, since it offers a deeper understanding of the usage of the resources at hand. Bourdieu's work provides an explanation of the relationship between structure and agency, in which structures are not static but a reflexive field (Threadgold and Nilan 2009: 53). In our analysis, we look at the micro-level of how our respondents made use of the different capitals during the transition process and how the capitals intertwined and how they were exchanged. Most of the capitals in Bourdieu's theory are not easy to detect and measure and we had to rely on our respondents' self-reflexive interpretations. We thus observed which capitals the interviewees themselves preferred to present and value, instead of judging their success by detecting the lack of some capital.

In our analysis, we first agreed upon predefined categories that we searched for in our data, relying on Bourdieu (1986), Bourdieu and Wacquant (2005) and James Côté (2002, 2007). Bourdieu has distinguished four types of capital: economic, cultural (education, cultural goods, long-lasting dispositions of mind and body), social (social networks and relations), and symbolic (legitimacy and prestige). Côté has conceptualized identity capital (meaningful self), which in many ways can overlap with Bourdieu's cultural or symbolic capital, but is somewhat different (for further discussion, see subsection 'The years of social transformation, Nikolai's case'). The transcribed, language-of-communication texts of the interviews were then analysed, identifying the use of those categories (mobilization, acquisition, and exchange of those capitals) in their life stories. After detecting passages in the interviews where the respondent appeared to talk about mobilizing or accumulating those capitals, we tested the relevance of those concepts to the life story and compared it with other analyses and critiques of those concepts in the literature.

Childhood and school

Toomas was born in Tallinn in 1975 as the second son of a couple who were both university-educated. His mother was a top executive in industry and his father was a researcher in the Academy of Sciences. Toomas's mother could be classified as managerial elite (see Eyal *et al.* 1998 for discussion) and his father as intelligentsia (for discussion, see English 2000). Both had a certain amount of symbolic and cultural capital, but had at times lacked material resources for material wellbeing. However, in a relatively egalitarian society economic capital did not matter so much and symbolic power or political capital had much more significance. According to Toomas, his family did not enjoy any of the privileges of the nomenklatura, but his parents' cultural and symbolic capitals seemed to help develop Toomas's own capitals indirectly and in many ways.

For Toomas, socializing and taking part in social life seem to be two of the most important aspects of life. Looking back on his early childhood, he recalled his first childhood home in a quiet suburb with lots of friends:

TOOMAS: I remember I had a very happy childhood. Up to the seventh year. Then we moved. I remember we lived… on […] Street [a quiet region with wooden houses – RN&AH] – and after that we moved to … [one of the biggest suburbs of apartment blocks, famous for its (relatively) huge buildings – RN&AH]. We had half of a house with its own garden and everything was very lovely and my own friends and … Then my childhood was like cut through… There, in … [the apartment-block region – RN&AH] I didn't make a single friend.[2]

Thus, for Toomas the most important childhood memories were connected with time spent with parents and friends. He did not recall any specific events (apart from moving to the apartment-block suburb) but only the social side of his childhood. When asked what he remembered of school and if he liked it, he also began with listing his social activities.

TOOMAS: In the school there was … I did a whole lot of things, I had tennis practice since first grade and then I had choir singing … […] and in order to sing in this boy choir, I had to go to music school, too. So I attended music school […] I studied acoustic guitar. And then through this music school, several bands came along, and … and finally, a brass band orchestra and … then there were additional choirs, several chamber choirs and … and finally I sang, like, in five choirs. And then … I quit, like, tennis. […] Then I concentrated more on music and then different kinds of sports activities came along … there was basketball and … I think I was back then the captain of handball, basketball, volleyball … in my school and … and I took part very actively at several kinds of sports days and I was the […] … Estonian champion of ball throwing … and skiing, and I did all this different stuff. I was like … like … very active. Very.

From this excerpt one can see how Toomas likes to represent himself: an active person who is always involved in multiple activities, who has large social circles and many talents. He mentioned a school concert where the director of the concert appointed him to act as compère since he was involved in 36 of the 50 performances in the programme. When asked about his social circles he said:

TOOMAS: Well, like today – when I whistle, at least 25 buddies come together. So well … quite a lot. How many of them could be considered as good friends, is another story. But well, the circle of people was very broad. Very…

Thus, Toomas had (and still has) a vast circle of friends and he was actively taking part in various highly social activities. According to Bourdieu, the accumulation of different capitals starts during childhood and capitals are acquired through an established habitus. In the case of Toomas, his active lifestyle during school began a pattern that he has followed throughout his life. One could say that he has acquired a habitus of social life that has helped him in his transition to adulthood as well as in his later social ascent as a businessperson. In this sense, he is a perfect fit for the model of a 'successful' transition to adulthood that is supported by heterogeneous social networks (Walther *et al.* 2005: 225). Such accumulation of social capital is also closely intertwined with cultural capital, because his hobbies (playing guitar, being good at sports) allowed him to secure a certain position among his friends (Bourdieu 1986: 249).

However, this kind of vigorous participation in extra-curricular activities during school is not a phenomenon unique to Toomas. During the Soviet era, social involvement was highly encouraged. Sports schools and music schools were accessible to virtually all children with the relevant skills. Toomas's family also supported his hobbies. Therefore the starting point of Toomas's habitus – being socially involved in cultural activities – emerged because the structural conditions of Soviet society promoted it, his parents supported and encouraged him, and his personality was disposed towards such a habitus.

Nikolai was born in Tallinn in 1972 as the only child of a working class family. He said that his mother is ethnically Estonian (but her mother tongue is Russian), and his father is an ethnic Russian. His home language has always been Russian and he does not speak Estonian very well. Thus, he can be considered a member of the Russian community. He spoke eagerly about his family origins, claiming that he has German and Swedish blood in his veins from his mother's side (according to Nikolai, his mother's family has lived in Estonia for 300 years but does not specify where the family originally came from). His father came to Estonia in the 1950s as the son of a military man. Nikolai also said that he knew the story of his father's side of the family up to his great-grandfathers. The knowledge of his ancestors served, for Nikolai, as a sort of symbolic capital. The presentation of his mother's ethnic heritage serves in a way as a symbolic resource to legitimate his roots in Estonia. The knowledge of his father's heritage can be seen as important in creating a feeling of continuity and a sense of belonging.

Although Nikolai described the origins of his family very thoroughly, it is noteworthy that he did not speak much about his childhood or his relations with his parents. We assumed that the laconic nature of the narrative was a consequence of the introverted nature of our respondent. Furthermore, during the interview Nikolai kept emphasizing his reticence on personal subjects and preferred to concentrate on his creativity, and on present rather than past activities. The absence of his parents from the narrative is probably not due to any problems in his relationship with them, rather the contrary. We can safely infer that his parents loved him and spent time with him because he mentioned that according to his mother, he was taught to read at the age of three. From that time on, he developed a deep interest in literature. At the age of seven, he wrote his first piece of prose, a fantasy story.

As a teenager, even as one with good grades, Nikolai began to protest against public morality, and tried to live in opposition to the existing Soviet social norms. When he was 11–12 years old the militia became interested in his demonstratively deviant behaviour. He declared in the interview that he has opposed society and social norms for most of his life:

NIKOLAI: All my life I was a hooligan. Starting at school. Even when I was in the second grade I was taken to the militia. [...] I have never been in sync with current age and society, even up to now. I cannot pretend that current age does not exist, [...] because I am more honest by nature. Secondly, I am – one can say – an anarchist. [...] With age people usually get more settled down. So to say, it takes different forms, but...

In other words, he reflexively prefers to represent himself as being opposed to society rather than being actively involved in social life. This reluctance to accept social norms and an effort to distance himself from social activity has become Nikolai's habitus, even if it has currently taken milder forms. However, as we see later on, this antisocial representation does not necessarily translate into antisocial behaviour. Thus, the habitus is more complicated in his case, as it is mainly expressed in his reflexive identity rather than his actual behaviour.

The years of social transformation

With the unleashing of perestroika at the end of the 1980s, the rigid Soviet system started to relax and a number of civic organizations emerged. Their initial aims differed with some demanding independence, while others fought for the preservation of the natural, architectural, and historical heritages in Estonia. Yet they all were opposed to the Soviet regime in one way or another. Toomas, like many of his peers, began to take an interest in politics and joined Kaitseliit (Defence League). The Kaitseliit in 1990 operated on questionable legal grounds claiming to be the legal successor of the Kaitseliit from the first period of independence (1918–1940). Toomas actively took part in its activities and also voluntarily took up security duty at events of national importance, such as the gathering of *Eesti Kongress* (Estonian Congress), which claimed to be the first democratically elected parliament, even though it legally never became one. Such close contact with the process of regaining national independence made him take a deeper interest in politics and led him to join a political youth organization.

For Estonian youth, the transition period and the perspective of Estonian independence was exciting (Vogt 2005; Nugin 2008). Toomas was involved in the process indirectly through the activities of the Kaitseliit as well as the political youth organization and he had a lot of good memories from that time due to his level of commitment. This experience significantly affected Toomas's identity, not the least because it happened during his formative years when social events have the strongest impact on one's personality (see for example Mannheim [1928] 1993; Erikson 1968; Inglehart 1997). He felt that he had done something for independence, even if he had not defended Toompea Castle during the *putsch*:

TOOMAS: I didn't take part directly in the defense of Toompea but I was there, somewhere ... ready to do it. [...] But ... you know ... there was a time when I even thought that I'd like to abandon school, since this thing [Estonia's struggle for independence – RN&AH] seemed the right one, that … the Estonian Republic stands on the edge of a knife and then … that everyone has to do like, something. Then in the name of that I gave up a lot of things, that…

This experience was not only a memory for Toomas, but had a symbolic value that shaped his generational identity. It can be transformed into symbolic capital in the framework of the discourse that those who lived during this time possess something that others do not:

TOOMAS: […] … I have … we like know how to value this, I think our generation knows how to value what we have right now, that … that a lot of young people don't … we are probably one of the last ones who remember this time like well … when there was nothing in the shops … and when there were food coupons and … I had to stand in the queue for butter … that … that well, these things like … they like help to value where we live right now. I am in this sense very-very … I wouldn't exchange this experience for anything, it's like a very, very good experience.

However, this high level of involvement in, and trust for his state and its purpose, has other aspects. Here we have to deal with the ambiguous concept of social trust, a term with poorly defined limits and usage, partly due to lack of research in the field (see also Schuller *et al.* 2000: 15; Allard 2005: 66). Our research confirms that social trust as a concept has an ambiguous nature, particularly during times of change. On the one hand, Toomas placed great trust in his country's future (i.e. the struggle for independence) and he truly believed in the widely shared (in the Estonian community) national goals and tried to contribute to the cause. On the other hand, he saw the corruption in the young state and decided to take no part in developing the institutions of the new republic:

TOOMAS: This was actually a very turbulent time … Then I realized how rotten the Estonian state actually was … that … I was absolutely sure that I would go to study law and … and … dedicate my life like to law enforcement and police work and … and then I realized, how rotten it actually is, that… that the corruption and … and all that took place in Estonia … that it was so mad, that … And then I thought, that I would bury my life in this unhappy hole while I can be useful to the Estonian state otherwise.

The same ambiguous level of trust in society during the transition period is also apparent in his business-related stories. Toomas started his first enterprise with a friend when he was 16 years old. The idea and goals of the business were a matter of coincidence. During a party the headmaster of his school confessed to him and his friends that the school needed renovating, but the budget would only allow for the repairs of the main hall. Toomas and his best friend promised to renovate the entire school within the budget limits and founded a company to do exactly that. That the headmaster favoured a newly established company of some of his 16-year-old students over professional contractors demonstrates a huge level of trust in Toomas and his friend (especially considering that Toomas had no experience at all in renovation projects and the company had been founded on the spot just for this purpose). On the other hand, it also shows how little faith the headmaster put in professional companies and their pricing policies. We could provide similar examples from the transition period. On the one hand, there was an extreme amount of interpersonal trust and even large contracts were often only verbal. Yet, on the other hand, the mistrust towards official documents was enormous. Social trust is closely connected with social norms (Putnam 2000). When the norms themselves are changing (as they were during the transition period), social trust easily erodes and becomes unstable. This indicates that social trust is very context-specific.

Toomas's first enterprise did not make much of a profit, but he was not disappointed in its limited success. He and his partner (his best friend) started to seek new challenges and other kinds of business: they talked to their classmates' parents and used the social contacts gained from those conversations. But they were also looking to co-operate with foreign companies. A breakthrough soon occurred: they found foreign partners and opened a small factory. After a while they sold their share of the factory to their partners and went into trading instead. Although that enterprise is still in business, Toomas has invested his profits into several others, such as real estate and restaurants.

Toomas presented his social contacts as the key to his business career. He went to a school where many of his friends' parents worked in influential positions in finance, state administration, and in the private sphere. He and his friends did not hesitate to go and ask for their advice, help, or capital (financial resources) and offered a share in their projects in return. He is a vivid example of someone who was able to convert their social capital into economic capital in a post-socialist society where contacts were sometimes more important than wealth (Eyal *et al.* 1998; Clark 2000: 444). His social capital, however, had a different characteristic as most treatments of post-socialist studies point out. He did not directly cultivate his own social network, but rather used the networks of his parents and his friends' parents. In other words, he was strongly motivated to use the social capital of the older generation of family and friends. The positive impact of parental social networks has been highlighted in other studies (Coleman 1988; Horvat *et al.* 2003), but children have commonly been depicted as passive beneficiaries rather than active initiators (for a critique, see Tolonen 2007: 32). This kind of agency and the initiative to make contacts were probably also a product of the transition period when the circumstances fostered a proactive attitude on the basis that everything was possible. The structural conditions of the society at that time were in a state of flux and the restructuring of the economy rewarded quick thinking and initiative.

As to his education, Toomas enrolled in one of the first private universities in Estonia to study finance. However, he never graduated due to lack of time, even though he restarted his studies on several occasions. A strategy combining studies with going into business was not rare in the aftermath of the collapse of the Soviet Union. The local market was yet to be fully established, and virtually anyone with enough initiative and some financial capital could start a new business. Founding one probably meant a great deal more than staying in school and so educational achievements became secondary, both personally and in the kinds of social circles Toomas frequented. Here, Toomas's acquisition of cultural capital (educational credentials) was closely intertwined with his social and economic capitals. His business partners financed his studies: in other words, his social capital (ties with business partners) contributed to his cultural capital (acquiring education), since business partners invested their economic capital to this cause. Conversely, it was also likely that Toomas's interest in cultural capital (education) contributed to his credibility as a businessperson (symbolic capital helping to acquire economic capital).

While Toomas told his story in a way that intertwined the transition years of Estonian society and his own, Nikolai's presentation of his life kept social events at a distance. He described many ways in which he opposed society while coming of age. After spending a year in university he was drafted to the Soviet army, but he evaded conscription by jumping over the fence of the place where the recruits were gathered. This escapade got him into even more trouble with the authorities. Yet, at that time, running away from the army did not carry a social stigma because of the many problems associated with military service. First, throughout the 1980s recruits could be sent to war zones such as Afghanistan or Nagorny Karabakh. The Soviet Army was also infamous for its *dedovshchina*, or 'Code Red'. In addition, escaping from the army could be seen as opposing the Soviet system in general and its military ambitions and particularly, on occasion, its ideology.

Although Nikolai's flight can be analysed in these terms, the main reason for doing so, as he stated himself, was being a pacifist and an anarchist by nature. Another way he expressed his anarchism was by joining the punk subculture, which was popular in the years of the perestroika. This subculture also possessed symbolic meaning in the context of the Soviet Union. The choice of being a punk meant resisting the social and political order of the Soviet Union and was therefore a form of political resistance at a time when such activities were still significantly persecuted. The local punk subculture, consisting of ethnic Estonians, actively supported the process of regaining independence and the dissolution of the Soviet Union. The ethnic Russian's punk subculture is largely unstudied, but it is probably safe to assume that its members had mixed feelings about abolishing all Soviet structures. While they might have welcomed the disappearance of the old oppressive system, the new developments were not exactly favourable to their ethnic group.

By being a punk, Nikolai developed what Tarja Tolonen calls 'subcultural social capital' (2007: 38; for subcultural capital see Thornton 1995). His social capital neither provided upward social mobility (he was unable to transform it into economic capital as Toomas did) nor promoted his social inclusion into the ethnic Estonian society. However, it did help him in his transition to adulthood in building an identity and in meaning-making (Zittoun 2007: 196). Nikolai reflects on his association with punks as *svyatoe delo* (holy business) as a means of finding friends who were opposed to the social order just like he was. This experience probably helped him accumulate what Côté has called 'identity capital', which 'operates to access and/or preserve group membership validation and personal definition' (2007: 68). In Côté's conceptualization, identity capital facilitates 'the person's movement through the life course, with or without any social class mobility' (2007: 68).

During that turbulent time, he had his close friends and social circles, but he does not emphasize them in the same way Toomas does:

INTERVIEWER: Did you have special places for meetings with like-minded youth?

NIKOLAI: One does not have to go anywhere. Why go? Friends are the same everywhere. We live in Tallinn, not Moscow. Why go somewhere special if everything can be reached in 30 minutes? We used to go to the Hill [Harjumäe hill in the center of Tallinn was a famous place for youth gatherings where, among other activities, foreign music records were sold illegally – RN&AH] at some point, yes, that was holy business.

While Toomas was enthusiastically starting his own business at the age of 16 by relying on social relations, Nikolai prefers to represent himself as part of the working class and describes his non-manual jobs as 'complementary':

NIKOLAI: There is no job I have not done. I was a loader, and … Mainly, I did the proletarian jobs. Although I have worked as a translator, too. To be honest, it was just *khaltura.*

This attitude probably stems from the working-class background of his family or the social circles he moved in. It is ironic that he defined himself at that time as a 'proletarian' rather than drawing on other, undoubtedly more intellectual activities. Due to the change of regime Nikolai's parents lost their previous jobs and had to look for new ones. In order to help his parents in a difficult situation, he held several jobs: loader, construction worker, carpenter, etc. Yet, as we will see, his other activities encompassed a considerably wider range of intellectual activities than just translating.

The topic of regaining independence is not entirely absent from Nikolai's story, but it is hardly something he regards as a determinant in his life. The Estonian mass media was full of negative stereotypes of Russians, and the collective memories of Estonian and Russian communities were divided. Public discourse depicted the Estonian youth as carriers of the 'new' order, while their Russian-speaking contemporaries were stigmatized. Thus, unlike Toomas, Nikolai regards the entire movement for independence as a type of entertainment which he did not have time for – he had to earn his living:

NIKOLAI: Well, my father is an apolitical person like me, but mum likes to talk. As a matter of fact, she is Estonian, so ... She is Estonian according to her passport and by origin, but her mother tongue is Russian. She likes ... She can be easily inspired. She actively participated in various pro-independence movements, but more for fun, but this is my personal view. As if she was interested in all that ... Dad was working at that time, and I was working too – we had no time for that, to be honest. She probably compensated for our indifferent political attitudes with her active involvement.

Nikolai actually had a positive attitude towards the social changes and independence of the country. But, naturally, since he belonged to the Russian community he was not enthusiastic about it because he did not feel included. We may speculate that not being a part of Estonian politics has accompanied Nikolai throughout his life, just like Toomas's active political participation did. We can conclude that, in this sense, ethnic identities operate in different fields in Bourdieu's terminology. For Bourdieu, fields are the domains of power, the spaces of conflict, competition, and creativity, and they exist to the extent the players believe in them (Wacquant 2005: 19). It seems that the Russian minority had its own players and its own space which they did not share with Estonians. The above excerpt demonstrates how Nikolai saw the struggle for independence as a separate field apart from his. It does not mean that ethnic identity determines one's attitudes entirely, but it certainly has an impact. The extent of this impact probably depends on the given individual.

As we mentioned earlier, this act of distancing himself from society has become a habitual representation for Nikolai who repeatedly underlined his continuous antisocial attitude, which he has kept up to date:

NIKOLAI: Look at me, look at me now [he still has long hair tied up in a ponytail – RN&AH]. To quote Zhvanetski: 'What does it mean to be 60? Terror in her eyes but the rest is just the same' As you see, everything is the same on the whole, only when I was younger [at the end of the 1980s – RN&AH] I was more aggressive. [...] You know, [...] in general I am an asocial person [...] I have not read papers in ten years; I have had no TV for over ten years now; I have never listened to the radio.

However, keeping his distance from the independence movement and picturing himself as antisocial does not mean that he has never taken up a social cause. Though he did not actively take part in the political transition, he still had an urge to improve society and to help people. He worked as a volunteer for a Help Line for three years where he demonstrated his empathic ability:

INTERVIEWER: Did you really feel a need to help people?

NIKOLAI: On the whole, yes. On the one hand, I am a tattler. On the other, I can listen to people, paying myself a compliment [i.e. Nikolai admits to himself he has a talent for listening – RN&AH]. As a matter of fact, my friends have for a long time been using me as a kind of 'helpline'. Then I thought, why not?

This work brought Nikolai a certain type of symbolic capital – acknowledgement – in the form of gratitude from the Help Line's callers:

INTERVIEWER: Did you get feedback too?

NIKOLAI: Yes, of course. Firstly, it is quite obvious that if you let the other person [speak] … this is a form of communication. I just try to talk less and to listen more. If somebody thanks you at the end of the conversation 'Thank you. It was very helpful' – how else should one understand it?

Thus, he distinguishes between public and private social spheres. His private sphere is not entirely personal affairs – society is not excluded. Being eager to express his indifference towards society, he still repeatedly revealed his concern for wider social issues. He constantly brought up his interest in human relations and human values in general. So his claims of lack of concern for the public sphere may also be just a part of his habitual antisocial self-representation and not necessarily expressed in everyday practice. While maintaining that he has kept himself away from the mass media for the past 10 years, he was still quite knowledgeable about the major events in Estonian society.

As to his education, Nikolai's experience was quite similar to that of Toomas. After graduating from high school at the age of 17, Nikolai was accepted into the Faculty of Information Technology of the Tallinn Polytechnic Institute. But he was dismissed for poor progress after the first year and, since he was no longer a student, faced conscription into the Soviet army. After his escape from the army and to avoid further drafting attempts, he re-enrolled for a second time, but in another faculty (the Faculty of Energetics). He worked and studied simultaneously for a year, because his parents had scarce resources to support him. Then he lost interest in energetics and left the university. Fortunately for him, the Soviet Union collapsed at the same time and conscription to the now extinct Soviet army ceased. The Estonian Republic established its armed forces and compulsory conscription practice in 1991, but even after passing the law about conscription, the young state was not consistent in its recruitment practices and many men born in the 1970s got away without serving in the newly established army. After leaving university, Nikolai deliberately began to compensate for his lack of formal education by reading various books and a variety of literature including fiction, philosophy, history, and natural sciences. His reasons for quitting university and becoming an autodidact may be somewhat influenced by his involvement with the punk subculture, of which the core slogans were anarchistic and not exactly welcoming towards Soviet higher education. The punk subculture probably stirred his interest in literature and music, since punk had its own literary and music styles.

We can conclude that both Toomas and Nikolai passed through the transition years, during which their lives were influenced by the transformation of society and by the symbolic order of the time. If we were to measure their performance in terms of economic capital and career advancement, it would seem that Toomas is the 'winner'. However, the reflexive recollections of both respondents show that they have led their lives in different fields. They have mobilized and accumulated social, cultural, and symbolic capitals in both fields but in different ways and both evaluate their accumulations differently, especially when it comes to social capital.

It is noteworthy that Toomas found his own way sooner than Nikolai and his transition was more linear, while Nikolai's was full of frictions and ruptures. Nikolai searched for his identity in the punk subculture, but grew out of that phase. He sought his calling by working in a multitude of temporary jobs (both manual and intellectual), and found his own way just short of the age of 30. His questing coincided with a turbulent time in society during which the entire local Russian community was looking for a stable identity. The collapse of the Soviet Union not only dissolved the illusion of shared social goals with Russia, but it also initiated a sharp economic decline and rising unemployment, not to mention causing a cultural shock in society. Nikolai commented on this as follows:

INTERVIEWER: Some people had a cultural shock when Estonian independence was proclaimed. How did it impact your personal values?

NIKOLAI: Not really. For me and my family it was a shock of a more ordinary kind because we lost our jobs. By the way, when Estonia became independent the situation became better. I mean that, in all respects, a small place is easier to clean than a big one. But I would not say that I had a shock. Simply I am an apolitical person, very apolitical. In those times, when I was 20, I was even more so. I have not noticed much [change]. One thing which I found irritating was that on my birthday – when there was the change from roubles into kroons – there was nowhere to buy sausage – everything was gone from the shops. This is what I could not understand at all. But otherwise I cannot say that I was seriously shaken in a cultural or social sense.

Yet, even though he denied any personal trauma or shock, he was part of a community that did experience one and we can speculatively assume that it had an impact on him as well. This is no doubt an assumption, but it is supported by the identifiable turning points in his biography, because since society stabilized at the end of the 1990s his life seemed to fall into the 'right track' as well.

Adulthood – a stabilizing society

Toomas still has a lot of leisure-time activities in addition to his multiple business ventures. One of his new hobbies is diving. Even though it started as a hobby, Toomas has gained such a level of proficiency in it that he is often asked to take part in various expeditions in Estonia, looking for lost ships or searching for drowned people. He still occasionally sings in choirs or ensembles (brought together temporarily for special occasions such as weddings). Recently, he has started to learn the skills of a 'barista' and attends their competitions. He is also involved in a right-wing political party.

The close intertwining of cultural, social and economic activities has continued up to the present. Even today, his use of cultural capital is connected with the social and economic spheres. His hobbies (diving, travelling) are costly, but also enable him to spend time with his friends and acquire new ones. They are often either current or potential business partners. He continues to accumulate cultural capital at the same time.

His multiple activities both provide him with opportunities for self-expression and function as symbolic resources, contributing to meaning-making in his life (Zittoun 2007: 207). Diving has gained a special meaning for Toomas, giving him mental balance and harmony:

> [About diving – RN&AH] TOOMAS: That … like … adrenaline … This is like…. Very relaxing activity…. To chill under the water and…. There's not this kind of brouhaha and noise and … zero gravity … And very lovely and beautiful … In Estonia it's not so beautiful. In Estonia, you have like adrenaline, if there's someone somewhere [drowned – RN&AH] … and to wander around somewhere there on shipwrecks and … and … and … to find there something maybe and … Or just to discover something or … we go and search ourselves a lot, you know…

His participation in diving teams and search operations has also provided Toomas with symbolic profits, since he has acquired a skill set that makes others treat him like a professional. He has participated in operations of international importance and media coverage. There are also other activities that have gained him symbolic capital (prestige). One example of such an activity is his membership of a political party, which Toomas feels helps him to take an active part in life and in the fate of his country.

Another hobby that brings him a symbolic profit is the art of coffee-making or being a 'barista' (coffee-maker). As he is very interested in this increasingly popular (but still elite-oriented) gastronomic art and wanted to test his own creativity, Toomas successfully took part in the World Barista Championships and is now proud of his place in the rankings.

We can say that Toomas has largely continued with most of the activities he started during the time of transition. Even though he has acquired new hobbies (diving and being a barista), the nature of these hobbies has not changed his life in general. Finding new hobbies and new friends has been in character for him since childhood.

The story of Nikolai, however, is different. During the years of political and social transformation, he was still looking for his place in life. He performed manual labour, mingled with his friends from the punk subculture, occasionally did voluntary work, and was a translator while reading a lot and educating himself. Yet the two main fields that he now considers to be the core of his identity entered his life much later when society was stabilizing and he was beginning to reach his thirties.

He joined the rock-climbing club when it was established in 1993. However, he stayed involved with it only for a short time and rejoined the club only at the end of the 1990s. Then he began to take his hobby with increasing seriousness until it became his main job. Now he is an accomplished rock climber and claims the activity to be his lifestyle. Like diving for Toomas, rock climbing also serves him as symbolic capital due to his prestige among those interested in this sport. He is among the best in the rock-climbing club and continues to achieve high placements in international and local competitions. Yet it also serves him as identity capital for him:

> NIKOLAI: I can tell that since I started to do rock-climbing I have changed a lot. This is because rock-climbing is a kind of sport that appeals to some inner deeper feelings. [. . .] This is a certain psychological state and in, some sense, a meditation.

Since Nikolai became a member of the rock-climbing club in the initial years after its foundation and therefore belongs to its group of 'veterans', he enjoys some authority over the beginners. Alongside the prestige rock climbing gives Nikolai is the freedom of choice and an opportunity to be engaged in a sphere valuable to him.

For his self-education, Nikolai has continued to read books on philosophy, psychology, and sociology, but also fiction and poetry. This intellectual quest for identity has led him to creative work, as around 1999–2000 he became interested in writing poetry of his own. His first attempts gained positive feedback and he has continued to write and has joined a literary community of Russian writers in Estonia. He is now a member of the editorial board of an online publication of that community. As a board member, he works with and accepts or rejects the literary texts in Russian of young poets and writers from all over the world.

His creative work gives Nikolai a symbolic capital through his audience which he evaluates highly:

> NIKOLAI: A writer can only make a statement through his art rather than by self-advertising. One has accomplished oneself as a writer as long as one has readers. This can be regarded as the only statement a writer can make. If one has no readers, this – sorry – means that one is a functionary of the Writers' Union rather than a writer. In my opinion, only readers can provide criteria by which literature is to be judged.

Relying on Russian culture and the Russian language, Nikolai uses his ethnic identity capital, which enables him to identify himself as a writer living in Estonia and writing in Russian. That capital can provide Nikolai with access to the young Russian-speaking intellectual elites of Estonia as well as of the world.

Conclusion

Transition to adulthood during uncertain times of social transformation is a task many young people in the post-socialist Baltic states had to face at the beginning of the 1990s. It is always appealing to look at the interrelations between individuals and society and the impact of social change on biographies. Numerous theories have been modelled to depict the complicated relationship between society and the individual and the scenarios about what happens when society changes. Yet, to point out the aspects of life of particular individuals and claims that one social development or the other has changed the person's habitus, or transformed their biography a certain way that would not have happened without the change, is a shaky argument. This chapter has contributed to the debate in sociology concerning individual agency versus social structures. It has attempted to reveal some of the aspects of the relationship between society and the individual. Toomas and Nikolai have showed us that the habitual dispositions and capitals acquired in childhood play a major role in guiding the life path through social change, although the acquired capitals are not always exchangeable and measurable. For an individual, moving forward and leading a meaningful life can be more important than moving upwards on the social ladder. This leads us to also question the division of the winners and the losers in social change. Searching for oneself at a time that your community experiences an identity crisis may or may not have negative impacts. However, the assumption that winners are those actively indulged in social affairs with a linear transition path to adulthood was not proven in our analysis. Having listened to our respondents' life stories we would be reluctant to label either of them a winner or a loser. They both lead meaningful lives, with their own ideals and their own habitus, and have both struggled through several phases of winning and losing.

Notes

1 Toomas and Nikolai are pseudonyms to protect the privacy of the respondents.
2 All translations are the responsibilities of the authors.

References

Adelman, D. (1994) *The Children of 'Perestroika' Come of Age: Young People of Moscow Talk About Life in New Russia*, London: Amonk.

Allard, A.C. (2005) 'Capitalizing on Bourdieu. How useful are concepts of "social capital" and "social field" for researching "marginalized" young women?', *Theory and Research in Education*, 3(1): 63–79.

Bourdieu, P. (1986) 'The forms of capital', in John G: Richardson (ed.) *Handbook of Theory and Research for the Sociology of Education*, New York: Greenwood Press.

Bourdieu, P. (1991) *Language and Symbolic Power*. Edited and introduced by J.B. Thomson, Cambridge, MA: Harvard University Press.

Bourdieu, P. and Wacquant, L.D. (2005) *An Inivtation to Reflexive Sociology*, Cambridge: Polity Press.

Clark, E. (2000) 'The role of social capital in developing Czech private business', *Work, Employment & Society*, 14(3): 439–458.

Coleman, J. (1988) 'Social capital in the creation of human capital', *The American Journal of Sociology*, 94: 95–120.

Côté, J.E. (2002) 'The role of identity capital in the transition to adulthood: the individualization thesis examined', *Journal of Youth Studies*, 5(2): 117–134.

Côté, J.E. (2007) 'Youth and the provision of resources', in H. Helve and J. Bynner (eds) *Youth and Social Capital*, London, Tufnell Press, pp. 59–70.

English, R. (2000) *Russia and the Idea of West: Gorbachev, Intellectuals and the End of the Cold War*, New York: Columbia University Press.

Erikson, Erik H. (1968) *Identity: Youth and Crisis*, New York: Norton.

Eyal, G., Szelenyi, I. and Townsley, E. (1998) *Capitalism without Capitalists: The New Ruling Elites in Eastern Europe*, London: Verso.

Gazsó, Ferenc (1992) 'Youth and the change of regime youth', in F. Gazsó and I. Strumpf (eds) *Youth and the Change of Regime*, Budapest: Institute for Political Sciences of the Hungarian Academy of Sciences, pp. 15–25.

Helemäe, J., Saar, E. and Vöörmann, R. (2000) *Kas haridusse tasus investeerida? Hariduse stratifitseerivast rollist kahe põlvkonna kogemuste taustal* (*Was it Worth to Invest In Education? The Stratifying Role of Education Based on the Experience of Two Generations*), Tallinn: Teaduste Akadeemia Kirjastus.

Horvat, E., Weininger, E. and Lareau, A. (2003) 'From social ties to social capital: class differences in the relations between schools and parent networks', *American Educational Research Journal*, 40(2): 319–351.

Inglehart, R. (1997) *Modernization and Postmodernization: Cultural, Economic and Political Change in 43 Societies*, Princetown: Princetown University Press.

Keller, M. and Vihalemm, T. (2003) 'Return to the "consuming West": young people's perceptions about the consumerization of Estonia', *Young*, 11(3): 195–215.

Lauristin, M. (2004) 'Hinnangud Eesti ühiskonnas toimunud muutustele' ('Evaluations on the change in Estonian society') in V. Kalmus, M. Lauristin and P. Pruulmann-Vengerfeldt (eds) *Eesti elavik 21. sajandi algul* (*Estonian Lifeworld at the beginning of 21st Century*), Tartu: Tartu Ülikooli Kirjastus.

Lauristin, M. and Vihalemm, P. (2009) 'The political agenda during different periods of Estonian transformation: external and internal factors', *Journal of Baltic Studies*, 40(1): 1–28.

Mannheim, K. (1993) 'The problem of generations', in M.A. Hardy (ed.) *Studying Ageing and Social Change: Conceptual and Methodological Issues*, London: Sage, pp. 24–60.

Nugin, R. (2003) 'Meedias kajastuv eestlaste kollektiivne mina-pilt 1991. ja 2001. aastal' ('Collective self-identity as reflected in media in 1991 and 2001'), *Acta Historica Tallinnensia*, 7: 162–173.

Nugin, R. (2008). 'Constructing adulthood in a world of uncertainties: some cases of post-Communist Estonia, *Young*, 16(2): 185–207.

Putnam, R.D. (2000) *Bowling Alone: The Collapse and Revival of American Community*, New York: Simon & Schuster.

Roberts, K. (2003) 'Change and continuity in youth transitions in Eastern Europe: lessons for Western sociology,' *Sociological Review*, 51(4): 484–505.

Rosenthal, G. (1997) 'National identity or multicultural autobiography: theoretical concepts of biographical constitution grounded in case reconstructions', in A. Lieblich and R. Josselson (eds) *The Narrative Study of Lives*, Thousand Oaks: Sage.

Schuller, T., Baron, S. and Field, J. (2000) 'Social Capital: A Review and Critique', in S. Baron, J. Field and T. Schuller (eds) *Social Capital: Critical Perspectives*, Oxford: Oxford University Press.

Steen, A. and Ruus, J. (2002) 'Change of regime – continuity of elites? The case of Estonia', *East European Politics and Societies*, 16(1): 223–248.

Tallo, A. and Terk, T. (1998) 'Erinevad generatsioonid üleminekuperioodi Eestis' ('Different generations in transitional Estonia'), in E. Terk, (ed.) *Eesti Inimarengu Aruanne* (*Estonian Human Development Report*). Tallinn: UNDP.

Thornton, S. (1995). *Club culture: Music, Media and Subcultural Capital*, Cambridge: Polity Press and Blackwell Publishers.

Threadgold, S. and Nilan, P. (2009) 'Reflexivity of contemporary youth, risk and cultural capital,' *Current Sociology*, 57(1): 47–68.

Titma, M. (ed.) (1999) *Kolmekümneaastaste põlvkonna sotsiaalne portree* (*The Social Portrait of the Thirty Year Olds*), Tallinn: Teaduste Akadeemia Kirjastus.

Tolonen, T. (2007) 'Social and cultural capital meets youth research: a critical approach', in H. Helve and J. Bynner (eds) *Youth and Social Capital*, London: Tufnell Press.

Toomse, M. (2004) 'Koolist tööle: millistelt positsioonidelt alustavad noored oma tööteed' ('From school to work: which positions do young people start their work paths from'), in R. Vöörmann (ed.) *Noorte siirdumine tööturule: probleemid, vastuolud, kitsaskohad* (*Transitions to Labor Market: Problems, Contradictions, Bottlenecks*), TPÜ RASI sotsiaalse stratifikatsiooni osakonna toimetised, vol 1. Tallinn: TPÜ RASI.

Vogt, H. (2005) *Between Utopia and Disillusionment*, Oxford: Berghahn Books.

Wacquant, L. (2005) 'Toward a social praxeology: the structure and logic of Bourdieu's sociology', in P. Bourdieu, and L. Wacquant (eds) *An Invitation to Reflexive Sociology*, Cambridge: Polity Press.

Walther, A., Stauber, B. and Pohl, A. (2005) 'Informal networks in youth transitions in West Germany: biographical resource or reproduction of social inequality?' *Journal of Youth Studies*, 8(2): 221–240.

Williams, C., Chuprov, V. and Zubok, J. (2003) *Youth, Risk and Russian Modernity*, Cornwall: MPG Books.

Zittoun, T. (2007) 'Symbolic resources and responsibility in transitions', *Young*, 15(2): 193–211.

11 Background for biographical research

Value change in Estonia, Latvia, Lithuania, and Sweden in 1991–2007

Indrek Tart

Introduction

Biographical research involves stories of life courses and interpretations thereof, usually told during and specific to a certain period of time. Many aspects may even be influenced by the particulars of a biographical interview. While interviews may not reveal 'how things really were' or 'what the truth was', the narrative is a biographical version of events told in a more recent context. The more remote the contexts are, the more their explanation depends on changes in and around the story-teller. Considerable societal, political and cultural adjustments to the change can manifest on both personal and cultural levels and thus provide a background to the lived life stories. Life stories referring to particular events may lose their significance over time as a consequence of later cataclysmic events. Changes may involve altered societal environments, but are also connected to variations in identities, basic values relationships, and habits (Eisenstadt 1998; Inglehart 1997). The corresponding processes may take place gradually over a lengthy period or can happen very quickly (e.g. military conquest).

The Baltic nations have experienced sudden changes on several occasions during the twentieth century. Most proved to be traumatic by nature and are now being revived in cultural memory through biographies and interpretations endeavouring to make sense of what happened and what is worth remembering. This does not apply only to the micro-level of individual experiences or destinies, but also concerns the macro-level of 'life-(hi)stories' of nations. Similar reflections on cultural developments at the macro-level are available through examining the changes over time in the highly aggregate concept of basic human values (BHV). Biographical research faces memory problems from disperse points of view: the reliability of an individual's memory; the degree to which their memory has been manipulated by the culture (including mass communication media); which types of memory are responsible for vivid, intimate, and cinematic stories and alternatively the types responsible for abstract, concept-based knowledge of societal processes. The everyday experiences and life stories reflected upon in this book do not take place in a cultural and social vacuum. They play out against the background of identifiable macro-cultural transformations, even if individual lives are unique and should also be analysed as such. The grand change of the 1990s influenced lives and their backgrounds in a highly significant way (Sztompka 1996; Szakolczai and Füstös 1998). Life stories themselves transform even more than simply the manners and modes of telling about living through past. Narrators not only found out and evaluated hitherto hidden corners of their memories, but also did so inside altered settings of their lifestyles and value orientations. In this chapter, the focus is on the combined cultural patterns of value stability and value change as a consequence of the societal transitions in the Baltic states during the 1990s. Finding adequate objective indicators for grand change is invariably problematic; nevertheless basic human values could provide a tool for estimating the overall trends and depth of societal change. The idea is to determine, in a comparison of several societies, which basic human values remain central to society and those which seem to become peripheral because the value change overall is slow and hidden. In our comparison of the three Baltic states, we involve Sweden, because any explanation of the changes in Estonia, Latvia, and Lithuania requires a referent society that has achieved enduring socio-economic stability.

The basic human values concept

Basic human values (BHV) have been chosen as the core, representative and extensively explored subset of many other equally emergent human value relationships (political, religious, etc.). The subset, gathered through opinion surveys, expresses the trends in the dynamics of certain highly abstracted and deeply internal levels of motivational beliefs inherent in most cultures, which have been useful in making quite complex theoretical analyses of human encounters with nature, within society, and between individuals. In our case, we will use the Baltic Value Battery (BVB), also known as the extended Rokeach value survey (Lauristin *et al.* 1997: 339–340). The data comes from 1991 to 2007 and allows us to bring out the basic value dynamics of the cultural communities of Estonia, Latvia, Lithuania, and Sweden. We chose Sweden not only for the characteristics of being a stable mature welfare democracy but also because significant communities of Baltic refugees emerged in Sweden after the Second World War. Thus, the BHVs inherent to Sweden's culture provide a comparative contrast to illuminate the BHVs of the Baltic states.

Sociologists expected general values to change quite fast in post-Socialist societies after communism began to collapse in 1989. Changes in BHVs have, however, been profound and much slower (Schwartz and Bardi 1997), whereas Swedish BHVs have been more or less constant. Furthermore, long-term data have higher correlations within each of the chosen Baltic communities than between any of the different countries. The overall Swedish results from data of different years form a tight cluster, while each of the Baltic countries has a linearly divergent chain of aggregate value rankings' correlations' starting from 1991. Essentially, the BHVs of Estonians, Russians in Estonia as well as Latvians and Russians in Latvia have followed a long trail of successive changes, each related to their beliefs in the previous data year and rarely returning to beliefs of earlier years. Lithuania lacks data for the 2000s, and is therefore not included in the comparison.

Figure 11.1 depicts the dynamics of the changes in BHVs in terms of overall correlations for the communities under investigation. Every data point's relative position represents correlations between value items rankings for each cultural community and each year. So the closer the positions are, the higher the degree of similarity there is in their total rankings. It is evident that the Swedish (SE) yearly aggregates for 1991, 1994, 2002, and 2004 are close together and quite distinct from those of Estonians (EE) for 1991, 1994, 2002, and 2007, Russian-speaking people in Estonia (RE) for 1991, 1994, 2002, and 2007, Latvians (LV) for 1993, 1994, and 2006 and Russian-speaking people in Latvia (RLV) 1993, 1994, and 2006. We have used a multidimensional scaling technique that construct measurements of similarity/dissimilarity between pairs of data as the distances of representative points in a low-dimensional multidimensional space (Borg and Groenen 2005); in our case in a two-dimensional model for visualization of the results. Dimensions themselves have no specific meaning but allow the embedding of data points in an impressive way into the chosen space. From that image we can sometimes conclude their connotations but not vice versa.

Although the trajectories of change for BHVs in Estonia and Latvia are quite different, the trajectories for the native populations follow parallel tracks, as do the trajectories for the Russophone communities. None of these four trajectories

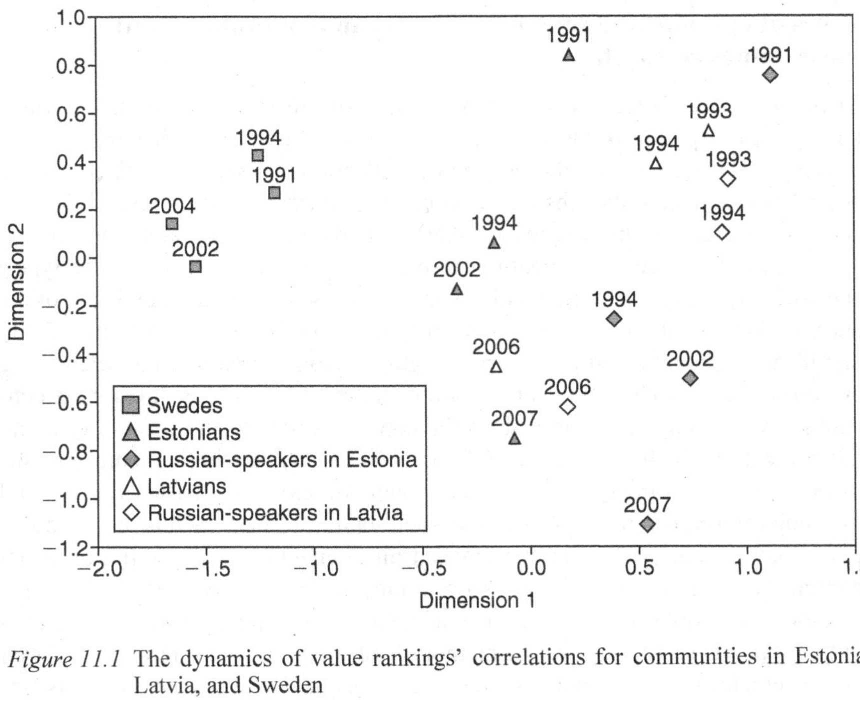

Figure 11.1 The dynamics of value rankings' correlations for communities in Estonia, Latvia, and Sweden

forms the same kind of tight correlation cluster as seen for the Swedish data, but rather advance linearly into separate positions over a relatively long measurement from 1991 to 2007. The two Estonian communities (EE and RE) are remarkably and consistently far apart between 1991 and 2007 demonstrating a steady and continuing difference in their basic value systems, or in other words a high degree of incommensurability between the cultures (Aarelaid-Tart and Belobrovtseva 2004). Notably the two Latvian groups are by contrast close and parallel to each other throughout the period 1993 to 2006. In all the cases, Estonia is closer to Sweden than any of the other three, which may reflect a European or Nordic characteristic which Russian Estonians lack or do not consider important. The relative closeness of Russians in Latvia in 2006 and the Russians in Estonia of 1994 and 2002 may mark temporality or just be an accidental coincidence. Overall, the important feature is how similar the value change trajectories are, which biographical interviews should perhaps reflect.

Some very interesting and valuable aspects from the point of view of biographical research are the trends in generational value change over the last 15 years. The younger age group (15–29) has a uniquely different perspective, largely free of pre-1991 socialist memories, whereas the middle age group (30–49) and the old age group (50–74) disclose and evaluate changes in the transition from the socialism period. Unfortunately, our data does not include the value changes in the republican generation (as described in Chapter 1), because the corresponding age ranges were omitted from the surveys of the 2000s.

Roles of episodic and semantic memory in biographical and basic values research

There have been attempts to determine how the results of quantitative value surveys correspond to those of qualitative interviewing (Vihalemm 1997). Tulving (1972) compared the personal recollections present in narratives (episodic memory) and the abstract notions (i.e. intrinsic social knowledge) of semantic memory, which is responsible for perceiving and maintaining meanings in a cultural context, creating abstractions concerning shared prototypes, schemes and experiences. Semantic memory represents human knowledge of the surrounding world while episodic memory provides recollections of personally significant events. Episodic memory is highly personal, relating to or referencing episodes that are connected to an individual's identity. 'Episodic memory is conceptualized as a system that enables the conscious recollection of an event and the context in which it occurred' (Gilboa 2004: 1336). Semantic memory seems to be personally timeless and connects with the external construction of and meanings attributed to linguistic and socio-cultural signs. While believing in one's internal memories is a most private truth, semantic memory relies on social consensus. Internal memory draws on immediate experience and the semantic memory uses symbolic language-mediated concept-based knowledge. In the case of biographical research, episodic memory is primary, while basic value research places emphasis on semantic memory by design, because survey items are abstract nouns or adjectives with a few added characterizations. 'According to its most recent definition, episodic memory refers to personal events recollected in the context of a particular time and place – the "what", "where" and "when" – and with some reference to oneself as a participant in the episode' (Piolino *et al.* 2009: 2314). Although this memory system seems to contrast with semantic memory, its operations rely on and even go beyond the latter.

As both types of memory interact within a person, this dichotomy makes it interesting to find out whether any elements of BHV relate to story-telling. Some efforts to compare qualitative interviews with corresponding value items have come to the assertion that: 'quantitative results of the Balticom value survey have mainly reflected the mediated and "processed" experience. We may thus assume that by applying Rokeach system we are measuring first and foremost the transformation of culture' (Vihalemm 1997: 278). Thus it is primarily the reflections of cultural change in BHV that are important to note and compare to the findings from biographical research.

Main results of previous Baltic BHV studies

Several research projects have been conducted using the extended Rokeach value survey and investigating their change and stability. These studies have mostly taken place in Sweden where there is an element of profound concern about the economic and political climate in the Baltic countries, particularly in Estonia. Free market and democratization processes flooded the re-independent Baltic countries after the fall of the Soviet Union.

> Democratization has brought not only political and economic reforms, it has also opened the borders to numerous cultural influences, bringing many new problems into focus. Paradoxically, many people living in the same country have experienced nothing more than culture shock as the result of global influences.
>
> (Björklund and Liubiniene 2004: 35)

Alongside specifically cultural changes, the results have focused on the individual collective axis. 'Many people have felt lost and isolated, unsure of how to act and sometimes frightened – a consequence of being outside the symbolic web of the previous Soviet culture that had joined individuals in social life' (Björklund and Liubiniene 2004: 36). On several occasions, change to the Western-like basic values ranking system has been marked as a rise of fierce individualism:

> Baby Boomers value individuality and youth and are self-absorbed. Baby Boomers were born between 1943 and 1964 ... the findings of our study showed that, although Lithuania was under a totalitarian regime for 50 years, both the terminal and the instrumental values of the Baby Boomers generation are very similar to those of the same generation in other countries. During 16 years of the Independence, there has been an on obvious

> transition in the scale of values from the socialist principle of equality and collectivism towards the principle of individualism.
>
> (Blazeviciene and Jakusovaite 2007: 4–5)

This survey was conducted for Lithuanian nurses in 2006, but covered only half of the items of the extended Rokeach survey. While this is a very specific sort of evidence of Lithuanian BHV change, it has been presented as generalizing.

Some more sophisticated research has found that:

> [T]he beginning of the 1990s in Estonia was characterized by a period of high social turbulence, when people's social positions and life trajectories could and did change rapidly. /–/ The duty of finding solutions and coping with the risks and contradictions produced by societal transformation was therefore individualized.
>
> (Kalmus and Vihalemm 2006: 99)

There is also emphasis on the need to rewire basic value relationships in order to maintain one's psychological balance and act according to the changed social environment. 'A new social hierarchy – "winners and losers" of transition – has emerged in post-Soviet Estonia: self-positioning within this imagined hierarchy correlates closely to attitudes regarding the changes in Estonia' (Kalmus and Vihalemm 2006: 99). The same kind of strategy of pursuing optimal solutions for a quite long period (perhaps more than 10 years) is present for BHV, where the younger, or people quicker to react, gain an advantage over the more conservative and traditional people. The world now consists of two nation-specific dimensions: internationally and internally. 'The global orientation in transitional society is a "thing in itself," without supportive cultural context … this "global pattern" also derives from the inertia of the utopian way of thinking characteristic of the Soviet culture' (Kalmus and Vihalemm 2006: 116). Within a value space this is represented by disparities between those values that are under a person's control and those that are not. There are some highly appreciated abstract and universal values (e.g. the 'world in peace'), while personal 'freedom', so important on Western value scales, is relegated to the background in all the Baltic countries' ethno-linguistic communities. 'In general, the transitional culture in Estonia can be characterized by three specific mental patterns we call "cultural templates": nostalgic resignation, a striving for success, and an escapist Western orientation' (Kalmus and Vihalemm 2006: 117). Basic values represent the most durable part of the cultural templates, and act as a tool for discovering and describing the hidden forces of culture through a construct that is simultaneously personal and collective. The personal decisions are deeply influenced by the internalized and instinct-like preferences for basic values.

Data management and age groups

In order to retain the possibility of comparative analysis in a diachronic perspective, we use the 25 value indicators, the system of measurement devised by

Rokeach (1973), employed in the Balticom value surveys of 1991–95 (Lauristin *et al.* 1997). Values were measured on a five-point scale (from 'not important at all' to 'very important'). Following Rokeach, single value concepts (words and expressions denoting values) are considered to be relatively independent items, not put into definite hierarchies, but which can relate to each other in various dimensions or clusters.

The analysis is based on collaborative and comparative surveys carried out in the four countries, covering people in the 15–74 age range. The studies in the 2000's used a self-administered questionnaire and a follow-up interview, with respondents drawn according to a proportional model of the general population (by areas and urban/rural division) using multi-step random probability sampling. Such rated extended Rokeach surveys of 25 items were carried out several times in a period 1991–2007, of which we use four surveys in 1991, 1994, 2002, and 2007 for Swedes (SE), Estonians (EE) and Russian-speakers in Estonia (RE); three surveys in 1993, 1994, and 2006 for Latvians (LV) and Russian-speakers in Latvia (RLV); and two surveys in 1993 and 1994 for Lithuanians (LT) and Russian-speakers in Lithuania (RLT). The RLT results are not statistically significant due to the small size of the age groups and should be treated with caution.

In order to manage the data in small, statistically easier to manipulate, selections and to preserve the data's original meaning by not performing any transformations before applying statistical analysis methods, we use three separate age meta-groups:

- young (15–29 years old): born 1962–1976 for the 1991 survey and 1977–1991 for the 2006 survey;
- middle (30–49 years old): born 1942–1961 for the 1991 and 1957–1976 for the 2006 survey;
- old (50–74 years old): born 1917–1941 for the 1991 and 1932–1956 for the 2006 survey.

This division is more aggregated and differs from the five generations presented in Chapter 1 of this book: (1) the Republican generation of those born in the 1920s; (2) the generation of children and teenagers from the 1944–1956 period of warfare and deportations who were born mostly in the 1930s; (3) the first true post-war generation that grew up under the conditions shaped by Soviet mentality who were born mostly in the 1940s and the 1950s; (4) the teenagers of the 1980s who were born around 1970), and whose formative years coincided with the destabilization and then the collapse of socialism; and (5) the children of the re-independent Baltic states who were born from 1991 onwards. The first two coincide with our old age meta-group, the third belongs mostly to the middle, the fourth overlaps both young and middle, and the fifth is not present at all. We have the option of following synchronic and diachronic change by comparing the same age groups at different points of time (young to young, middle to middle and old to old) or by following changes going from one meta-group to another over the time (young to middle, middle to old). In the first case we have a change of generations, in the second the change inside a generation, i.e. what happens to basic values when people grow older and move into another age group; do they change or stay the same during their whole lives? With the data available to us, we can follow value change best for the third and fourth generations, the forced builders of Socialism and their blasé children who are sincerely disinterested in their surroundings, introverted and withdrawn from a mundane world. Nevertheless, both cohorts were tightly involved in the Baltic singing revolutions of 1991.

General description

The Table 11.1 lists all the 25 basic value items presented as rank data averages (all rankings for each item in every separate year summed and divided by the total number of communities involved over all the years) separately for Sweden and the Baltic countries, and more specifically for all the age meta-groups in both. The purpose of this process is to find values that clearly distinguish the Baltic countries from Sweden, transition countries from welfare states, and to see how similar such aggregations are in this division.

In addition to presenting the means, value items are arranged in groups corresponding to the six clusters found out by K-means cluster analysis of Baltic countries' overall configurations that provide a more reliable background for analysis. As we will see, those overly aggregate means of basic values actually do hide more than expose any differences.

There is a significant dissimilarity between the Swedish and Baltic BHV clusters. For example, the Swedes appreciate 'freedom' and 'honesty' much more than the Baltic nations, placing those in their first cluster instead of the second or third, 'wealth' is comparatively deeply underrated in Sweden and 'inner harmony' together with 'mature love' switch places with 'national security' and 'happiness' in the second and third clusters of different societies. This reflects the principal differences in BHVs. Those values that are relatively higher placed in Sweden represent personal rather than collective or abstractly normative aspects of societal being. They not only symbolize an individualistic way of life, but certainly also emphasize the profound significance of personal decisions and experiences which make up a person's biography that stems from the depths of episodic memory. Such attitudes are among the foundations of a welfare society, where solidarity functions on behalf of peoples' responsibilities. It also marks the differences between older and newly re-established capitalist world views. Central and eastern European societies expect first and foremost governmental protection and security, downplaying individual initiative. The long-term changes in the Baltic countries' BHV have continued the trends that appeared in 1991.

There is a notable age-group discrepancy, with some items shifting upwards by three ranks. Most of those cardinal differentiations are shared by Swedes and Baltic nations, indicating a purely age-based effect, e.g. older age groups prefer 'world at peace', 'national security', and a 'clean environment', while younger ones favour 'happiness', 'mature love', and an 'exciting life'.

Our particular question is: which of those basic value items are more relevant to the episodic memory that is used for biographical endeavours? Admittedly, it is more event-centred than the purely educational knowledge-based semantic memory, but we should still be able to identify some basic value items that relate better to exploring one's personal past. Some values evoke vivid pictures from the past that are associated with its meaning, while others remain only abstract notions that merely relate to other abstract concepts. In many cases the latter functions slightly like legal norms or rational options. But the former, more connected with one's private world, possesses the flavour of personal involvement. This may be where basic value configurations and their change over time could help to interpret biographical interviews – do changing times and values influence the interviewee? Do they have a burden of already changed value worlds on their shoulders while talking of the past events? While it is not always easy to tell them apart, some notions have more political than personal emphasis, e.g. 'freedom' and 'equality' versus 'health' and 'salvation'. We will attempt to extract the degree of episodic memory in our value items by following their changes over time. Due to the blurriness of available criteria there will not be an exact balance between those that are more individual and those that are purely concept-based knowledge.

The first, fourth, fifth, and sixth clusters are quite uniform with similar-ranking BHV means in each of them. On the other hand, the first three may be semantically classified as universal indicators of environmental and security conditions and markers for personal cognitive welfare. The other three are mostly concerned with technological matters of self-realization and hedonistic ways of life, manifesting in lifestyle choices such as 'pleasant-comfortable-exciting lives' or quite institutionalized (or at least pictured as such) 'salvation' and 'power'. For Sweden, the exceptions are 'wisdom' and 'self-respect' which fall into the lower clusters and 'world of beauty' with 'equality' that go up into the upper half. Those first three clusters could be said to be more functional, and the others more static background values. This certainly raises many points for discussion and it is not easy to see which ones emphasize episodic memory. As has been expected, the young meta-group considers 'exciting life' more important as items in extended Rokeach value surveys are formed on the basis of the terminal not instrumental sets of values.

If we look at those values that all the countries in question share, we can see both abstract, knowledge-based, and episodic, individual memory. Three items form the ultimate top ('health', 'family security', and 'world at peace') and two make up the definitive bottom ('power' and 'salvation'). Those seem to form the border between outside influences and someone's private world. Such values of deep impact are always present and need no special awareness; they are already predetermined to be at the top or bottom. The most consistence can be seen in the universally low ranks of 'power' (the possibility of directing and controlling others), 'social recognition' (respect, approval), and 'salvation' (purification of

Table 11.1 Value item means' ranks and clusters, in total and by age groups in Sweden and the Baltic countries in 1991–2007

	Swedish means	*Age groups in Sweden*			*Baltic means*	*Age groups in Baltic countries*		
		15–29	*30–49*	*50–74*		*15–29*	*3–49*	*50–74*
Cluster I								
Health	1.5	4.4	2.0	2.0	1.0	2.2	1.4	1.3
Family security	5.3	7.0	5.6	5.5	3.1	2.8	2.5	4.3
World at peace	2.8	6.5	3.8	1.5	2.8	5.4	3.3	2.2
Cluster II								
Clean environment	9.8	11.5	10.8	8.5	4.3	7.7	4.9	4.2
National security	12.0	13.8	12.5	6.5	6.3	10.4	7.4	4.8
Honesty	3.0	5.3	3.5	2.8	7.1	11.7	8.4	5.3
Justice	6.5	9.3	8.0	5.8	8.0	9.2	8.5	7.5
True friendship	8.3	7.3	9.0	9.5	9.1	5.5	10.1	9.6
Happiness	11.3	4.1	9.0	12.3	7.3	5.8	7.1	10.2
Cluster III								
Freedom	3.0	2.0	2.4	4.3	10.2	8.8	10.0	10.9
Wisdom	16.5	18.5	16.8	17.8	12.4	12.9	12.7	11.7
Self-respect	16.5	20.3	16.3	16.1	12.6	12.1	11.5	12.3
Inner harmony	8.8	9.5	7.5	9.0	12.8	13.6	10.9	12.8
Mature love	6.5	1.8	5.3	10.8	12.4	7.0	9.8	15.9

Cluster IV								
Technical development	18.3	20.8	19.5	16.6	18.2	18.2	17.7	18.1
Self-realization	18.8	17.0	18.0	19.3	17.8	14.0	16.7	19.0
World of beauty	14.3	14.3	14.5	14.3	14.5	15.8	14.7	11.9
Wealth	23.0	23.0	23.0	23.0	16.6	17.9	17.2	16.4
Equality	14.5	14.0	14.5	13.3	18.1	19.6	18.7	15.5
Cluster V								
Pleasant life	16.8	14.5	16.5	18.5	20.7	18.8	21.5	21.4
Comfortable life	16.5	12.8	15.8	17.5	20.1	19.7	20.2	20.5
Exciting life	20.5	16.8	20.0	21.8	20.3	15.9	19.2	21.5
Social recognition	22.0	22.0	22.0	19.8	22.2	22.4	22.9	22.4
Cluster VI								
Salvation	25.0	25.0	25.0	25.0	22.2	22.8	22.6	20.2
Power	24.0	24.0	24.0	24.0	25.0	24.9	25.0	25.0

the soul). The respondents seem to have little appreciation for both religion and external pressure, as remote as they may seem at first glance. The same could be said of 'family security', 'health', and 'world at peace', which are less preferred by the younger generations but still demonstrate high average ranks across all age groups. Since those mostly involve some kind of (social) security, they are not that important for personal networking that makes up the basis of much of biographical research. They are more environmental, similar to cultural and linguistic traditions and life-long skills that are slow to change and intuitively appear at various moments. Whether they are considered positive or negative depends on the situation at hand, as is the case with any instinctive but relatively low-impact basic values and basic needs (Maslow 1954).

The rankings of the other 20 vary more, especially the lifestyle items such as 'pleasant life' (pleasing, offers enjoyment), 'comfortable life' (without problems, prosperous) and 'exciting life' (stimulating, active). They even switch relative positions in some surveys ('pleasant' versus 'comfortable' in Sweden in the 1990s and the 2000s; also for the Russians in Estonia in 1991 and 2002). As expected, the young meta-group considers 'exciting life' more important. While it has been suggested that there may be hedonistic and other post-modern trends hidden within it, the available data does not confirm the existence of any such strong influence. They do not achieve outstanding rankings of any sort and a closer look reveals that they also change rather inconsistently. The 'world of beauty' (the beauty of nature and the arts) and 'technical development' (more efficient equipment) seem to be in neutral positions, regardless of whether their usefulness is doubted or merely taken for granted.

In the context of post-socialist change, the second and third clusters regain their rank-up importance with items like 'honesty', 'justice', 'true friendship', 'happiness', and 'freedom', 'wisdom', 'self-respect', 'inner harmony', and 'mature love'. Of these, 'freedom' and 'honesty', in particular, are near the top for the Swedes. We take a brief look at how they change their positions of influence for episodic memory in the following sections.

Basic values change in Sweden, Estonia and Latvia

In addition to the total rankings, we can also follow the changes over time in specific value items that the aggregated data does not reveal. The table in Table 11.2 presents the overall variations in rankings from the first year of survey to the last in all available surveys of the period. The more evaluated important items are mostly in the upper and the less important ones in the lower part of the table. If the more recent data prevail by more than three ranks then it is presented by a plus (+) sign, in the case of minus (–) sign the previous periods prevail.

If we look at the values for Sweden, we see that in only one case have the items gone up or down more than three ranks; namely, 'pleasant life' and 'comfortable life' have switched places. The majority have either not changed ranks or moved only one rank away from their original position. The first and last clusters, which could be regarded as some kind of security characteristics, are nearly

Table 11.2 Value items going up (+) or down (–) at least three ranks for all the respondents from the 1990s to the 2000s

	SE 2004–1991	*EE 2007–1991*	*RE 2007–1991*	*LV 2006–1993*	*RLV 2006–1993*
Cluster I					
Health					
Family security					
World at peace		–	–		–
Cluster II					
Clean environment			–	–	
National security		–	–		–
Honesty		+	+	+	+
Justice			–		
True friendship		+	+		
Happiness		+	+	–	+
Cluster III					
Freedom		–	–	–	–
Wisdom			+		+
Self-respect		+	+	+	+
Inner harmony					
Mature love				–	
Cluster IV					
Technical development		–	–	–	–
Self-realization			–		
World of beauty				–	–
Wealth		+			–
Equality					–
Cluster V					
Pleasant life	–		+	+	+
Comfortable life	+		+	+	+
Exciting life		+			
Social recognition					
Cluster VI					
Salvation		–			–
Power					

static and most of the upward adjustments have taken place in the second (societal relationships), third (personal freedom), and fifth (hedonistic impulses) clusters, with downward changes happening in the fourth (self-realization).

In almost all the cases, the Estonian and Latvian communities have moved in the same direction. The most prominent features are:

1 lost ranks: 'world at peace', 'national security', 'freedom', 'technical development', and for Latvian communities 'world of beauty';
2 gained ranks: 'honesty', 'self-respect', 'pleasant life', and 'comfortable life'; 'happiness' (except for the Latvians), 'true friendship' in both Estonian communities, 'wisdom' in both Russian groups.

In the case of 'technical development' the drop takes place early on between the first and second surveys and does not change much later. 'Freedom' on the other hand falls among the average in the mid-2000s (see Table 11.3).

Most of the items that moved up in rank seem to be more likely connected with situational memory and thus may provide valuable background information for biographical interviewing. We can also conclude that the values at the level of cultural communities have been overall just as stable as the theory predicts and the changes were selective rather than encompassing. But it is not yet clear whether this has any impact on the generational or age meta-group levels, since aggregation may obscure the relevant discrepancies. In the following, we try to look into this and compare the middle age meta-group of the 2000s with the young age meta-group of 1991 (members of which were 15 years older by 2006 and therefore comprise three-quarters of the corresponding middle age meta-group).

BHV changes in different age groups: the 1990s versus the 2000s

In 15 years, the young age meta-group largely transformed into the middle age meta-group with three-quarters of the latter moving on into the old age meta-group. This gives us an opportunity to look at the hypothesis that basic values are stable in a full adult life cycle and see whether this stability changes under the societal transformation from post-socialism to capitalism. What is different and characteristic of those who were young in the 1990s? Do the corresponding high-ranked values carry over to their new age group? Are the Swedish patterns the same as for Estonians, Latvians, and Russian-speaking populations in Estonia and Latvia? The table in Table 11.4 presents the basic value change patterns for these groups.

Somewhat surprisingly, we have found that the relative rankings have changed synchronously for young meta-groups of the 1990s in both Sweden and the Baltic communities. This may be evidence of globalization tendencies in the youth of the Western world.

We are interested in discovering which kinds of changes in basic values we should expect from those middle-aged or older people who are telling their life

Figure 11.3 Changes in the ranks for technical development and freedom in 1991–2007 by community

Item	*Group*	*1991*	*1994*	*2002*	*2004*	*2006*	*2007*
Technical development	SE	19	18	18	18		
	EE	9	18	19			22
	RE	8	20	19			23
	LV	16	17			22	
	RLV	19	19			22	
Freedom	SE	3	4	3	2		
	EE	8	10	9			14
	RE	10	13	9			15
	LV	7	8			10	
	RLV	9	11			14	

stories now, compared to what they believed in the 1990s when the events they are recalling actually happened. Do they maintain their former world views? We can conclude from the data in Table 11.4 that even for the Swedes there are several changes to be taken into account. Nevertheless, the period effect is also obvious: 'honesty' and 'self-respect' have changed positions in a similar manner for all the communities. We can also say that the changes do not preserve the relative patterns of the young meta-groups of the 1990s, but have a more community-based character and may even go in the opposite direction of where they were at the beginning. The prominence gained by 'self-respect' and 'honesty' needs special attention, since these indicate an increasing trust in 'seeing and believing only your own eyes' and 'what I am saying is the one real truth' that are important in biographical story-telling. There may also be a global background, since several items have experienced changes in the same direction and of the same magnitude for both the Russian speakers in Estonia and the Latvians ('world of beauty', 'social recognition'), indicating transnational value change. Most of the adjustments have nevertheless happened within Estonian and Latvian groups. As could be expected, common values to have gained ranks are 'honesty' and 'self-respect', which speak of the growing importance placed on self-perceptions and personal opinions of the surrounding world. The appreciation of 'freedom', 'technical development', and 'world of beauty' declined in all cases, as something already put into its right place beforehand by natural forces. Of noteworthy non-shared changes, we should mention the decreased ranks of 'national security' in Estonia and 'mature love' in Latvia, 'wealth' going up in both countries, and 'clean environment' and 'self-realization' going in different directions in the two Latvian communities. Overall, there is significant and diverse transformation on the BHV scale between the earlier young and later middle meta-groups, focusing on individual adaptation to new circumstances. We must be aware of that change in value constellations due to age as well as renovation of society. It is an obvious and vital background for biographical research – events in the past, happening along with one basic value system and told in another, alter value conditions.

Table 11.4 Value items going up (+) or down (–) at least three ranks for the middle group of the 2000s when compared to the young group of the 1990s

	SE 2004–1991	*EE 2007–1991*	*RE 2007–1991*	*LV 2006–1993*	*RLV 2006–1993*
Cluster I					
Health					
Family security	+				
World at peace		–	–		
Cluster II					
Clean environment			–	–	+
National security		–	–		
Honesty	+	+	+	+	+
Justice		–	–		–
True friendship	–		+		–
Happiness		+	+		
Cluster III					
Freedom		–	–		–
Wisdom	+		+	–	+
Self-respect	+	+	+	+	+
Inner harmony				+	+
Mature love			+	–	–

Cluster IV					
Technical development		–	–	–	–
Self-realization				+	–
World of beauty			–	–	–
Wealth		+	+	+	
Equality					
Cluster V					
Pleasant life	–	+	+	+	+
Comfortable life	+			+	+
Exciting life	–				
Social recognition			–		
Cluster VI					
Salvation					
Power					

Conclusion

From the point of view of basic human values, the societies in question have changed over the last 15 years with respect to both the actors' needs and motivations due to aging effects and social transformations. The more ideologically coloured values have lost importance and their places have been taken by those that are more personal or individual, which may be taken as a trend of individualization in the post-modern world. In biographical research this means that the respondent's point of view should be shifting from what it was when the events being narrated happened towards more personal values. We had looked for and found significant changes in several BHV, but many others have concurrently moved very little in overall rankings, vindicating the theory that basic values tend to be quite stable.

In the life stories of this book (all related in the 2000s) we could notice that for the older respondents abrupt changes in their lives also exist in their narrated stories (Chapter 3); how an individual man throughout his quite long working life, substantially under the Soviet regime, finds adjustment to changed societal demands (Chapter 5) or how Russian speakers' experiences reveal some sort of helplessness after the crash of their previous semantic framing. The emergence of new semantics could be felt in the life stories narrated by the younger generation (Chapters 9 and 10). It may be efficacious to look at the narratives from two perspectives: what the narrator has taken for granted from the semantic point of view and how the specific emotionally loaded and episodically remembered life relocates into it. In pivotal times, conceptualized knowledge and emotional thought may turn out into conflict (Szakolczai and Füstös 1998). Any essential shift in background basic values will give us a life story in a renewed key. Methodologically finding out this division will allow in life stories/narratives analysis to break each of these into semantic and episodic components and accordingly evaluate possible basic value constellations supporting occurring detail choices and style of speaking out.

In contemporary research, little or no attention has been paid to the taken-for-granted side of told stories. The notions of situational and semantic memories that embody personal and abstract worlds of human action should prove useful in biographical research:

> An event happens, a person experiences it, memory traces are laid down representing the event, the past vanishes and is replaced by the present. The memory traces of the event continue to exist in the present, they are retrieved, and the person remembers the event.
>
> (Tulving 2002: 19)

Basic values provide one possible reliable background for understanding and interpreting life stories and their semantics.

> Episodic memories are summary records of experience. That is to say that they are experience-near and correspond to experience but they are not

> literal records of experience. In certain special cases, memory for highly self-relevant self-defining moments for instance, they may contain fragments that are close to being literal, veridical, records of experience.
>
> (Conway 2009: 2305)

Basic values, on the contrary, are a highly sophisticated artificial instrument used for searching for hidden latent variable(s) that take notice of the extent of knowledge in socio-cultural literacy of respondents and thus helps to understand episodes for which one has no solid operating principles or unambiguous landmarks.

References

Aarelaid-Tart, A. and Belobrovtseva, I. (2004) 'The (im)possibilities of Estonian–Russian dialogue in the conditions of cultural trauma', in A.P. Klemesheva (ed.) *Na Perekrestke Kultur: Russkie v Baltiiskom Regione. II*, Kaliningrad: Baltiiskii Mezhregionalnyi Institut Obchcestvennyh Nauk.

Björklund, F. and Liubiniene, V. (2004) *Value Change Related to the Process of Democratisation in Lithuania, Latvia and Estonia*, Research Reports 2004 (1), Stockholm: Södertörns Högskola.

Blazeviciene, A. and Jakusovaite, I. (2007) 'Value priorities and their relations with quality of life in the Baby Boomer generation of Lithuanian nurses: a cross-sectional survey', *BMC Nursing*, 6(10): 1–6.

Borg, I. and Groenen, P.J.F. (2005) *Modern Multidimensional Scaling: Theory and Applications* (2nd edn.), New York: Springer.

Conway, M.A. (2009) 'Episodic memories', *Neuropsychologia*, 47(11): 2305–2313.

Eisenstadt, S.N. (1998) 'Modernity and the construction of collective identities', in M. Sasaki (ed.) *Values and Attitudes across Nations and Time*, Leiden, Boston and Köln: Brill.

Gilboa, A. (2004) 'Autobiographical and episodic memory – one and the same? Evidence from prefrontal activation in neuroimaging studies', *Neuropsychologia*, 42(10): 1336–1349.

Inglehart, R. (1997) *Modernization and Postmodernization*, Princeton, NJ: Princeton University Press.

Kalmus, V. and Vihalemm, T. (2006) 'Distinct mental structures in transitional culture: an empirical analysis of values and identities in Estonia and Sweden', *Journal of Baltic Studies*, 37(1): 94–123.

Lauristin, M., Vihalemm, P., Rosengren, K. and Weibull, L. (eds) (1997) *Return to the Western World: Cultural and Political Perspectives on the Estonian Post-Communist Transition*, Tartu: Tartu University Press.

Maslow, A. (1954) *Motivation and Personality*, NewYork: Harper & Bros.

Piolino, P., Desgranges, B. and Eustache, F. (2009) 'Episodic autobiographical memories over the course of time: cognitive, neuropsychological and neuroimaging findings', *Neuropsychologia*, 47 (11): 2314–2329.

Rokeach, M. (1973) *The Nature of Human Values*, New York: The Free Press.

Schwartz, S.H. and Bardi, A. (1997) 'Influences of adaptation to communist rule on value priorities in Eastern Europe', *Political Psychology*, 18: 385–410.

Szakolczai, A. and Füstös, L. (1998) 'Value systems in axial moments', *European Sociological Review*, 14: 211–29.

Sztompka, P. (1996) 'Looking back: the year 1989 as a cultural and civilizational break', *Communist and Post-Communist Studies*, 29: 115–29.

Tulving, E. (1972) 'Episodic and semantic memory', in E. Tulving (ed.) *Organization of Memory*, New York: Academic Press.

Tulving, E. (2002) 'Episodic memory: from mind to brain', *Annual Review of Psychology*, 53: 1–25.

Vihalemm, T. (1997) 'Changing discourses on values in Estonia', in M. Lauristin, P. Vihalemm, K. Rosengren and L. Weibull (eds) *Return to the Western World: Cultural and Political Perspectives on the Estonian Post-Communist Transition*, Tartu: Tartu University Press.

Glossary

Aizsargi (Latvian, *guards* in English), National Guards paramilitary organization, established in 1919 with the aim to combat crime, to maintain the civil order, peace, and the national state. In the spring of 1940 the organization had approximately 68,000 members.

Beets and radishes The colour analogy of red (the colour of communism) referred to the difference between true communists: red on the surface and all the way through (beets); and lip-service pseudo-communists: red on the surface but white inside (radishes). Estonia had the same analogy – except there were no beets in Estonia!

Blat (Russian language) denotes the use, in the Soviet Union, of informal agreements, exchange of services, personal connections, Party contacts, or black market deals for personal benefit and advancement.

Bronze Soldier A monument that became a hotly contested issue in April 2007 between Estonia and Russia once its removal was introduced into the Estonian Parliament. The monument for Estonians symbolizes victory of the occupying power over their nation while for Russians the monument symbolized victory over Hitler. The intention by the Estonian government in 2007 to remove the monument, and the subsequent move from the centre of Tallinn to the nearby Tallinn Military Cemetery caused two nights (26–28 April 2007) of mass protests and riots. Since then the 'Monument of the Soldier-Liberator', which pays tribute to those Soviet soldiers who perished at the hands of Nazi forces in Estonia has become the figurehead of the complicated relationship between Estonia and Russia.

Cekomol ('ce' for Central; 'ko' for Committee; 'mol' for Youth). Primary organizations, the basic organizational unit of the Komsomol, were subordinate to a Komsomol committee for the corresponding city, rural, or city district. At the top of the Komsomol structure, which mirrored that of the Communist Party in the Soviet republic, was the Central Committee.

Chekists Members of The Cheka (ЧК – чрезвычайная комиссия *Chrezvychaynaya Komissiya*, Extraordinary Commission: Russian pronunciation: [tɕɛ. ˈka]).

Corvée Intermittent labour, often unpaid, imposed by aristocrats or nobles on peasants residing on the aristocrat's land. Because corvée labour for agriculture tended to be demanded by the lord at exactly the same times as the peasants needed to attend to their own plots at planting and harvest, corvée caused serious resentment.

Dedovshchina/Code Red A practice of extrajudicial punishment in Russian armies, initiated by soldiers and not officially authorized by army officers.

Destruction battalions (Russian *istrebitjelj*) Consisting of ideologically trusted communists of the local populaces of Estonia, Latvia, and Lithuania, they were initially formed in 1941 to destroy anything of value before the Werhmacht arrived, and were re-established in 1944 with the task of helping to defeat the 'forest brethren'. The Latvian destruction battalions were disbanded in 1952.

Forest brethren (Guerilla war 1944–1953) Partisans who operated from hideouts in the forests of Estonia (14–15,000 partisans), Latvia (10–15,000), and Lithuania (50,000). They were not a unified force.

Kaitseliit (Defence League) Originally created in the Republic of Estonia 1924 and re-established in 1990, the Defence League is a paramilitary organization enshrined in law and based on volunatry participation.

KGB The common abbreviation for the Russian Komitet gosudarstvennoy bezopasnosti or Committee for State Security. It was the national security agency of the Soviet Union from 1954 until 1991, and its premier internal security, intelligence, and secret police organization during that time.

Khaltura Either or both overtime and illegal work of all kinds for the purpose of gaining additional income in the Soviet Union.

Kolkhoz Form of collective farming in the Soviet Union that existed along with *sovkhoz* (state farms).

Komsomol Vsesoyuzny Leninsky Kommunistichesky Soyuz Molodjozhy or the All-Union Leninist Communist League of Youth was colloquially referred to by the first syllables of Kommunisticheskiy Soyuz Molodyozhi (the Communist Union of Youth). Komsomol was the youth division of the Communist Party of the Soviet Union (CPSU). Between 1918 and 1922 the CPSU established three youth organizations to prepare future adults for membership of the CPSU: Oktyabryonok (Little Octobrist) for children aged 9 or under; Pionery (Pioneers) for children aged 9–14 and Komsomol for youths and young adults aged 14–28. Komsomol was the dominant organization overseeing the activities of the younger movements.

Latvian Voluntary Waffen-SS Legion Formed in 1943 (Estonian Legion was formed in 1942) after an order by Adolf Hitler. The word 'volunteer' was included in the Legion's title in order to get around the Hague Convention of 1907, which forbids the compulsion of the inhabitants of occupied territory to swear allegiance to a hostile power. The majority of legionnaires were conscripted (March 1943 to August 1944).

Memory archives In Estonia life stories have been actively collected since 1989. The Estonian Life Stories Association was established in 1996 and started to organize life story writing campaigns.

In 2000 and 2001, the Estonian National Museum also collected memoirs about Soviet everyday life (questionnaires 'Life during the Soviet period' and 'Working life and working in Soviet Estonia'. Only a year earlier the Estonian National Museum had made a study of the post-war years and the impact of war on everyday life (questionnaire 'Post-war village').

- The Estonian Literary Museum, as a result of several contests spread over the mid-1990s, hold more than 5000 life stories (Estonian Cultural History Archives (ECHA).
- The Estonian National Museum hold over 3000 life stories.
- The Latvian National Oral History (LNOH) archives holds 3000 life stories.
- The Lithuanian Genocide and Resistance Research Centre hold 250 audio and video-taped life stories of former partisans and their supporters.

MGB Ministry for State Security.

Militia Soviet name for police.

Nagorny Karabakh (Nagorno-Karabakh Autonomous Republic or Artsakh Republic). An extremely tense flashpoint zone between Armenia and Azerbaijan. Predominantly Armenian-populated, the region is adjacent to Armenian state borders in the west and to Iran in the south, bordering with Azerbaijan-controlled territory in the north and east (http://en.wikipedia.org/wiki/Armenian_people).

Nomenklatura (etymology – Latin: nomenclatura – list of names). The CPSU possessed an 'appointment authority'. Every CPSU committee and department from All-Union level through to regional, city, and district levels prepared two lists: The basic list (osnovnaia) detailed positions in the political, administrative, economic, military, cultural, and educational bureaucracies that they were responsible for filling. The registered list (uchetnaia) consisted of the people (CPSU members) suitable for the osnovnaia positions. In order to appear on the uchetnaia list, a patron was needed.

Old Believers (Starovery) became separated after 1666–1667 from the hierarchy of the Russian Orthodox Church as a protest against church reforms introduced by Patriach Nikon. Old Believers continue liturgical practices, which the Russian Orthodox Church maintained before the implementation of these reforms. The first Old Believers in the Baltic area fled severe religious persecution in Russia proper and settled in the Baltics from the late seventeenth century onwards. There are currently tens of thousands of Old Believers in the Baltic states, some of them living in small, quite isolated villages in the eastern border areas, others in big cities like Tallinn and Riga.

Putsch (1991) Derived from a Russian word meaning *coup d'état*, and marks the attempt to overthrow Sergei Gorbachev, the head of the Soviet Union, and to establish a new regime in the Soviet Union. In order to secure their position, the conspirators sent military forces onto the streets in Moscow as well in several Soviet republics. People in Moscow as well as the Soviet republics conducted massive demonstrations against the military presence. The conflict ended with the defeat of the conspirators and the dissolution of Soviet Union.

Russian-speaking community Estonia's ethnic minorities consist of representatives of different nationalities: Russians, Jews, Ukrainians, Belorussians, Armenians, etc. who are the bearers of their national culture, as well as the Russian culture and often their main language of communication at home and between peers is Russian.

Sąjūdis Lithuanian Reform Movement. The Sąjūdis Initiative Group was formed in June 1988 and was the catalyst in encouraging Lithuania to declare independence in 1990. The movement refused to become a political party but did provide active support for non-communist candidates in the elections of February and March 1990. Sąjūdis-backed candidates won an absolute majority in the Supreme Council of the Lithuanian SSR, also known as the Reconstituted Seimas, which proclaimed the independent state of Lithuania.

Setos (*Setu* in English) are a Finno-Ugric people, numbering approximately 15,000 who are indigenous to the area around the confluence of the borders of Estonia, Latvia, and Russia (close to the Russian town of Pskov). Seto culture can be said to form a link between Estonian culture (through their vernacular language, which is a dialect (or variant) of south Estonian, a Finno-Ugric language (also called võru-setu)) and Russian culture (through their religion, Russian Orthodoxy). Religious practices, especially those of celebrating patron saints' holidays and visiting family graves at cemeteries, also firmly connect Setos with the Russian side of the border where many of their most important churches and graveyards are located.

Index